Martha Frances

W9-BVK-543

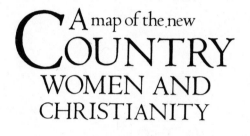

A map of the new
COUNTRY
WOMEN AND
CHRISTIANITY

A map of the new COUNTRY
WOMEN AND CHRISTIANITY

Sara Maitland

ROUTLEDGE & KEGAN PAUL

LONDON, BOSTON, MELBOURNE
AND HENLEY

Grateful acknowledgment is made to the following
for permission to reprint:
Excerpts from The Awful Rowing Toward God by Anne Sexton.
Copyright © 1975 Loring Conant Jr.
Reprinted by kind permission of Houghton Mifflin Company,
Chatto & Windus Ltd and Anne Sexton.

First published in 1983
by Routledge & Kegan Paul Ltd
39 Store Street, London WC1E 7DD,
9 Park Street, Boston, Mass. 02108, USA,
296 Beaconsfield Parade, Middle Park,
Melbourne, 3206, Australia, and
Broadway House, Newtown Road,
Henley-on-Thames, Oxon RG9 1EN
Set in Linotron Bembo by
Rowland Phototypesetting Ltd, Bury St Edmunds, Suffolk
and printed in Great Britain by
St Edmundsbury Press, Bury St Edmunds, Suffolk
© Sara Maitland 1983

Library of Congress Cataloging in Publication Data

Maitland, Sara, 1950–
A map of the new country.
Includes index.
1. Women in Christianity.   2. Ordination of
women.   I. Title.
BV639.W7M26 1982   280'.088042   82–13142

ISBN 0-7100-9326-8

'But it is time you recalled that, though I am a servant,
I am not your servant.'

Ursula le Guin, *A Wizard of Earthsea*

CONTENTS

PREFACE

◆◆◆

To Anne Scheibner,
New York, USA

My Dear Anne,
  I told you in New York last summer that I would dedicate this
book to you, and here it is with much love and many thanks.
  When I made that promise I had very little idea of what I would
end up offering you. Or, rather, I had a clear idea and it was nothing
like this. This is not the same book as I thought it would be. I am not
even sure that I am the same person. Personal change is not very
comfortable: there have been periods in the last year when I have not
only loathed the book, but also felt extremely antagonistic towards
the people who have challenged me through it. You have not been
exempt from this. However, change, and I believe growth, have
only been possible because of the warmth and love and support that I
have received from so many women, and especially from you.
  I started work on this book in 1978 shortly after I had finished a
novel. I thought it would be a quick and fairly calm way to earn a
breathing space before going back to writing fiction. If I had known
it would take two years and so much of my whole self I would
certainly never have started. Back then I managed to be a good,
orthodox Anglo-Catholic and a good feminist too: now I am
neither. That is to say I am still an Anglo-Catholic and I am still a
feminist, but neither party finds me good or orthodox. I find this
difficult. I would find it impossible if it were not for the fact that I
have found so many other women with the same problem, in one
form or another.

ix

I first got involved in the Women's Liberation Movement in about 1970 – it was my first ever 'conversion experience'; it was wonderful and exhausting. Imagine my horror when two years later I got 'converted' over again: this time to Christianity. The Church was very much my 'Mummy' – Christianity made me feel safe and virtuous when I returned from fine moral effort in the 'outside world'. I never applied the radical thinking of the Women's Movement to the conservative and ritualistic religion that I so much enjoyed. For nearly six years I managed to keep two of the most important things in my life rigidly separate. Obviously, as that division was the basis of my security I should never have started on this book, but I did not know what I was doing. Because of my careful divisions I knew no 'Christian feminists' – if I thought about them at all I would have said, as a feminist, that they could not be very good feminists; and, as a Christian, that they could not be very good Christians: such complacency is asking God for a lesson!

I did, however, know that there were individual women within Christianity who were doing some interesting work in a changing social context. Frequently they were taking traditional jobs and raising them to a new dimension. I was fascinated, for example, by what I knew about post-Vatican Council nuns, and wanted to understand more about them. I started to see the work of Christian women artists of vision and strength. There were individuals too whose political commitment sprang directly out of their Christianity; like Dr Sheila Cassidy. At a more domestic level there were women struggling against discrimination to do traditionally male jobs – like the Free Church ordained ministers. I thought of a book that would be a series of interviews with individuals, that would allow their voices to be heard and would present a picture of what Christian women were up to in the Church today.

As soon as I began to talk to women and to search them out, I became aware that there were massive underlying questions about the whole structure of institutional Christianity – problem areas that kept emerging, in different forms, over and over again. I realised that to examine the work of individuals without being prepared to examine these questions was not only pointless, it was wrong. I realised that the nature of the issues, as well my own integrity, demanded that I work on a book that was at least open to these serious questions and the underlying assumptions not of the Christian past, but of the Christian present. It was still an objective questioning; I still had no personal doubts or problems.

Then I came to the USA for seven weeks of interviewing. Away from my own haunts and thrown off balance by a Christianity and a feminism profoundly different from the English varieties laid me open to new influences. But, more important, it was the women I talked to, and you especially, who, by their openness, by their willingness to talk and share and work on being Christian feminists, forced on me a personal involvement with the subject. Not because they were necessarily right, but because they cared, and articulated that caring, and expected me to respond. Quite violently, and far from the stabilising influence of home, the questions became my questions. The whole subject of women and Christianity mattered to me in a profoundly important way. I could not return to my own complacency. I found too that I could not return to the Church, which I loved, and love, without engaging myself in some way to change it. Who was the God that I worshipped? How could the Church show forth that divinity in something nearer its fullness? It was not just a question of women any more: the oppression of femaleness (in the Church and in my heart) was just a symbol of the divided, dualistic, un-just, un-caring way in which we all carried on. I had to find some answers, or at the very least I had to look for some. When I came home I found that these feelings did not go away, as I had half hoped they might. I also found that now I knew what I was looking for England too was full of Women of Spirit – that discovery has been one of the redeeming factors of this last year.

Of course I have not found any answers. But I had to change the book that I was going to write. Not just because the old book was no longer very interesting to me, but because the detached, objective author no longer existed. The book had to be a personal exploration, a journey for me as much as for any reader.

In the light of all this I find it easier to say what this is not going to be. It is not authoritative – it does not pretend to be. It is very personal, selective and partial. I have only pursued those things that seemed potentially valuable to me. It is based on my own vision and hope, not on some objective standard of 'balance'. The Women's Liberation Movement has authorised this personal voice in a particular and liberating way: we have discovered that when each woman speaks from her own experience we can begin to hear a collective voice and form a collective understanding. I hope lots more people will join their personal voices to mine.

This book is not about Super-Women. Or, in more theological language, it is not about Saints. I know that there are saints around – I have met some – but the book is not about them. It is about the collective mass. It is therefore unashamedly about politics: about structures and the way Churches work and the practical consequences of these. It is about money and jobs and party-groupings and power and trade-offs and wheeling and dealing – as well as about prayer and love and creative energies.

The book is not about religion or spirituality in general; it is about Christianity. I am a Christian – I live and work and love inside the Christian community. The problems here are mine; if I wrote about Jews, or Hindus, or Wicca it would be an 'outsider's' book, which is just what I do not want to write. I now send my love and prayers to the women who are there. I send them especially to the women who are defining for themselves a specifically feminist women-only spirituality; and particularly to those who define themselves as 'post-Christian feminists'. I would have liked to have written more about them, because they have been so useful to me. Their ideas have been immensely creative and formative even for those of us who do not wish to go out there with them, and there is so much coming and going on the boundary where there is a real love and exchange. Some of the women whom I have used in my work may feel that they really belong on the other side of the line; I apologise to them. The reason I have decided not to write too much about these women is because it is an insult to them. They have decided to leave: it would be impertinent of me to drag them into a book about Christianity.

Finally this book is neither history nor theology, I am not properly equipped for either. There are lots of women who are and they are working hard on both. The results are exciting. Although obviously I mention both they are not my focus. This is an attempt to gather together some contemporary events and try to look for emerging patterns in them.

On my best days I would like to think of the book as a combination of journalism and prophecy. In more modest moods I think it might be a sort of text book to be used when people ask, either from within or from outside the Christian community, 'what is all this fuss over Women and the Church ABOUT?' But what the book really is, is cartography, map-making. There is a fundamental Christian journey which has always been the same and always will be: the journey out of Egypt and into the painful freedom of the wilderness; out of Babylon and exile back to our true home; out of sin, through death, towards the difficult experience of free life. It is a journey that cannot be made alone and cannot be made on anyone else's behalf. Until the comfortable compliance is recognised for what it is – both slavery and disobedience – the journey cannot be at all. Just as the Daughters of the Exodus often longed to be back in Egypt, so the women of the New Covenant do not always want to be free. But some women have set off again on the Freedom Trail. Cartographers are not pioneers, but they can be useful to the women who come after them. I would like this book to be a map of the new country; indicating the sign-posts that the women who have already gone have set up for us, pointing out the danger areas and the best camp-sites. The first maps of the New World in the sixteenth century were frequently very inaccurate, but they were inspirational: they encouraged other people to go there too. As a map it has been useful to me anyway, this two years of talking to women who have dared to set out: it has encouraged me to want to go to the New World myself.

The women who have already started on this exploration have been generous to me. Although you have been so often my special 'native guide' in the new territory, you have not been alone. I want to thank more people than is really practical. Some gratitudes are like the National Debt, you never even pretend you can pay it back, you cannot even remember who made the loan in the first place. In this book particularly my overall intellectual debt to Rosemary Radford Ruether will I hope be clear to all who know her work; likewise my debt to St Benedict whose vision of a unified human community founded in love, prayer, work and discipline does not seemed dimmed by 1,500 years.

I want to thank everyone who has spoken to me about their lives – either formally, with my tiresome tape-recorder, or informally. I have tried to acknowledge every individual contribution I am aware of, but I have doubtless absorbed many people's ideas so naturally that I think they are my own. (This is another reason of course why this book should be dedicated to you: I cannot possibly hope to make formal acknowledgment of every contribution you have made.) It is important to recognise that many women opened themselves to me in ways that entailed considerable risks to themselves; they have often expressed themselves, their doubts, difficulties and pain. I pray that I have treated them with the respect they deserve.

It is usual in the acknowledgment section of a book to absolve one's friends and colleagues of all responsibility for the content. In one particular case I cannot do this: I hold Sr Anna Cooper MSC, who was once my agent, directly responsible. The book was in very many ways her idea, and though I thank her energy and commitment which made it possible, I also want – with gratitude – to implicate her in the final result. After she left her agency to follow another vocation she was replaced by Chris Green, who picked up the pieces, bullied me into producing something concrete, and whose wit, knowledge and healthy ideas about how much alcohol is needed at lunchtime have been invaluable.

It seems strange that most of the people whom I need to thank personally are not known to you. I welcome the chance to do some introducing. My dear friend, sister and comrade Michele Roberts made my life possible while I was writing this book – I thank her. Also Jo Garcia who makes me laugh as well as making me think; Meinrad Craighead whose work is a constant inspiration and whose friendship is precious to me; Monica Furlong who has kept me safe in many storms, but also put me firmly back on the road to self-knowledge and honesty; Helen Sands whom I met as a direct consequence of the book and whose friendship has been a real reward; Alison Webster, whose quality of loving attentiveness is remarkable; Ruth and John Matthews who were a light in a dark place and may not know how much that meant to me; Mandy Merck, Matt Hoffman and Michelene Wandor whose affectionate detachment about what I was doing has helped to keep me sane; Fr Peter Cobb who kept Christianity tolerable for me at times when that seemed impossible; Frs Donald Lee, Stuart Wilson and Christopher Colven who may not feel that their attempts to keep me orthodox have been very successful, but whose efforts are none the less much appreciated.

I thank my mother and friend The Blessed Virgin Mary and my mentor and sister St Teresa of Avila for their love, prayers and support. I thank my mother Hope Maitland and my daughter Mildred Lee for existing. These are all people who appear little or not at all in the text but without whom it would not have been possible. That is also true for every woman whom I do mention in the book and their naming there must be read as a real thank you.

Last I thank you, Anne, and ask you not to be too cross about the things we disagree over, nor about the inadequacies of this book after all your efforts and love. This is not a conclusion, but a starting point for me; confusions are inevitable. But I have a vision of which we will not be made ashamed. A vision of wholeness, humanity and unity; a balance between past and future; graceful order and apocalyptic freedom. I believe this vision can be brought nearer to its concrete reality through love and honesty and sisterhood. So much of that vision, that hope, that possibility has been given to me by you – there is no recompense except love, which I send you always, Sara.

From Sara Maitland
London

NOTE ON BIBLICAL QUOTATIONS

❖❖❖

I was brought up on the King James Bible. Although I recognise the superior scholarship of the New English Bible and the forceful, clear language of the Jerusalem Bible, scriptural references always come to my mind in the King James version. I have therefore compromised somewhat and used the Revised Standard Version as my principal text. Where a less 'male biassed' translation has been available in either the Jerusalem or the NEB I have used that (although interestingly the NEB is actually worse in this respect than the older translation). I have, however, frequently altered texts myself, for example usually using the word 'God' for 'Lord'. In some instances these alterations are only acts of retranslation: where New Testament texts are concerned I have tried to check that the Greek permits an open, non-sexist translation, e.g. using 'human' instead of 'man' only when the generic rather than the gender specific word occurs in the Greek. With Old Testament texts I have not been able to do this, as I read no Hebrew. In a few cases, however, I have gone further and actually imply a non-sexist use which the original writer did not intend.

Where the text is markedly different from the RSV I have indicated in the notes what translation I am following. There are now 'non-sexist translations' of the whole New Testament available, but I have not found any of them satisfying enough to use exclusively. I have tried where possible to avoid using any gender referent for God – both in quotation and in my own text – and have not used either 'man' or 'he' in the generic sense. In extending these principles to the Biblical texts I have taken a liberty, but not one without usefulness, I believe.

CHAPTER I

ROOTS AND BEGINNINGS

---------- ◆◆◆ ----------

Let a woman learn in silence with all submissiveness. I permit no
woman to teach or to have authority over men; she is to keep
silent. For Adam was formed first, then Eve; and Adam was not
deceived, but the woman was deceived and became a
transgressor.

(1 Timothy 2: 11–14)

Jesus said to her, 'Mary.' She turned and said to him, in Hebrew,
'Rabboni' (which means Teacher). Jesus said to her, 'Do not hold
me . . . but go to my brethren and say to them, I am ascending
to my father and your father, to my God and your God.' Mary
Magdalene went to the disciples and said, 'I have seen the Lord';
and she told them that he had said these things to her.

(Gospel of John 20: 16–18)

1946: The World Council of Churches, at its headquarters in Geneva,
established a study commission on the position of women within
Christianity. By 1954 this had evolved into the permanent Department for the Co-operation of Men and Women in the Church,
commonly known as 'The Women's Desk'. Its original chair-
woman, Dr Kathleen Bliss, published the first organised critique of
the discrimination against women in twentieth-century Christianity.[1]

1959: The Roman Catholic Church, under the leadership of Pope
John XXIII, opened the Second Vatican Council. Although there
were no women delegates and only one woman – a US nun, Sr Luke
Tobin – was invited to address the Council, the whole theological

I

bias of the Council was felt by women to be encouraging to their desire to play a new and larger role in the church.

1967: The Rev. Ruth Matthews became the first Baptist minister in Great Britain to continue her ministry after getting married; although the Baptist Union insisted that she left their pension scheme, she found a congregation that called her and her husband jointly so that she was able to continue working when her children were born.

1968: The Presbyterian Church of Scotland, the most tightly organised bastion of Calvin and Knox's misogyny in the West, allowed women to become Elders within their congregations, and thus enabled them for the first time to have a voice in the central management of the church.

1970: For the first time the Episcopal Church of the USA allowed women delegates to be full members of the General Convention – the governing body of that church.

1970: The two major Lutheran churches of the USA voted to ordain women. By this action the full ministry of 'word and sacrament' became a legal possibility for all women in the main Protestant churches in the USA. In the following decade the European Protestant churches all followed suit.

1971: Hong Kong. The Bishop of Hong Kong (the only surviving diocese in the Anglican province of Southern China) quietly ordained to the priesthood The Rev. Jane Hwang and the Rev. Joyce Bennet, Deaconnesses, the first women to be ordained priests by a church with a sacramental symbol-of-Christ theology of priesthood.

July 1974: The Church of the Advocate, Philadelphia, USA. Before a congregation of over 2,000 people, Bishop Daniel Corrigan, without the consent of either his fellow Bishops or the governing Convention of his church, ordained to the priesthood the Rev. Jeanette Piccard, Deacon. He, and three other bishops at the same ceremony, ordained a further ten women Deacons to the priesthood.

Those eleven women, in receiving ordination that was certainly irregular, and possibly invalid, at the hands of four Bishops who had no authority to licence them after the ordination, were making a radical claim about the standing of women, not in the eyes of their particular denomination, but in the eyes of God.

1977: USA. Maria Cueto and Raisa Nemikin, two social workers employed by the National Episcopal Church Center to minister to Hispanic Americans, laid claim to the privilege of 'ministers of religion' not to answer a Grand Jury on matters that they had learned in confidence. The judge ruled that the priest-penitent relationship could not exist as they were not ordained. Although unsupported by the Episcopal Bishops both women went to prison rather than breach confidentiality.

1979: The Bishop of Newark, New Jersey, licenced for experimental use the 'Mother Thunder Liturgy':[2] a service for Holy Communion prepared by an all-women group which used only 'non-sexist language': that is language which avoids using male words for either the people of God, or for the Godhead itself. Such language has been used for prayers inside women's groups for a while, but the Mother Thunder Liturgy was the first to receive an official recognition of this kind.

October 1979: The National Shrine of the Immaculate Conception, Washington DC, USA. In the middle of his tour of the USA, Pope John Paul II had arranged to meet and speak to representatives of the women's religious orders. Sr Theresa Kane as president of the Leadership Conference of Women Religious, was invited to deliver a speech of welcome. Instead of the anticipated pious platitudes, she unexpectedly demanded that the Pope 'be mindful of the intense pain and suffering which is part of the life of many women', and that he allow 'the possibility of women as persons being included in all the ministries of the Church'. Around the shrine about sixty nuns rose to their feet, wearing blue protest arm-bands, to identify themselves as part of the struggle against sexism in the Roman Catholic Church.

More nuns stood by when the Pope, who continued his speech without acknowledging the protest, said that Christians should have the courage of their convictions.

3

1980: Sonia Johnson, a life-long member of the Church of the Latter Day Saints (the Mormons) who brought up her children and organised her personal life in line with the strict disciplines of her church, was excommunicated because of her support for ERA (the proposed constitutional amendment which would endorce equal rights for women in the USA). The Mormons appear to have objected not so much to Sonia Johnson's active support of ERA, but to the fact that she challenged her own church to live up to and campaign for equality as a Biblical duty.

These scattered incidents from the last twenty years are only some of the more visible signs that women within Christianity, along with women elsewhere, are not only demanding, but are actually achieving, very radical changes in their status. It is increasingly unlikely that these changes will be brought about without disrupting the structures of Christianity, in a number of ways. Something is happening; and appears to be happening at an ever-accelerating speed. The difficulty is knowing quite what it is, where it came from and what it can possibly mean for the future.

The debate about women in the churches is not a new one. As the quotation at the beginning of the chapter makes clear, the discussion started practically with the start of the Church – the writer of the epistle to Timothy would never have had to speak with such fervour against women if it had been a purely abstract matter. Again and again throughout Christian history – and usually at times when unrest was most prevalent – women have asserted their god-given right to participate at different levels in the affairs of their denominations. This present phase, however, is different both in degree and in kind. It is more visible because high-speed communication and the increase of literacy enable isolated national phenomena to become part of a larger picture much more quickly than ever before. It is different in kind for a number of reasons: the growth of the secular Women's Movement, especially in areas where even ten years ago it seemed unlikely to have much impact, has made the churches look old-fashioned and foolish, adding to the pressure applied to them. But the principal difference in this round of 'women's demands' is that the basis of the demands themselves is different – women on the whole are no longer demanding simply a right to their fair share of the cake, they are saying that the churches got the recipe wrong in the first place, the cake is not worth the eating, and that a new deal is

4

necessary – not merely to give women what they want, but to serve God as God wants. This new consciousness among women is not an isolated idea, but is shared in the demands of the black and national liberation movements. Where thirty years ago oppressed groups were defining 'freedom' in terms of what the oppressor was seen to have, there is now in every field a much more reasoned critique of what white, First and Second World male society has to offer.

Christian women are no longer saying to their churches, 'we want to be allowed to do what men do, have what men have'; but are instead saying something much more challenging: that they are called to prophesy to the churches in the Old Testament sense of that word. There is a duty incumbent on the prophet to recall the community to its own roots to its central truth.

As Christians our central truth is not some set of laws or magical formulae. It is Jesus of Nazareth: an historical person who lived in an obscure province of the Roman Empire in the middle of the first century AD, *and* our resurrected, glorified saviour who promised that he would be with us always, even to the end of time. As a token of that presence he promised that people who believed in him would receive the Holy Spirit, who would lead them into all truth, so that our reflection on Jesus' person and life would not be static but dynamic. He also promised that Christians would have a particular and concrete knowledge of the divine – not through magical rituals, nor through secret knowledge, but through observing Jesus himself. As he put it, 'Everyone who knows me knows the Father who sent me.'

Thus Christianity, from its earliest beginnings, was mandated not to philosophise abstractly, but to look at Jesus, and learn the truth about God. Christian women, observing both that they are treated as less than human by their churches *and* that Christianity throughout the world does not seem very successful in fulfilling its mission of love, freedom and peace, have to look again to see what Jesus may be saying.

Because the Gospels themselves are not simple reportage but the first attempts at theology, this is not easy. For as long as Christianity has existed there have been conflicts about what is the central message of Jesus' incarnation. There are similar disagreements about where the authority for interpreting Jesus' life lies – in the Gospels, in the Church, in the individual. However, there are points of agreement: Jesus was born, suffered and died to reconcile humanity to

God – to bridge again the gap between creator and creation, between eternity and time, between self and Other. Moreover, in declaring that God loved all of humanity Jesus acted out a special preference for the poor and oppressed: for outcasts, 'sinners', and all those whom society regarded as outsiders, of less value. He also urged his followers to do likewise – stressing the high value that God placed on voluntary service, humility and self-denial on the one hand and on mutual love, respect and community on the other. In his life he demonstrated this preference markedly not just in his teaching but by selecting as followers not the learned, the powerful or the respectable but precisely the reverse. One of the notable ways in which he did this was by giving women – who in his society were not even regarded as competent legal witnesses – key roles in witnessing to his identity and mission. Mary was the first person to learn of God's intended intervention into history; Elizabeth the first to recognise what was happening; to a Samaritan prostitute Jesus first revealed himself as the Messiah; to his friend Martha he first declared himself as 'the resurrection and the life'; and to Mary Magdalene he gave the first demonstration of that life, as well as the first charge to proclaim it. In every case these were private experiences so that it was the women themselves who felt called not 'to be silent' but to teach others. In the case of Mary Magdalene, John makes clear that Jesus commanded her to speak. Jesus does not seem to have chosen these women because they were holier or better than any one else around, but because they were members (like the Jews themselves, or like tax-collectors, or the poor or lepers) of a group that society felt entitled to despise and discount. God declares in Jesus that 'what God has cleansed, you must not call unclean.'

The writer of the Epistle to Timothy wrote before John's Gospel was written, so it is not fair to ask why he chose to contradict Jesus' own words. The salient question is, rather, why did the Christian Church, from the third to the twentieth century, *prefer* to remember and quote the Epistle when deciding about the role of women, rather than Jesus' own explicit command to Mary – 'Go and tell' – and implicit respect for women that marked his whole mission? Why does organised Christianity remember the line about women being saved by childbirth, and Eve being the source of human sin, rather than Jesus' clear response to the remark, 'Blessed is the womb that bear this and the breasts that gave thee suck', which was, 'No, blessed rather is she who hears my words and keeps them.' Why, finally, are so many Christians, of both sexes, made uneasy and even aggressive when these readings of the texts are pointed out to them and they are asked to act on their own commitment to just and loving dealings with their fellow human beings?

The early theologians of the Church were clear in theory. God is the absolute Other, who cannot be described or contained in any human terms. It is wrong to assign to that Absolute any qualities whatever (and male and female are explicitly such qualities): to do so is to attempt to limit God, to make an idol of the Infinite, to remake God in our own image. Any of the ways in which we may try to describe God are only images, analogies which may be useful but have no real truth.

However, as the early Christian movement expanded outwards from its Palestinian roots, it came into contact with the sophisticated world of the Roman Empire. Here the language of philosophy and theology was not the same as the Jewish idiom, based in community, history and law; it was rather the Hellenic language of abstract systems and anti-materialism. Inevitably the Christian community absorbed this new idiom, despite Paul's sensible realisation that Christian truth was bound to prove 'foolishness to the Greeks'. Although the Church attempted to fight dualistic tendencies in Gnosticism and later Manicheanism, the Jewish legal understanding of male-as-superior gained a justification and sanctification from the Greek philosophical concept of human beings as binary – a body part in which the spirit/soul/divine element was trapped. This is a psychologically comforting as well as an intellectually attractive idea as it allows a person to identify everything about the self that is dark and painful as being part of the bodily order, to be discarded when the spiritual part is freed from it. In a society where men have already gained ascendancy in the intellectual, legal and social life, and where asceticism is felt to be the way in which the spiritual-human can overcome and dominate the material-human, it is all too easy to project the dark, bodily, dangerous and uncontrolled elements of life on to women. Women are therefore dangerous, alien, other; they are also not what God is: good, orderly and, in terms of imagery therefore, male.

This emphasis on good and God as male was of course increased when Christianity allowed itself to be adopted as the religion of the Roman Empire. The Empire was built by military victory, and increasingly civilisation, as the Roman world understood it, was defended by military might. A God who is on our side, because our side represents all that is civilised, gracious, must and will fight with us against the barbarians. Therefore he is a God of military power, and therefore he is male.

Once the divine is securely identified as male, however subconsciously, women become less divine than men; and for Christianity that also meant less human. Whether they are despised as 'carnal' or exalted as 'inspiring' they no longer have to be treated as though they were fully human people, made in the image of God.

History tells the same tale; gradually the power and influence that women had exercised in the early church was disciplined and channelled by the church. The creation of women's communities, where they could live freed from the social and legal restrictions of marriage, allowed the Church to suggest that this was the best, and later the only way in which it was proper for women to serve – they could be excluded from practical authority within the active community. Later the elevation of Mary did little or nothing to improve the actual status of other women; she presented an impossible model – Virgin and Mother. Every real woman could be judged as failing to live up to her standard, and with the best will in the world it was impossible to achieve both. While Jesus could be seen as 'a man just like men', Mary could not be experienced as a woman just like women.

The history of women throughout the 2,000 years of Christian history has been worked on in detail and this is not the place for it.[3] There are just two general points that I wish to draw out.

First, the effect of not having to regard women as fully human means that their experiences, complaints and joys do not have to be given the same validity. Male experience is declared as normal; female alternatives to this experience are perceived as deviant. This applies most directly in the field of sexuality: because women are regarded as less fully human than man, male exploitation of women is seen as separate from women's experience of that exploitation. Prostitution, for instance, has been seen as a more or less serious moral offence at different times, but it has always been considered in the light of what using prostitutes might mean for the moral fibre of men and of their society. Thus Augustine could write 'remove prostitution from human affairs and you will unsettle everything because of lust' (men's lust, presumably) and Aquinas could agree, 'Prostitution in cities is like the sewage system in the palace. Do away with it and the palace will become a place of filth and stink.'[4] Sexuality – in all forms from birth to procreation is the place where men are most obliged to recognise that women are different from them, are the Other, and are potentially lovable – necessary and real. Here male society has to be most careful not to confront women as whole and human because it would be too threatening. So much of the abstract structured misogyny that women encounter from their churches seems to be based on the deep fear that those in authority have of meeting face to face with the object of all projections and finding her lovable. Historically it was not until women had developed enough autonomy to articulate their own sexual experiences, and society had developed to a point where it could permit the subject to be talked about at all, that women's claims for justice from their churches could confront the reality of the problem.

Second, of course, many women throughout Christian history have emerged from this state of silence and laid claim to their own experience. Every century has seen women, often even praised by their own churches, who have been able to take a stand. Some, like Joan of Arc have paid very heavily. Others, like Catherine of Siena, have wielded real political power at the heart of the system. It is interesting that these women are most likely to emerge at times of conflict: for example, during the reformation and again during the evangelical revivals of the seventeenth, eighteenth and nineteenth centuries women claimed and were allowed to exercise ministries of real authority. It was at these times that the men they were involved with were themselves making stands of 'radical obedience' – proclaiming that the Holy Spirit gave them an authority and a legitimacy higher than that of any social institutions. At the Reformation the Roman Catholic Church claimed that they had the complete authority from Christ: the Reformers claimed that there was a higher and freer authority, the Holy Spirit who 'bloweth where he listeth', and it was on the basis of that authority that they were allowed, even obliged to act. Outlaws and exiles from the existing authorities, they had no interest in denying that the Spirit could endow anyone with charismatic graces. Women took a strong hold on these ideas; often they were leaders, even initiators, of new sects. Quaker women, for example, were immensely bold and fearless in their evangelical fervour. But Quakers went further than almost any other group in declaring that there was no human source of authority whatsoever, and thus it was particularly hard for the men to sanctify any attempt they might have made to discipline their women.[5] On the whole charismatic authority in women was suppressed as soon as the group was sufficiently established to start exercising its own authority. George Eliot makes this point clearly in *Adam Bede*; women preachers were eliminated almost as soon as Methodism was able to create an organised structure.

Exceptional women have not always worked to the advantage of the rest of us. Just as people will tell you now that there is no more need for a women's liberation movement because Margaret Thatcher became Prime Minister, so Christians will say that there cannot be anything wrong with the position of women because of St Teresa of Avila or Julian of Norwich. Leaving aside the irrelevance of this answer (if it is couched in the terms of black oppression the inanity is clearer: 'Black people are not disadvantaged because the Queen of Tonga had a royal carriage at the Coronation, or because Muhammad Ali won the World Heavy Weight Boxing Championship' for instance) this also takes little account of the psychological penalties paid by these women to achieve what they did. Perpetua, martyred in North Africa in 302 AD, was a well-educated woman living early enough for her still to be allowed to be a leader within her Christian community despite being married and having a child. None the less she records that in her dreams she identified herself as a man before she could enter heaven.[6] Teresa of Avila was constantly under the eye of the Inquisition; Joan of Arc was burned as a witch. Elizabeth Young, burned under Mary Tudor for distributing Protestant tracts, conducted herself with such courage under trial that she had to endure the added humiliation of having public bets taken as to her true sex.[7] Of course most of the great saints have suffered at the hands of the world, but for women there have also been additional burdens – the limited choices of life-styles, the humiliation of being less worthy than men, and the gruelling choice between personal and public lives. Since St Monica, in the fourth century, whose main claim to canonisation appears to have been the holiness of her son, Augustine, the Roman Church has not declared any woman a saint who was not a nun or a queen – with a few exceptions for virgins who came to painful ends, Joan of Arc and Maria Goretti, for example. This is hardly encouraging to the majority of women, and moreover suggests that in the eyes of the church sexual womanhood and holiness are incompatible.

However, until the end of the eighteenth century the discrimination against women and the ideology that gave this discrimination its authority was, to a very great degree, unconscious and unavoidable. Aquinas, for instance, built his theological position on gender on totally erroneous foundations. The fault was not his but his scientific contemporaries who taught and believed that women only provided a suitable nurturing place for the already complete human being contained in the male sperm and so a child owed no part of itself to its mother: this scientific error led to an understanding of God's creative power as masculine and also inevitably tied tighter the link between women and nature. The attitude of the churches after the nineteenth century has a very different quality from the longer period that precedes it. The developments of the nineteenth century, both in Church and society, have led directly to the contemporary situation and must therefore be looked at in more detail.

Throughout the eighteenth and nineteenth centuries there was an increasing secularisation of political life and a corresponding privatisation of religious experience. The passionate 'religious politics' of the sixteenth and seventeenth centuries died away, their final demise trumpeted by the explicitly atheistic French Revolution – the theological idiom was no longer adequate to describe political experience. Religion was increasingly confined within the home, a domestic matter. With the Industrial Revolution, however, religion was joined – in the culturally dominant middle-class family – in its domestic seclusion by women. Women, at the height of the nineteenth century, were regarded as too pure for the secular rough and tumble of men's lives, and became the guardians of men's souls, held responsible for the moral tone of the nation.

Separating completely the spheres of influence along gender lines had a series of curious effects. Although it eliminated women from public life in a more complete way than ever before it also made them a new and separate 'interest group'. The response to the demand that they should 'guard the nation's life' was taken seriously: if morality was their field they would expose the immorality of men's world: it was their holy duty to do so. Women started by 'meddling' in a large number of philanthropic causes, from missionary work to the position of sweated workers, from temperance to anti-slavery. In this they were encouraged by the clergy of all denominations who saw that their influence on the world could be most fully worked out through well-organised, under-employed women. However, in trying to exert moral influence women were forced to realise just how the social structures of their era discriminated against them. The suffrage struggle, for example, was born at least in part out of the struggle against slavery: women found that they were hampered in their good works by being disenfranchised themselves, and moreover were attempting to win for another group a privilege that they themselves did not enjoy.

At the same time the enforced leisure of middle-class women was having another major effect. Freed from domestic labour, many women turned to intellectual pursuits. Throughout the nineteenth century women proved themselves capable in a wide number of tasks and professions that had previously been regarded as 'biologically impossible': Florence Nightingale in England and Roman Catholic nuns on the Continent demonstrated that nursing could be both a rewarding and a respectable career; Elizabeth Garrett Anderson not only showed that women could be doctors, but that they could be doctors and still be satisfactory wives. At the very end of the century Helen Fawcett proved that even mathematics were accessible to 'the inferior female brain' by being listed after taking the final exams at Cambridge University as 'above the Senior Wrangler' (a title given to the undergraduate who scores highest in the Mathematics finals). Women were becoming successful writers, artists and performers, thus invalidating the popular idea that women could not be creative. Working-class women, despite the gruelling disadvantages under which they laboured, proved themselves capable of organisational and educational skills, and demonstrated in trade union struggles and in 'all-women' organisations like the Women's Co-operative Guild that they could indeed co-operate with each other and with men. Although the professional standing achieved by some remarkable women did not immediately change the plight of the vast majority of well-socialised 'angels in the home' or women sweated workers, it did dent the assumption that women had to be protected and cossetted because they were physiologically incapable of independent thought or autonomous action. The churches' refusal to grant women any sort of leadership, or even partnership roles, began to seem increasingly reactionary – a fact complicated by the divine inspiration that many women were claiming for their progressive activities.

Throughout the same period a number of very different changes were taking place which would make the explosion of 'women's theology' possible nearly a hundred years later. The churches, despite passionate rearguard actions, were forced gradually to assimilate a number of scientific discoveries. Darwin's discovery of evolution and the effect that it had on the authority of Biblical accounts is perhaps the best known of these discoveries, and its effects were shattering. But biological evolution was only one aspect of the intellectual impact. The new schools of Biblical scholarship, which started in Germany but spread throughout Europe, had an even more devastating effect on Christian understanding, particularly as the scholars were often convinced Christians and could not be dismissed as 'enemies of the faith'. The basic impetus behind this scholarship was to look at the social and historical context of the Biblical texts, an activity made possible by the development of archaeology, and linguistic and anthropological studies. The understanding that the Gospel texts, for instance, were not eye-witness accounts, or that the history of the Old Testament was not in accordance with literal truth, opened up new possibilities for interpretation, undermined Christian fundamentalism, and brought the possibility of change within the imaginative grasp of Christians.

The development of economic theory – whether by Marx or Adam Smith – revealed the immense complexity of historical and ethical issues. The work of Freud undermined the understanding of free will, and therefore of sin and guilt on which so much of Christian theory and practice was built, still further. The increase of democracy, and in many countries the total abandonment of monarchy in favour of republicanism, destroyed the core of much traditional Christian imagery. Not just women but all sorts of Christians were increasingly realising that they could not, in conscience, back the political status quo against the just desires of the oppressed. Although these were diverse and isolated elements, and it is important to recognise that many people were quite untouched by them, none the less they produced a current of unease, and an openness to new possibility throughout all the churches. The success of both Methodism and the Catholic Revival in Britain, the explosion of evangelical and pentecostalist sects in the USA, and the divisions of the Roman Catholic Church throughout Europe and the USA can, in retrospect, all be seen as signs that Christianity was being deeply affected by apparently 'secular' developments of the nineteenth century.

The first half of the twentieth century saw these unsettling currents accelerate. The privatisation of religion at the beginning of the nineteenth century and the ethical concerns thrown up by the industrialisation of much of the Western world led in some cases to a reaction in favour of a more 'social gospel' – the idea that Christians had particular duty, which should take priority over private and independent salvation, to identify with the oppressed and involve themselves in social and political action. As a further development progressives began to adopt political analyses of oppression and identify themselves clearly with political stances, often socialist and communist. This led to a new school of theology, known as 'liberation theology'. Although liberation theology explicitly grows out of specific situations and therefore lacks a single coherent creed, it is a powerful tool for those who desire social change. Often, as in South America, it is closely connected to Marxist doctrines and its drive is to face up to the implications of political reality. If it is true that Christians have a natural identity with the oppressed, and if economic analyses of poverty and oppression are correct, then traditional philanthropy is no more than self-indulgence and actually helps to maintain oppression. Hence, liberation theologians argue, it is the duty of Christians to ally themselves with those groups who seek to end oppression by political means. Living on a hope of 'joy after death' or in the conviction that Christ has already won the victory so that class and economic oppression do not matter any more are unacceptable positions in the face of the gospel mandate. Liberation theology stresses a gospel priority of justice and freedom over the more traditional images of a God of peace and gentleness. (Often these qualities are subsumed into definitions of love itself – a point often ignored by critics of liberation theology.) A vital tenet of liberation theology is that the understanding of the Incarnation commonly held by the Western churches is seriously inadequate. The humanity of Jesus means the solidarity and identification of all Christians not just with each other, but more importantly with all oppressed, enslaved people. Traditional theology has reduced the significance of God becoming human, and still applauds a passive waiting for an Old Testament God to swoop down and do 'the liberating' for and to his people – probably after they are dead. On the contrary, argue liberation theologians, the Incarnation put both the responsibility and the power to transform the world into the hands of human beings, who therefore have an obligation to act in the most affirmative ways. Enduring passively any deprivation of liberty or dignity is thus changed from being a virtue worthy of future reward into a serious breach of Christian duty – a sin itself. The implications of this for women are clear.

In the 1960s many of these apparently disconnected ideas came together explosively. Even with a whole decade now separating us from the 1960s there seems to remain a feeling that it was a time when some things really happened: from the birth control pill and the Beatles, to the Paris student riots, the USA race riots, and the final collapse of the Western dreams of empire. A major, world-wide challenge to Western cultural dominance was launched from a surprisingly wide range of sources. Students, racial groupings, the economically oppressed, the ecologically minded on behalf of the natural universe, and towards the end of the decade women on their own behalf expressed their disillusion with those in authority, and a belief that things could be changed.

The Christian churches, suffering from declining numbers, loss of self-confidence, and genuine self-criticism, began a move towards their own renewal. This took many forms – an increasing recognition of the spiritual values of other faiths, a new commitment to ecumenism, a re-assessment of their organisational and ministerial structures. Perhaps the clearest outward and visible sign of an inward regeneration was the calling of the Second Vatican Council by the Roman Catholic Church. That most unchanging of the major denominations expressed its willingness to re-examine everything, both theologically and in practice, with a commitment to change.

Simultaneously, the growth of 'liberation' movements – groups of people who felt that their prime commitment had to be to their own self-development and freedom – of many types inspired certain women to re-examine their position and the progress they had made over the first half of the century. The Women's Movement was re-born, but this time with a significant and fundamental difference, from its previous manifestations. Women no longer demanded parity with men simply in the traditional fields of civil rights; they began to demand a total change in the whole structure and ideology of society. The movement saw itself as autonomous, independent and potentially-revolutionary, whether in alliance with the organised left (socialist/Marxist feminists) or completely separated from all other tendencies (radical/revolutionary feminists).

On the whole the Christian renewal movement and the Women's Liberation Movement had little or nothing to say to each other. The churches, heavily male-dominated at every level – except membership – were not much aware that there really was a 'women's question' that they needed to address themselves to. In hindsight three petitions that were presented to the Second Vatican Council – one suggesting that Thomistic theology was obsolete when dealing with questions about women because of its erroneous biological basis; another requesting the admission of women to the priesthood and diaconate; the third asking for the elimination of 'male-only' language from the official liturgy of the Church – seem prophetic and significant, but the truth is that they were little commented on and were lost under the wave of changes which were generated. The Women's Movement paid even less attention to the Church, except to analyse its historical record and declare that 'The Church is the Enemy'[8] – the perfected tool for the oppression and subjugation of women.

This was particularly true of the European Women's Movement. With a stronger socialist bias than the movement in the USA, and yet more easily able to see the 'enemy at home' than the Third World movement, it was less interested, and has remained less interested, in spiritual and metaphysical arguments. Following Marx's idea that 'religion is the opiate of the masses' it has consistently rejected not just formal Christianity, but many other cultural and individualistic considerations. These all surfaced more easily in the USA where the Women's Movement has always been more likely to stress individual and cultural advances. The Women's Movement in the Third World is different again because women there have a different history, and because they have a clear common cause with progressive man against an *external* oppression. The idea of proposing a *separate* list of women's demands (as opposed to a more holistic, unified liberation platform) is less immediately necessary or desirable. The particular impact of Christianity on Third World countries is also complicated: it has frequently been a special vehicle of oppression, but it has also, as in South America, proved a dynamic inspiration for change.

Gradually over the last twenty years, however, women's demands are coming more and more into direct confrontation with Christianity. This is partly because the ideas inherent in feminism have spread very much more widely than might at first be thought. Women who would hotly deny that they had any connection with 'women's lib' none the less have totally different expectations for their lives than they did thirty years ago. Inevitably this expansion has involved women who have deep commitments to their churches – a place where middle-class women particularly have had considerable scope to exercise their talents, albeit within a restricted sphere. Such women often very much want to stay within their churches if it is at all possible, but at the same time are obliged, in the light of their new understanding, to demand certain changes from those churches. Many, however, want to go further than that; it is not simply a question of making the churches tolerable places to live, grow and worship. There is also the crucial business of prevailing on the churches to be true to themselves and to their mission – which seems, in the light of the insights of the women's movement, to require deep-rooted change.

There is a final element that was necessary before Christian women could turn to their own organisations and demand radical change, collectively and determinedly: Hope. The heady optimism of the 1960s provided that. It was vital. Their church for most committed Christians is a place of love and support: to turn one's energies to struggling with it needs a great confidence that change is possible and is really likely to improve things. I was a student in 1968; years later it is easy to see that we were frequently wrong and even feckless. But it is more important to understand the chaotic creative optimism which allowed us to believe that change was not only possible, but practically certain. All things could be and would be made new. We could fly to the moon, stop the US government fighting the Vietnamese War, end class and gender divisions, conquer poverty and sexual hang-ups with the Pill, save the whales and (if we wanted to) still believe in Jesus.

The importance of this optimism is not that it was wrong or right, but that people believed in it. True Hope is the power for transformation – which is why Christianity has always regarded it as one of the three great virtues. Without that hope energy cannot be released into action, nothing can be created. Once there is hope everything becomes imaginable; if something is imaginable it is worth fighting for.

The 1960s created that sort of hope for many different people, including women, the churches and women in the churches. The collapse of that optimism does not change the fact that a wave of energy was released. In the cynical, morning-after feeling of the 1970s the new ideas still had a veracity which could not be denied just because they were not going to be realised immediately. There was no going back to where we were before.

The awareness that there was some discrepancy between the teachings of Christianity and its actual treatment of its own women members was not invented in the 1960s; but many of the buried issues surfaced into popular consciousness then. What had appeared as isolated injustices were now understood to be connected parts of a complex pattern called 'sexism', which would not really be eliminated by piecemeal reforms. In 1968 Mary Daly, then a respected Catholic academic, published a book called *The Church and the Second Sex*[9] which outlined the grim history of women in Roman Catholicism and optimistically called for some basic improvements in the light of the Second Vatican Council. The added dimension of this book, and what made it a turning point, was that it described sexism in a coherent and detailed way – not picking on individual discriminations, but showing the underlying anti-woman bias of Christian theology.

In 1970, with the secular Women's Movement beginning to attract increasing public attention and with women genuinely beginning to change the way they were thinking, another book was published, again in the USA, edited by Sarah Bentley Doely, called *Women's Liberation and the Church*.[10] Daly's book had been expressly about the Roman Catholic Church and had been intellectual and philosophical. Doely's book contained seven personal essays describing the painful experiences of women from assorted denominations. Common to every essay was the idea that the admission of women to 'visibility' and equality was not merely a matter of 'individual freedom of choice', but vitally necessary for the churches to fulfil their self-proclaimed mission. One of the contributors, Davida Crabtree, went further by suggesting that sexism was not simply disabling and constraining for individual human beings, but was actually hampering society in all its 'justice' efforts, particularly in its attempts to deal with war, pollution, poverty and racism. The agenda, so to speak, was set.

Women, with their consciousnesses raised by the new Women's Movement, felt that those attributes commonly designated 'feminine' – and dismissed, despised or punished – were godly, god-imaged, and had to be incorporated into, and manifested by, any organisation that claimed to be the Body of Christ. Understanding the authority of baptism, the gospel that Jesus preached and the clear teaching of the early Church, women were genuinely surprised and appalled at the deep resistance they encountered from their churches. They were forced to look theologically at the reality of sexism, both in the present and in the history of the Church, to discover what possible value it held that could lead to its passionate defence.

Theories and applications proliferated throughout the 1970s, but there now seems to be an emerging consensus that the root of the problem is a very ancient Christian heresy. Dualism, for all the different ways it is structured and all the different names it is given, means splitting the wholeness of God's creation into divisions labelled 'good' and 'bad'. The Hellenistic model, on which so much Christian theory was based, was deeply dualistic – that matter (reality or flesh) was inferior to spirit, which sought to escape from the bodily trap. Jewish culture, from which Christianity sprang, was at its best deeply un-dualistic: it did not believe in a difference between soul and body, classically it did not even believe in an 'after-life'. It did not believe in a real division between a person and society, or between God and God's work – shown in creation and in history. God was not known by mystical contemplation of abstracts, but in the history of God's people. For early Jewish Christians the Incarnation of Jesus, fully human, fully divine, reasserted that matter was good; that the life of the community was not antithetical to individual liberty, and that all contributions and talents were of equal value to the whole. Dualism asserts the opposite – as soon as one begins to believe that certain qualities (nature, body, weakness, disability) are bad and opposed to God there is the desire to project them outwards, away from oneself. Dualism is a fundamental *ground of oppression* – the ability to assert that me and mine are better than that which is Other, and justifying this by making God, the ultimate Other, over in one's own image. It is worth noting that people do not create dualistic systems which put themselves, or their own group at the bottom of the division. Dualism means the emotional and intellectual justification of elitism: theoretically that need not be true, historically it always has been so.

Feminist theology perceives that dualistic splits are the cause not just of sexism, but of racism, classism and ecological destruction. This is why, at its core, the feminist struggle within the churches is of crucial importance, and especially in the West. Sexism is not only one of the primary symbols of division (God as male, nature as female, for instance) it is also the one mode of dualism which the

First World is obliged to confront. The West has effectively distanced itself from the threat of the Other – as represented by poverty, powerlessness and even to a degree of race. It is possible for most of us to muddle through without being too directly confronted by the real humanity of these groups. It is not so possible to avoid the Otherness, the division between men and women. Male hierarchical systems must resist the claims of women to be fully human, fully divine, because labelling women as lesser is the protection from Other that they need. Women, however, through the history of the last twenty years have increasingly faced up to the fact that it is in themselves that Dualism lurks, that we have assimilated all the projections into self-hatred, self-abnegation, self-assertion, the denial of sexuality, the safety and comfort of projections, both as protagonist and victim.

Of course the way that sexism operates in society is more complicated than this, precisely because women are members of every class; the cultural bias that symbolises God as male does not stop there, it is a bias in favour of seeing God as male-ruling-class; not as male garbage collector, but as a male king or elite warrior.[11] In trying to bridge the gap between male as central and female as aberrant, women hope that they will force the Christian churches to recognise the dualism that is buried in all of us, and which distorts our relationships, not only to each other but to the whole world.

Against this dualistic tendency women oppose various models. For most of this book I shall be looking at the specific issues on which women are attempting to challenge the existing models. I turn to specific issues because as a Christian it seems to me that this is the way we are supposed to proceed. The Incarnation did not happen 'out of the blue'; some theoretical guidelines were laid down, hence the Christian respect for the Old Testament; but nor did it have to wait until everyone had grasped the analytical background. God acted, did something, and left us with the responsibility of drawing conclusions and meaning from the act itself. Jesus did not wander round Palestine with *The Encyclopedia of Christology* under one arm; nor at Pentecost did the Holy Spirit whizz in and lay six volumes of *Canon Law and Ecclesial Polity* on the table before retreating to a heaven 'up above'.[12] The word was made flesh and acted (lived) among us.

None the less I only take specific issues because I believe that they reveal the underlying challenge, which is a prophetic one: the task of reminding the churches of their basic calling – to act on behalf of the oppressed, to lay claim proudly to our identity with the oppressed, to realise that it is God who is Other, and we, the whole created order, who are united.

The women's issue raises for the churches a challenge to their whole model of 'ministry'. Since Jesus was clear that it was service, ministry, that counted, the way in which we perceive ministry is important. The Christian churches carry round a crippling mis-understanding of ministry as something done *by* one person *to* another. This division into subject/object, active/passive, or as the traditional imagery of Christianity expresses it male (God, Jesus, the priesthood) and female (the Church, ministered *to* by the priest-hood), is a perfect example of how dualistic division works. Moreover, the identification of Christ as both king and servant has helped in the corruption of his own model of ministry. An example of this identification is the description of the Pope as 'the Servant of the Servants of God', coupled with the fact that he is infallible. A servant is precisely not infallible, a servant is one who does what she is told. Very often Christians who act the *kingly* role of Christ (one that he was extremely reluctant to act himself) claim that they are acting the servant role, whereas in fact (like the medieval monarchs who with spices pressed to their noses descended among their poor one day a year to wash their feet) they are just kings play-acting.

This model of ministry is very bad for everyone involved. Too frequently the active 'ministers' develop inflated egos, a sense of being indispensable. They may also tend to be less and less able to relate to other people as people, rather than as objects for their activity, and are cut off from fellowship. Moreover, since they have reduced themselves, as well as their objects, to a set of functions they often become alarmed if these functions are threatened. Meanwhile those on the passive side become just that – passive, dependent, childlike and often seething with resentment which has no way to express itself as they do not have a framework which might allow them to assert that they are as 'good' as the person who is making them feel so 'bad'.

Not only is this an unhealthy model, it is also a non-Christian one. Jesus says that it is 'more blessed to give than to receive'. This means that anyone who is in a position to be 'ministered to' – able to express their needs to another – and accept that ministry is also and equally 'ministering' in that they are allowing the other person to gain some of Jesus' promised blessedness. In parts of Hindu India tradition dictates that if you give money to a beggar *you* should thank the beggar, since by begging he has given you an opportunity to do a good deed. Here there is a glorious circularity. The question must be asked – who is 'ministering' to whom? And the answer is that this, like all other loving exchanges between people, is a case of mutual ministry – we are ministering to each other, serving one another. The Bible gives innumerable examples of such mutual ministry: the Old Testament story of Ruth and Naomi is a powerful instance: Naomi, by being willing to free Ruth from her social obligations, allows Ruth also to give her one of the most beautiful expressions of love that we know of. But perhaps the finest example of all is in St Luke's story of the Visitation. Mary, newly pregnant in rather complicated circumstances, rushes off 'with great haste' to visit her middle-aged cousin. Mary thus initiates the cycle; but 'as soon as the voice of her greeting' sounds in Elizabeth's ear, it is she who moves to affirm Mary's vocation – 'Who am I that the mother of my Lord should come to me?' This is the first time that Mary has received any confirmation or support for her curious and isolated vocation. Now they are ministering to each other – Mary by coming, Elizabeth by affirming Mary. And in this mutual exchange of love and support Mary can go further, she is able to rejoice in her special vocation. To the angel she indicated consent, now she exults – 'My soul magnifies my God . . . my spirit rejoices in my saviour . . . all generations shall call me blessed.' And from the core of her own joy she can prophesy to the joy that God wants to give to all 'the servants in their lowliness' – the hungry will be filled, the humble exalted.

This last point is important. It is too easy for mutual ministry to degenerate into an excuse for the poor and oppressed to remain poor and oppressed so that the rich may be ministered to by giving them a chance to minister. We have to accept absolutely Mary's realisation, unambiguously expressed in the *Magnificat*, that

> in liberating humanity God functions with a bias on the side of those who have been humiliated, in order to create the transformation by which everyone can indeed be accepted as equal. Everyone cannot be accepted as equal in the present system. If you say that God loves the rich and poor *alike* you are not saying what Mary says.[13]

All of this is not meant to be an abstract sermon on ministry. The experience that women have *now* of coming together and finding strength there; of organising in a way that is deliberately non-hierarchical, non-judgmental, non-dualistic; of structuring corporate activities according to need and affection, rather than along some pre-given lines of efficiency, or tradition, or propriety – is precisely the model of Christian ministry which most of the churches seem to have lost sight of. Of course there have been other models of this: Scots Gaelic, for example, does not have a word for *servant*: the balance of authority and responsibility was so well integrated in the clans that individuals did not perceive themselves in a 'servant' relationship to their chief. I am talking about a precise moment in history – in which women, emerging, have found a model *now* to meet a need. It is of course not any innate superiority in women which has given them this rôle, but an historical chain of events.

Not only has the model of 'servant' been debased by play-acting, but the model of 'brotherhood' seems to have gone the same way. What populist anthropologists have chosen to call 'male-bonding' (a quality that most of them insist is markedly lacking in women) has been shown up, by themselves, to be governed by aggression, territorial imperatives and the need to subjugate other groups. Additionally most service roles have been designated as 'feminine'. Brotherhood has thus become a concept rather alien from the mutual ministry and loving service espoused, at least nominally, by Christians. Now the word 'sisterhood' better describes the true model of Christian ministry: mutual and non-dualistic. Sisterhood is a way of relating to other people which has existed, despite being ignored and insulted, for generations, but which now is both proclaimed and practised within the women's movement.

For Christian women the consequence of this understanding must be active. In obedience to God there is no escape from this engagement: with the tradition itself in terms of study, history, theology; with the present – both with the worshipping life of the community and with the political realities and specific issues. We are committed to this engagement because we cannot ask our churches to minister to us; in the light of the understanding of mutual ministry we have also to minister to them.

The Body of Christ (as Paul does *not* say) is a pregnant body; pregnant with the new birth, the New Creation, pregnant with

Salvation. Throughout the Church's history, group after group, and individual after individual from within the Christian community have been called upon to be the midwives to this pregnancy. Now it is women who after centuries of repression (of talents, symbols, values and authority) are demanding their place in the body that sought to exclude them. As a group which is seen as Other by those with power, we can act, if we will, as a guide to the ultimate Other – God. People are not comfortable experiencing Other-ness: the normal response is either to deny its value (as has been done to women, coloured people, other cultures and classes) or to incorporate it, to deny its Other-ness. In standing up to claim that women (as one *sign* of all such groups) are in the image of God, we are not merely claiming 'rights' for ourselves but expanding the imagination and knowledge of everyone who will look and listen. It is in this sense that feminists are right when they claim that the Liberation of Women will lead to the liberation of men also. On a simple level this is a con trick, a lie – women are demanding that men give up their power and authority. It is only when the religious aspects of all this are recognised that men can hope to profit by expanding the recognition of what is both normal and holy to embrace women – and other groups. Giving up power is not easy, recognising that the things you have labelled as Other are not only fully human but are part of yourself is not easy; it is easy to hear and not to understand, to see and not perceive.

But the situation is now extremely serious. Two-thirds of the world are undernourished, while the remaining third kills itself with obesity; there is an ecological crisis of, as yet, unimaginable proportions; an international war economy and war psychology daily threaten the world with extinction. Almost every human being who has breath to spare from the struggle to survive at all is so eaten up with loneliness, guilt, self-loss, alienation and bondage that mutual love is little but a sentimental utopianism. Anything that offers any hope for real change cannot be other than beneficial.

The demand that women are making of their churches and of the world, for full humanity, is – or can be – the prophetic voice crying in the wilderness for a return to God, to adventure and to hope.

CHAPTER 2

WOMEN TOGETHER

-------- ◆◆◆ --------

In a large modern hotel room outside Atlanta, Georgia, USA, about a dozen women are gathered. One of them, an ordained United Churches of Christ minister, is telling a story:

> There was a small rural congregation which for the first time ever had appointed a woman minister. This congregation had a tradition whereby the two senior deacons always took the new minister out for a day's fishing – as a friendly greeting and a way of getting acquainted. With some trepidation they extended the invitation to their woman minister. Once they had rowed their boat out into the middle of the lake, she realised that she had left her rod on the shore. Apologising, she stepped over the side of the boat, walked across the surface of the water, picked up her rod and started back. One deacon turned to the other and said – 'Now isn't that just like a woman – forgetting her rod like that.'

The women roar with laughter; an astonishingly rich and healed laughter. Most of the weekend is spent laughing – also drinking, eating, swimming in the pool, talking and singing. The group of women is very mixed, in age, background and life-style: the oldest is in her late sixties, the youngest her early twenties. Some of the women are married with children, some single, some gay – there are two couples there. One woman is black. All have left extremely busy lives, and in some cases dependent families, for the simple pleasure of being together for the weekend. There is no 'business', no agenda, no work to be done – apart from a desultory conversation about mothers (interesting because some of the women speak from the standpoint of being mothers with grown-up daughters as well as being daughters while some are daughters only) and an eagerness for me to tell them about the Women's Movement in Britain, there are no 'serious' discussions. This is not a meeting, it is a time for being together and loving each other. The only thing that these women have in common is being women and being involved, as women, with their churches. About half are professionally employed by the institutional churches: two are ordained ministers; one woman is the personal secretary to one of the ministers.

The group has taken a long time to build. Normally they meet about once a fortnight in the houses of the members. Because of their different life-styles and professional commitments it is quite rare for everyone to be at a meeting. They do not feel that this matters, the group was there for the individuals, not the other way around. During the course of the week-end someone read a letter she had received from an ex-member of the group who had moved to another part of the country: the letter expressed both a real sense of loss – the writer missed both the group and the individuals in it – but it also expressed the hope that what she had experienced in Atlanta could be reconstructed elsewhere; because she had learned what everyone in the group clearly recognised: the need that women have for each other and a willingness to make time for that as a priority in her life.[1]

This is the alternative model of organisation that women want to offer to the Christian denominational churches. A model of mutual ministry which at its best is no less efficient than the old hierarchical model, but which is more supportive of the talents of all the individuals concerned, more open to change, and more loving of the individual members of the organisation.

Interestingly Christian women were among the first to organise in 'women only' groups. The Feminist Movement of the 1960s and 1970s did not invent them. From the nineteenth century women in the churches have demonstrated the falseness of innumerable myths which continue to beleaguer the Women's Movement. The mythology which says that women cannot work together; cannot co-operate; are petty-minded, tyrannical, bossy and incompetent; lack a sense of humour and the ability to 'bond'; are gossipy, treacherous and boring, has been absorbed by most women from our childhood. Pauline Webb reports her own experience when the World Council of Churches' Women's Desk proposed its first Conference on Sexism, in Berlin in 1974:

I must confess that when people first discussed it I pressed very strongly that it should be men and women together; but the other women resisted this. In the end I bowed to their wisdom but inside myself I thought, 'How awful spending a whole week just with women.' I think it's my conditioning, I've been taught to think that I can't really enjoy myself unless there are men around, let alone have a good conference.[2]

But the historical facts are quite the opposite; the 'prodigious influence' of autonomous Christian women's groups was commented on the 1842. This long history is something that Christian women have to offer the secular Women's Movement as much as the other way around. I remember a National Conference of the Federation of Women's Aid – the British organisation which campaigned against domestic violence, and for the rights of Battered Women. There was an acrimonious debate about whether or not men should be allowed to attend the meeting. Finally a woman said that she could not understand the problem; she had been brought up in a middle-class household where her mother was a committed member of the Mothers' Union (an Anglican women's organisation) and there had never been any question in the minds of the women that, of course, women met and worked alone, without men. She could not understand why Women's Aid, a supposedly feminist organisation, should have doubts and problems about something which the Mother's Union had solved in the nineteenth century.

In the USA Virginia Baron, the Communications and Interpretations Officer for Church Women United – a grass-roots ecumenical women's organisation – developed this idea even further:

I've been involved in the secular and the Christian women's movement. From the earliest days with the secular movement I'd come home from meetings with a splitting headache, because women were literally screaming at each other – everything tore us apart. In the churches we have this very ancient heritage, going back before the emancipation movement, to the missionary societies of which our great-grandmothers were a part. Then our mothers came along in the church women's organisations – service organisations mostly – but they learned how to work together, how to organise together. Women in the church have provided a great deal which hasn't perhaps been recognised, but the women who come out of those backgrounds know so much better how to keep things together. We know that it isn't easy; but it's in your blood, in your growing up that *of course* women can work together with other women.[3]

This ancient heritage is now joining with the newer, more conscious theories of organisation models which the Women's Movement has developed. 'The consciousness-raising group' is the basic structure of the Women's Liberation Movement. Such groups have built into themselves a series of assumptions which are frequently, and sometimes wilfully, misunderstood by those outside the movement. With certain variations all these groups reject leadership and hierarchy, and specifically reject tightly organised structures and channels of command; they proclaim the absolute parity of all members and believe strongly in blurring the distinction between the personal needs of individual members and the aims or business of the group. Within such groups there is a move away from majority rule in favour of seeking a consensus opinion: this is coupled with a theoretical willingness to devote hours of time to finding and consolidating that consensus rather than utilising the democratic short-cut of the vote which will inevitably polarise the participants and can too often mean that issues are not discussed with an open mind. Another noteworthy characteristic of these women's groups is the combining of the social and the business aspects of a meeting. When the theory behind the structure of these groups is coupled with the current Christian struggle against the dualities of hierarchy/mass, clergy/lay (shepherd/sheep), active/passive, the God-out-there/the sinner-down-here, then the possible implications of the feminist-structured group become clear.

There is sometimes a superficial tension between these new radical Christian feminist groups and the older, often highly organised, denominational church women's societies. It is too simple to see these two groups standing in opposition to each other while the institutions get on with the real work of Christianity. It is easier to emphasise the differences than to recognise the fact that both sorts of groups are places for women to exercise their own authority and skills and to evolve their own patterns of administration. In the case of the denominational societies their opposition to their own bureaucracies is not always conscious, and indeed is frequently denied. But the reality is there and it is becoming increasingly recognised. Thus my mother, Hope Maitland, a National Vice

President of the Church of Scotland's Women's Guild wrote to me in a letter:

> Dad said that under your influence I had become much more women's lib in my attitudes. Certainly you have made me more aware of the difficulties faced by women, but *Church of Scotland Ministers have really taught me what discrimination is all about.*[4]

When the historical knowledge that 'of course women can work together with other women' is combined with the new experience, women can build a base from which they can demonstrate new patterns of mutual ministry.

I have suggested already that the confining of middle-class women to the home, and simultaneously giving them the 'moral' responsibility for the state of the nations, led to rapid developments in their self-awareness. One of the forms this took was the founding of societies and organisations which were understood as a natural extension of women's domestic role into the family of the Church, and indeed the family of the world. For women otherwise trapped at home with domestic affairs the effect of being able to associate with others for 'holy' purposes must, apart from anything else, have provided a considerable social outlet. The number of societies that women found to join witnesses as much to their isolation and boredom at home as it does to their spiritual and philanthropic zeal. On her death in 1826, which was before the boom in women's church societies really developed, a Mrs Susan Huntingdon in Boston was a member of the Female Orphan Asylum Society, the Graham Society (founded by Isabella Graham for the relief of widows and orphans), the Female Society of Boston and Vicinity for Promoting Christianity among the Jews, the Female Bible Society of Boston, the Widows' Society, the Boston Female Education Society (for educating ministers, incidently, not females), the Old South Charity School Society, the Boston Female Tract Society, and the Boston Maternal Association.[5]

Although the aims and functions of these societies were seen, even by their members originally, as being only a small extension of the 'woman's natural role', and they were kept firmly under the guarding hand of the clergy, these societies had two very important effects. First women were there able to learn skills to which they had no other access: handling money, publishing appeals to the public, running meetings and making speeches. Moreover, and more significantly, the members of these philanthropic organisations found 'their sympathies and thoughts became active and enlarged far beyond the bounds of hearth and nursery' and by the middle of the nineteenth century some women began to apply 'the zeal and strength of newly exercised freedom' to the cause of women's rights[6] while arguing throughout that they were only doing the Lord's work.

The radicalising effect of these associations of middle-class women also worked in another direction; they increasingly recognised that their own interest, as women, lay together, and sometimes in opposition to their duty to their homes and to men. This mutual support allowed them considerable reflection on the whole role of women in their society. One organisation resolved that its members were 'never to make an illiberal remark . . . respecting the performance of any of the other members; neither shall they report abroad any of the transactions of the society to the prejudice of any of its members.'[7] Thus women who had been confined to the home on the grounds that they were the purer conscience of the nation took their role extremely seriously and throughout the century harrassed men and male institutions with precisely this God-inspired conscience.

In America, however, the abolition movement, and in Britain the growth of the labour movement, began to draw the most energetic women out of the church organisations altogether. As more opportunities were opened up to women the churches ceased to be the only place in which they could exercise this role; very often the women who remained within the church structures were rendered increasingly nervous of being identified with the feminists and began to turn their attentions elsewhere. The second half of the nineteenth century saw the great rise of the women's missionary societies. Women of energy and skill, denied admission to the authorised ministries of their churches, took their vocations overseas where they were able to exercise leadership and ministerial authority; and women at home increasingly saw that they had at least a vicarious ministry in supporting, training and funding the women missionaries.

By 1900 the sixteen major women's missionary societies in the USA were supporting 856 single women missionaries, 96 doctors and 389 working wives of male missionaries. They were also responsible for numerous orphanages, hospitals, schools and dispensaries all round the world. Perhaps more significantly they were also responsible for the missionary training schools: although these were not technically confined to women they were particularly attractive to women who were barred from all other forms of theological training. Although the courses in these schools were intensely practical, rather than theoretical, they were almost entirely taught by women as well as attended and funded by women. The women's missionary societies worked under enormous difficulties of a practical sort, as well as against the prejudices and limitations inevitably attached to them during that period. One of the principal difficulties was their obligatory autonomy: they were not recognised by the denominations to which they belonged. This meant, for example, that they were generally prevented from raising money in congregational meetings or at general missionary boards which were run by the church establishments.

The success of the women's missionary societies, however, did not work entirely to their advantage in the long run. By the beginning of the twentieth century they had demonstrated to the denominational churches the effectiveness of single missionary women, whom the official missionary societies had resisted. They had also demonstrated that women were experts at raising money and disseminating religious and mission materials, at involving children and youth in the work of the Church, and that practical training courses were a better use of resources than the academic approach preferred by the seminaries. The institutional churches in the first decade of this century began the work of incorporating the women's societies into their own structures. Superficially these consolidations appeared to give the women's missionary societies the recognition they had desired and to herald a new period of 'full co-operation between men and women'.[8] Similarly, the amalgamation of the women's missionary schools with the men's seminaries seemed to give women access to the superior education that men received, particularly as elements of the women's practical approach were incorporated in the new curricula. But women quickly realised that the advantages were frequently outweighed by the loss of autonomy. As early as 1911 one woman mission society leader commented that these amalgamations would only work if women truly received equal standing in the new integrated bodies, but she personally doubted that men would be 'emancipated from the caste of sex so that they could work easily with women, unless they be head and women clearly subordinate'. And so it proved – women were not accepted in the seminaries as teachers, nor did they enjoy even as students the special women's programmes and emphases that they had gained in their autonomous mission training schools; women did not find themselves appointed trustees and governors of the new schools in anything like the proportion that had been used to. And even when the mission organisations committed themselves to protecting women's jobs and preserving a clear role for women's work, they themselves were answerable to the denominational churches, none of which allowed women into the overall structures of leadership. So that even if the proposed merger guaranteed executive positions to the individual women incumbents, on their retirement they were very often replaced by men. Where the new constitutions guaranteed a proportion of executive posts for women – as the Methodist Church in Britain still does – they became a minority, with less authority and independence than before. The number of women in executive roles within the church organisations actually declined from the end of the First World War until about 1970.

The disaffection of women with these new amalgamated mission societies was so quick and so noticeable that the Presbyterian Church in the USA actually commissioned a report in 1927 into 'The Causes of Unrest Among Women of the Church'. The investigating team noted that:

> Among thinking women there arose a serious question as to whether their place of service could longer be found in the church when a great organisation which they had built could be autocratically destroyed by vote of male members of the church without there seeming to arise in the mind of the latter any question as to the justice, wisdom and fairness of their actions. . . . So long as there was a service into which they could put their strength and affection, the women were willing to ignore the disabilities that faced them in general church work.[9]

There were other factors too that led to the decline in the involvement of women with the mission societies. One was the increasing professionalism of the church bureaucracies, and with this the opening of jobs for women. The number of women ordained in those Protestant churches where it was possible – Baptists and Congregationalists for example – rose slightly but significantly in the 1920s and 1930s. Most denominations opened or extended the diaconate or other lay ministries to women during the same period.[10] Outside the churches too there were more professional opportunities for women. This changed pattern led to a decline in the importance of voluntary women's work. Increasingly the common denominational model for women's organisations became the 'women's auxiliary': large organisations, under the control of the denominational structure, whose role was understood as 'separate and not-equal', and whose principal functions were mutual amusement (fellowship) and fund-raising for the church, with little control over how the money they raised was spent.

These sorts of women's organisations now find themselves in a difficult position. The role of auxiliary, or help-meet, is no longer one that women, collectively, are as comfortable with as they were. Over the last fifty years the denominational women's organisations have been places where women of energy and talent have been able to exercise themselves; within their constitutional limits they have also been places where women have been able to be together without the direct interference of the male hierarchies; and, as in the early nineteenth century, they have been a base from which women have been able to develop administrative and institutional skills. But these types of organisation, which exist in every denomination, are now being challenged to redefine themselves in the light of new understandings about women in society at large and in Christianity in particular.

It is worth looking at these organisations and the pressures that they are responding to in some detail, because they reflect so many of the opportunities, difficulties and ambiguities that women, individually, are facing in every other field of church affairs, and because they offer the largest and most coherent group of organised women in the world. The Mothers' Union alone, for example, is the largest single voluntary organisation existing. In order to clarify these points I have chosen two organisations to look at: the Episcopal Church Women of the USA and the Women's Guild of the Church of Scotland.

Episcopal Church Women was founded in 1871 as the Women's Auxiliary to the Board of Missions. It never had the sort of autonomy that other women's mission societies had. It was highly and tightly organised in diocesan chapters and was directed from a national headquarters. Until the 1950s it saw its role, reflecting its title, entirely in terms of service and support – implementing programmes determined by male clergy, at both the parochial and diocesan level. At the national level the Auxiliary had two principal functions. First it ran a delegate conference every three years – The Triennial – which met simultaneously with the National Convention, the executive body and the ultimate authority of the Episcopal Church. These women discussed and voted on the issues as the National Convention and reported their findings to the Convention, though in an advisory capacity only. Throughout this period there were no women delegates to the National Convention, and therefore the Triennial was the only way in which women's views could make themselves heard in the Episcopal Church. Second it organised the United Thank Offering – money contributed by members' donations. This is entirely separate from parochial giving, and is specially designated as money for the missionary activities of the Episcopal Church. Over the years this has developed into an enormous fund, now running to over a million dollars a year, and has financed a large proportion of Episcopalian out-reach programmes both in the traditional overseas mission fields and for domestic developments.

In 1958 the Triennial eliminated the name and assumptions of Auxiliary, and along with that the tight control from national headquarters. This was replaced by far more autonomous diocesan groupings who saw their principal role as developing lay ministries of many varieties. One of the consequences of the shift from the auxiliary model to the autonomous one was that the dioceses, in need of the Episcopal Church Women's organised support for their various programmes, began to find official places for representatives on their executive councils.

With this new structure the Episcopal Church Women, particularly in the Triennial, demonstrated a dynamic progressive approach to social problems, and a willingness to explore and accept change. It moved ahead of the National Convention in its desire to commit the church to affirmative social campaigns. In 1967 the entire United Thank Offering was turned over to Bishop Hines's (the then Presiding Bishop) fund for combating racism and urban poverty – known as the General Convention Special Program. The Triennial's support for this progressive campaign was considerably more uniform and practical than the support given by the institutional church in general and clearly reflected the priorities of Episcopal Church Women. At the same time the Triennial maintained a special interest in women's issues, and here too took a stand often considerably in advance of the

National Convention. At Houston in 1970 and at Louisville in 1973 the Triennial voted overwhelmingly in favour of the ordination of women, although National Convention did not take a vote on the issue the first time and defeated it in Louisville. The Triennial also expressed a special concern for women on a wider basis, for example supporting abortion, and making low-paid domestic workers a special concern.

However, the progress that Episcopal Church Women made in the 1960s created new problems for them in the 1970s. At the General Convention of 1970 women were seated as delegates for the first time. Women in ECW were faced with a difficult choice – either they could maintain a women's voice though without power or they could involve themselves in a male-dominated executive. Some women decided to try for both – Marge Christie, the Newark Diocesan President of the Episcopal Church Women was a delegate both to the Triennial and to the National Convention at Denver in 1979 – but this solution is not a comfortable one. Sue Rich, of the Washington Diocese, decided that she would rather remain within the Triennial structure, partly because she believes strongly in the value of a strong women-only voice. From her own experience she feels that women still find it very difficult to function militantly within the denomination's structures. Both these women, like many others, are caught in a real bind. They have positions of genuine authority within the established women's machine, and a driving commitment towards women's rights and status within their denomination and within Christianity generally. On the other hand they have the feeling, quite common in the USA, that younger women now coming into the institutions do not have the same understanding of sexism and discrimination that their bitter experience has given them and that despite the obvious gains there is a danger that a special and clear 'women's voice' will be lost while it is still badly needed. Younger women are far less ready to become active in Episcopal Church Women than they were, because neither the radicals nor the new conservative women appreciate what the organisation has and could achieve. Martha Blacklock, who is the Archdeacon for Women's Ministries in the Diocese of Newark, sympathetically summed up the problems facing the Episcopal Church Women:

In theory it is an organisation to which every woman belongs, but in fact it's often more like a Guild. They do very interesting things, but they feel most acutely that there are no new women coming in. They are women in their 40s, 50s and 60s and they ask 'where are the others' and there aren't any others.

You can see in the kinds of programmes at the diocesan level that they're interested in the things that the church at large is going to be interested in in a couple of years. They're way ahead. They're certainly ahead of the clergy but you'd never know it, because most of the clergy think 'O yes, the Ladies' and minimalise their contribution. They feel keenly that though they know they're working on ministry, no one else recognises it.[11]

To some extent this dilemma is increased by the admission of women to the priesthood, despite the fact that the ECW has supported this for years. Episcopal Church Women has endeavoured to project a strong image of lay ministry in opposition to the clericism of the church. Now many of the women whose personal authority and charisma used to support that image are themselves becoming priests. There is a danger that the ordination of women will only, in the long term, serve to increase the dichotomy between lay and ordained, rather than eliminate it. Martha Blacklock, herself ordained, experiences many of the same doubts and explains:

If I had spent 20 years of my life in the church as a lay woman and was knowledgeable about all the issues and then some 23-year-old could vote in Diocesan convention as of right and I still had to seek election, I'd wonder, 'Is this going to be of benefit to me or is it not?' and I would wait and see – I think that many women are doing just that; asking 'are the ordained women going to be aligned with the clergy or with women? Are they just going to be more of the same old thing, or are they going to be something different?' Certainly the lay women who worked for ordination did it in the hope that it would really make a difference. That it was really going to be an affirmation of every woman's ministry – and not just symbolically.[12]

The future role of the Episcopal Church Women will undoubtedly be affected seriously by the 'performance' of the new ordained women. The autonomy won in the 1960s is thus undermined by its own success, as was the case with the Mission Societies of sixty years ago. It will also depend on the development of the newer style 'underground' explicitly feminist groups which are appearing. But the 'wait and see' period is none the less extraordinarily frustrating to women who have given so much energy and talent to the Episcopal Church Women, which has provided a vital bridge between the late-nineteenth-century feminism and the Women's Movement of the 1970s

The difficulties of the transition are eased in the USA by the wider spread of the American-style Women's Movement. It was very strange for a British feminist like me to hear rich, middle-aged women with Scarlett O'Hara accents slam their Bishops as 'male chauvinist pigs' and come out strongly for the ordination of gay women. This makes American church women less worried than their British equivalents about take-overs by dangerous radicals. It also gives them a perspective from which to recognise discrimination and understand the value of maintaining a separate women's position – even if the Triennial is technically powerless.

In the Church of Scotland Women's Guild the history is similar but the tensions are more acute, and the solution harder to imagine. The resistance to an explicitly feminist analysis is very strong. The Church of Scotland also presents its Women's Guild with some special problems of its own. While all the denominations in the UK endured (and are probably still enduring) a very difficult period of escalating inflation and declining membership, the Church of Scotland has been worse struck than almost any other. In addition the Church of Scotland is the child of John Knox's interpretation of Calvinism, and formed at a time of political unrest: from these beginnings it has inherited a constitution designed to prevent change. The Church of Scotland was created against a background in which the cultic influences of Roman Catholicism presented a political as well as a spiritual threat and its whole ethos is deeply opposed to feminisation of any sort. Its structured inflexibility combined with its tradition of gospel purity makes any radical challenge extremely difficult. The inbuilt clericism of the Church of Scotland is impressive and designed to keep as much power as possible in the hands of the ordained ministers. Individual congregations are gathered into groups called presbyteries. All ministers, even retired ones, are members of the presbyteries; they sit for life. Elders are supposed to represent the laity on the presbyteries, but they sit in rota and for limited periods. This makes it hard for them to develop the allegiances and political skills which the ministers have. Moreover all elders of a congregation are affirmed in their office by the congregational minister (thus while technically it is possible for women to be elders, ministers who disapprove of this can prevent it happening in their parishes). To complete the conservative orientation ministers need the approval of the presbytery before they can be 'called' by a congregation. Only ministers and elders are eligible for National Assembly and they are appointed by the presbytery.

In the face of this system any struggle for autonomy by the Women's Guild is hard. There is a branch of the Guild in every congregation and these are interconnected at the presbytery level with an overall National Organisation. The congregational Guilds are controlled in two interlocked ways: they are under the authority of their local minister and governed completely by the binding, detailed and restrictive constitution. The constitution covers every imaginable eventuality and includes, for instance, the precise formula for presenting a motion; the sorts of 'service' suitable for a congregational Guild to undertake (the first suggestion, incidentally, is 'collecting flowers, eggs, etc. for hospitals', which is hardly inspirational); and the exact form on which the annual report shall be filled in. This sort of constitution makes it well-nigh impossible for the Guild to import new understandings of administrative structure that grow up in other women's organisations. Moreover the prescribed organisational format is rigidly hierarchical. The fundraising duties of the Guild are made clear, but the branches have extremely limited control over their own spending. The minister and elders can veto any cause that a branch might want to support; and the *maximum* amount that a branch can give to any charity, local or national, is limited to £3.00 per year.

At the national level the Women's Guild is run by a Central Committee which is answerable to General Assembly. The Central Committee cannot initiate new policy programmes nor change the constitutions without the consent of General Assembly. In many ways the Women's Guild is in the position that Episcopal Church Women was before 1958 when its 'auxiliary' status was still clearly defined. In the meantime, however, women's position in the rest of the Church of Scotland has developed much as it did in the Episcopal Church. In 1965 women were officially admitted as elders, although fifteen years later they remain seriously under-represented, and in 1968 were for the first time allowed to be ordained to the full ministry. In the case of the Church of Scotland, moreover, there has always been a full-time professional ministry open to women. The order of Deaconesses not only managed to survive throughout the 1940s, 1950s, and 1960s, it is also a women-only ministry – until 1979 there were no men Deacons. The Women's Guild in the light of developments also added to its problems by creating the Young Women's Groups: these, although the Constitution makes clear that they are a part of the Women's Guild, none the less have some independence. The upper age-limit for the Young Women's Groups is presently forty, and there is also a ten-year limit on membership. Although the purpose of these groups was originally to give younger women a chance of exercising administrative and authoritative roles it may have served only to protect the 'main' Guild from an influx of progressive younger women.

The Guild is now trying to reflect the social development of women and break away from its 'fund-raising and bottle-washing' image, but the difficulties confronting it in this task are enormous. Like most national women's church organisations the work is all voluntary, and this inevitably means that the national executive is substantially composed of middle-class, non-working women. These women in Scotland, unlike their counter-parts in the USA, generally do not have the same popular feminist culture to inform their need for autonomy. The present National President, Daphne McNab,[13] is a minister's wife with a now grown-up family. She is an elder of her local congregation and also a delegate to the National Assembly. More importantly she is an immensely experienced church politician. She was the first woman on the Home Missions Board; she worked on the Deaconess Board during the time that the ordination of women was a political issue. She was a member of the Committee of Forty (a progressive group in National Assembly who proposed major constitutional reconstruction); and she was the first woman convenor-member of the governing body of St Colin's College, the centre for professional lay training. She is well aware of how the discrimination against women works in her church, and is also a person empowered by vision as well as energy. She herself feels keenly the need for women to increase their autonomy and authority and knows that this cannot come just through constitutional changes, but through a raising of consciousness about the way women are oppressed and oppress themselves. She was doubtful about becoming the National President because of what she called 'the obvious relief' of the people she had worked with that she would be withdrawing from wider church affairs, but at the same time she felt that women did have a separate interest and special concerns which the Guild might be able to represent. The ordination of women to the ministry, in her opinion, had achieved less than nothing for women in general and because of the low ideological value the Church of Scotland places on ordination, 'symbolic' victories have little meaning. She felt that the ordination happened too soon in the sense that there was no collective sense of a women's victory, just professional advancement for some individuals. Most of the women ministers, she believes, have identified with ministerial structures instead of with women's oppression. She is convinced that women in the Church of Scotland and especially within the Guild are still over-identified with a service ministry and are therefore not laying claim to their prophetic voice, which is not only theirs by right but is the sole hope for the Church of Scotland at this extremely difficult point in its history. However, she is in an isolated position on most of these matters, and especially in her belief that women must have a better self-understanding before they can serve the church in a realistic and useful way. Because of this isolation she takes up positions that are sometimes peculiar and even counter-productive: after telling me with obvious sincerity that the grass-roots members of the Guild had to stand up and lay claim to their own autonomy, and be challenging about women's social position, she then maintained that the £3.00 rule about donations was neces-sary because women were too easily moved by emotional appeals and could not be trusted not to give all their income away to unworthy causes. It is impossible to dole out liberation from above and the Guild's senior officers seem more determined to 'liberate' the members than the members themselves desire.

The declining membership, with withdrawal of more radical women from the Guild, the existence of the separate Young Women's Groups, plus outside factors like the rigidity of class structures in Scotland, the puritan heritage which prefers good deeds over self-reflection and the narrow dissemination of Women's Movement understandings all combine to make the serious radica-lisation of the Women's Guild extremely improbable.

One of the National Vice Presidents, Hope Maitland, from a much more conservative understanding of the problems confront-ing women, but aware of all the present difficulties, sees a completely different answer to the dilemma – to disband the Guild altogether. She sees it as all too often providing nothing but a slightly self-important ghetto for women like herself who are thus able to escape from the obligations of wrestling with the 'real' church and being brought face to face with the exclusion of women. She feels that at all levels the sort of women that the Guild now attracts are using it as a refuge rather than a dynamic way of confronting both discrimination in the church and other issues of social justice. If the Guild were disbanded women would be forced to look for other ways of exercising both their ambition and their genuine desire to serve God and the world. Moving from a holy clique into specific interest groups would both increase Christian participation in other secular organisations and improve the impact that women would have in General Assembly and elsewhere in the church.[14] It is interesting that with these views both women have accepted office in the Women's Guild, rather than organising radically outside its inflexible structures.

In order to do this they and other women like them would have to take much more seriously the whole detailed analysis of sexism and its implications and they would have to believe in the potency of the alternatives. The idea that women would be better engaged – more pleasantly, more soundly theologically and more effectively – in forming small, unstructured, totally autonomous groups is a discovery that is emerging among Christian women. Rather than try and gain crumbs from the denominational masters in exchange for playing by their rules, women are moving out of the denominational women's groups and forming their own.

Christian women's 'loyal opposition' groups have been around since the 1920s: the International St Joan's Alliance and the Interdenominational Society for the Ministry of Women in the Church are two organisations which have been functioning since the 1920s. Both are reformist groups struggling to gain for women positions within the existing hierarchies, and in that sense are products of the nineteenth-century women's emancipation movement. Groups like these tend to be strictly issue-oriented – and in that sense see themselves as provisional. Over the years their definition of the issues has developed: the St Joan's Alliance did not speak about ordination in its early days, only about the representation of women within their church's decision-making processes. But the approach remains essentially the same: rational, gradualist, and educational.

These groups do not, on the whole, present a critical analysis of the whole structure of the institutional churches' administrative machinery, but rather ask for women to be given a larger slice of the cake.

Other women's organisations like the American Church Women United go further than this. They pick no quarrel with the denominational churches, but simply organise ecumenically for co-operation among lay women in spreading both a social gospel and a shared spirituality. Church Women United have maintained their autonomy almost militantly, including separating themselves from the National Council of Churches under whose umbrella they once sheltered. In some ways women, who have always had less to lose, find informal ecumenical contact far easier than men within the bureaucratic hierarchies do. Deprived of money and outside the legal, property and power structures, ecumenism has a very different context from the high-powered interdenominational talks and schemes. Church Women United do not work on systematic legal amalgamations of denominational structures but rather on free association. They are one of the few ecumenical organisations which have managed to involve the members of the Eastern Orthodox denominations at an active level. One of the products of Church Women United's approach is the Women's World Day of Prayer: although they no longer organise this, as it has developed a separate machinery of its own, it was the brainchild of this group and says much about their methods. One Friday in the spring of every year women throughout the world gather locally and pray the same service which is prepared by a national committee: the committee for the year can pick their own theme and develop it as they see fit. Nationally it is translated and distributed and at the local level readers, preachers and service leaders (all women) are chosen. The massive administrative machinery of this international activity appears to move very quietly and close to the ground, using the women's denominational organisations where necessary, and local ecumenical groups where possible.

Because of its complete separation from all denominational and 'official' machinery Church Women United does hold together almost invisibly a vast network of concerned Christian women in a very different 'service' role from the one demonstrated by the denominational women's organisations. Here the service in question is direct – both to projects and to fellow members, there is no sense of 'servicing' the denominational organisations. Because of the type of structure that Church Women United have chosen for themselves they do still have certain aspects of the older women's organisations: they concentrate on outward-looking good works, and to a specific women's role in performing these good works. Although the issues that they take up – like ecology, women's religious art, pacifism – may not be the same objects as the nineteenth-century women's organisations adopted there are certain similarities in approach – being quietly at work at the roots of society to transform them into holiness.[15]

The newer women's groups repudiate this role altogether. Taking their basic structure from the secular women's movement, not from any Christian model, they deny that they meet as women because women have a separate role. Their claim is that women have to explore their own roots, develop their own theological understandings and create their own forms, both of spirituality and of organisation, because the male model is both alienating to them and unchristian. There are two types of the new women's groups – although it is important to remember that not only do individual women work in both types, but that a group itself may shift its whole focus either temporarily or permanently. There are the 'issue groups', set up to campaign publicly on an issue or collection of issues, which believe in having a public face and confronting the outside world. And there are the more private 'supportive groups' whose function is to explore privately and intimately areas of direct concern to its members.

The gathering in Atlanta, which I described at the beginning of this chapter, is an example of this latter type. Groups like this exist throughout the USA and are springing up increasingly in the United Kingdom also. In Britain many are loosely connected through networks like the *Christian Feminist Newsletter*.[16] This cyclostyled news-sheet is not a policy document but an information service, used for reporting the existence of groups, airing opinion and sharing information. By the very nature of these autonomous cells, there can be no policy; each one has its own pattern, purpose and formulae. Because of this diversity it is hard to say anything general about them collectively.

One of the longest established groups meets in Oxford.[17] This particular group is probably more intellectually oriented than many and also, Oxford, being the sort of town that it is, is fairly homogeneous in terms of the age, class and life-style of the members. It has been meeting for about four years (which makes it older than the average Christian feminist group); they started meeting after two of the current members met at a Roman Catholic ordination and fell into a discussion about whether, were it possible, they would want to be ordained into the existing Roman Catholic institution. Thus they started out with a radical criticism of the institutional Church. They now meet 'slightly more often than once a month' in the house of a member: it is usually the same house because of the baby-sitting problems of one individual. They were positive about this restriction, however, as they felt it had given them a certain useful stability. There are about twelve or fifteen members altogether, although some attend much more regularly than others. They recognise in themselves a range of functions: academic discussion – when I visited them they had been discussing a paper by one of the members on the positive contribution of feminist theology to wider feminist theory; political debate – most of the members are deeply concerned in radical politics, Marxist, Trotskyite and anarchist, and although this had not been a primary concern of all the members they had discussed it extensively; personal support and feminist consciousness-raising. In common with many such groups a great deal of their talking had been about ethical concerns, particularly sexuality, and other forms of exploitation. Because Western ethical positions on sexuality have been formulated almost exclusively by men, and because concerns of sexuality are an area where the differences between men and women are obvious, a great deal of feminist discussion deals with this area. Christian women are no exception; indeed so much guilt and sense of sin has been generated within Christianity around sexual activity it is particularly a Christian concern.

This group has practically no public face at all. They once collectively wrote a long article for a Christian periodical on Christianity and sexism and found that this combined activity in explaining themselves to the outside world was a valuable exercise.[18] Another attempt to do something active and externalised precipitated a very difficult period for them. In response to the 1978 Anglican vote not to ordain women, they decided to initiate a monthly 'women's worship service'.[19] They discovered that their own denominational differences and strategic perspectives differed widely and the attempt to develop these monthly meetings tore the group apart. This problematic honesty about denominationalism is much more likely to emerge in Britain than in the USA where the overall deficiency in ecclesiology makes ecumenism far less challenging. I formed the strong impression that the women in Oxford, unlike many women in the USA, did not identify the group as their 'church', but rather as a place of love, support and strength from which to challenge their own denominational structures and the sexism in society at large. However, the warmth, caring and sisterhood which were abundantly apparent, is in itself a challenge to most of the congregations in which women worship.

This particular example in Oxford is only an example of Christian feminist groups. Just as they denied that there was any such thing as a 'typical meeting', so too it would be impossible to claim that they were a 'typical group'. What they all have in common is a strong belief that efficient and established institutional ways of working are counter-productive, and that it is worth losing out in the race to influence people 'outside' in the short term if that leads to the fuller participation and self-development of the members. They also share a conviction that, as women have been discounted in all the orthodoxies of the Christian tradition, there is no need to assume that what is laid down represents the fullness of truth.

Such groups as the Atlanta and Oxford ones I have described leave open almost all speculative doors. Because the lack of structure and public stance means that the groups do not have to produce a coherent 'position' there is no threat in having members who disagree theoretically, even quite seriously, about issues: 'heresy' is not a dangerous problem, but an interesting idea. After the emotional and intellectual experience of working in this sort of unstructured, anti-hierarachic group, established ideas about the necessity of order, procedure, and protocol appear simply nonsensical; and the hold that traditional methods of organising have over women's imaginations is loosened. The special feminist blend of love and theory can (when not too self-indulgently applied) create a model of sisterhood which is inevitably in opposition to the ways in which the churches currently run themselves. This model seems not only more useful and practical but also infinitely nearer to the most orthodox Christian teachings on community and ministry.

Unfortunately real difficulties are likely to arise when people informed by this understanding try to deal directly with church politics. Groups form around specific issues: ordination, or homosexuality, or contraception, or feminist theology – but in order to have any chance of 'winning' tactical battles they have to go out and confront the organised churches. The institution is dominant in these struggles; they are the status quo and can set the agenda, demand the 'proof' and deny the standing and authority of those who challenge them. Because of this it is too easy to compromise on what is the most important thing that women have going for them – the practice of non-discrimination, of sisterhood.

The women's ordination platform did indeed win the vote at the General Convention of the American Episcopal Church at Minneapolis in 1978. The Women's Caucus, which had formed around the issue and had been defeated in 1973, allowed itself in the intervening three years to be reformed on much more conventional lines, in order to be 'better organised', more attractive to voting delegates and generally more respectable. The overall women's perspective was lost. There was even a serious threat that the Philadelphia and Washington uncanonically ordained women priests would be sacrificed in the drive to appear unthreatening to the established church. Somehow it was forgotten that it was precisely *to threaten* the established church's sexism that the issue of women priests had been taken up in the first place. There is a feeling among some women involved in that fight that less was gained for women in general than might have been, simply because women abandoned their own organisational perspective in order to ingratiate themselves with precisely that structure which they were supposed to be challenging.

Ordination is just one visible issue. The danger of accepting existing structures is a real one as women move out of small-cell groups and try and organise on a larger scale. A better understanding of our own history would be useful here: single-issue campaigns have seldom really worked to women's advantage. The suffrage struggle, for instance, demonstrated convincingly the danger of seeing any single issue as being of such primary importance that other issues are sacrificed for it. Because wider women's concerns were jettisoned in the pursuit of the vote, a heavy price had to be paid in the reactionary use to which the new voters put their privilege, and in the elimination from practical politics of almost all women's concerns for the next thirty years.

There are of course numerous attempts to expand the small-group method of working into larger-scale activities. The Women's Project of the Student Christian Movement, along with other Christian feminist groupings, have organised conferences and events which reflect this way of working. Although the apparent lack of structure on these occasions can be very alienating for women whose first experience of feminism these are, they remain vitally important events. There have been several conferences which have used the open group structure as opposed to the more traditional pattern of lecturer, audience and mediating, controlling chairperson. There have also been very exciting occasions at which the feminist organisation model has been used as the basis for worship – but these will be discussed in the last chapter. One organisation which is trying to carry a feminist approach into a national organisation is the Christian Women's Information and Resource Service. Although grossly underfunded, CWIRS is attempting to run an efficient national information service, including a resource centre, without losing the feminist perspectives on which it is founded. The Ecumenical Women's Center in Chicago attempts the same thing in many ways but it maintains a strong central leadership, whereas CWIRS is attempting to be a group of groups. The secular women's movement is becoming experienced in the conflicts that inevitably arise when a structure that depends on personal trust and respect has to cope with people who not only do not know each other well, but may have good political reasons for distrusting each other strongly. The difficulties that this imposes are not a good reason to abandon the whole vision.

For the Church, as much as for the secular women's movement, it is important that these difficulties are confronted openly and courageously, because it is against the tendency to compromise and isolate that the autonomous women's groups can take a valuable stand. When more people have lived, worked and loved inside such alternative structures it will become clearer that we neither want nor need the existing power monopolies. The exploration of what it means, and the prophetic insight into what it could mean, to be a Christian woman in the widest possible sense; of what it means to love and be loved by, to support and be supported by, ministered to and ministering to other people as equals – these are the experiences which militate against compromise with clericism and dualism. I do not mean that specific campaigns do not have to be fought and won. But unless women are very clearly aware that they have a special access to something which lies at the very heart of Christianity, the individual victories will prove shallow. The history and the present development of women's groups within Christianity say very loudly that women united in sisterhood are not asking the institutional church for any favours, but on the contrary are offering them a gift and a vision. This vision, curiously, was recognised, though without acknowledgment, by the Roman Catholic Church in England in its major study document *A Time For Building*.[20] Here it proposed that the Church of the future could have a completely different institutional appearance: instead of the enormous and often impersonal congregations the local manifestation of Roman Catholicism would be small, closely knit cells of around twenty individual Christians who could mutually minister to each other, and form a base of loving, joyful concern from which to evangelise. *A Time for Building* was variously greeted as visionary or Utopian; but there was little evidence that Christians generally were aware that what this official document was dreaming of was already a reality in the lives of many women. If that fact is grasped the underlying meaning of the apparent confused proliferation of little autonomous women's groups becomes clear. Sisterhood is an institutional model that is already becoming a historical, material reality. The established denominational churches are beginning to seek for that model; women with the experience of it can now offer it to the whole body. That is our service, our ministry, our collective vocation. That model must not be compromised for small gains from a bankrupt bureaucracy.

CHAPTER 3

COMMUNITIES
OF FAITH

------------ ◆◆◆ ------------

Since to err is only human
There's a whole lot on the slate
That I'll have to make account for
When I reach the golden gate;

But then I'm not aworrying
About the deeds I've done;
I'll just whisper to St Peter,
'I'm the Daddy of a nun.'[1]

There is one group of women who have been living for the last 1,700 years with this vocation – the call to be a self-determining women's group living in a close and *useful* relationship with their institutional churches: simultaneously creating something that is exclusively female, and offering back to the Church and the world the fruit of their labours. These are the nuns. They deserve a chapter of their own for a number of reasons.

They are the largest group of 'professional' women Christians in the world; there are over a million of them – mostly Roman Catholic, but a substantial number who are Orthodox or Anglican.[2] They are a genuinely international group; with the possible exception of China (whence there is no evidence) they can be found in every country in the world.

They have a very long and complicated history; for almost as long as organised Christianity has existed women have been organising ways of living which have brought them into conflict with the other structures of the Church. The different attitudes towards them, and the ways in which they have been incorporated, described and regarded by the institution has been a way of understanding how the Church has felt about women more generally. At times they have been the only organised unit which has demonstrated a special and separate role for women, and this has been used both by them and by the hierarchy to define a proper sphere of female activity.

In the last twenty-five years or so they have played a very particular role in the renewal, particularly, of the Roman Catholic Church. The sweeping changes that they have undergone have brought them into conflict both internally and with the ruling authorities of their church, which are of course almost exclusively male. In a sense nuns are a paradigm for the whole argument of this book.

Finally nuns exercise a curious fascination for all sorts of people. They are the group of Christian women who are genuinely 'visible' to the world. This fascination expresses itself in a multiplicity of forms. They suffer from the most outrageous idealisation. Wordsworth, for all his free-thinking agnosticism, still wrote in awed tones of the nuns 'who fret not at their convent's narrow room'. The worldly Alexander Pope, to whom the follies and foibles of everyone else were an open book, wrote:

> Grace shines around her with serenest beams
> And whispering angels prompt her golden dreams . . .
> To sounds of heavenly harps she dies away
> And Melts in visions of eternal day.[3]

While the sentimental trivia of the angelic nuns in *The Sound of Music* or Ingrid Bergman's performance opposite Bing Crosby in *The Bells of St Mary's* present the same picture. The quotation at the beginning of the chapter, apparently worn with a picture of the daughter on the back by some Catholic fathers, makes the point even more clearly. Anyone who has thought at all about the images of women will recognise in exaggerated form the idealised sexless virgin who will work men's salvation for them and love it. While at the other end of the line is the popular image – from Langland's *Piers Plowman* to modern hard-core pornography – of the nun as whore. One of the major aspects of this pornography (and there is plenty of it about) is the sadistic element, complete with whips and jack-boots. At a less overt level this image of nuns as authoritarian, and cruel in their repression, shows up over and over again: the novice mistress in the *Song of Bernadette* and infinitely more sympathetically in Antonia

White's *Frost in May*. This element too is simply one extreme presentation of the popular mythology about women: dangerous, seductive, insatiable and malicious. Cruel, both to themselves and others – frustrated spinsters, and sadistic whores. Coupled with these two elements is the complementary one of 'unnaturalness': living apart from men and assuming roles of authority the nuns of contemporary fantasy are seen as petty, obsessed with rules, humour- less and authoritarian – unwomanly, but failures in a man's world.

Nuns, precisely because they do not belong – as daughters, wives or mothers – to any individual man, can be used safely as a projection of a misogyny which is far more general. I stress this because if nuns carry so much of the weight of an image that is applied more subtly to all women, the ways in which they change and protect themselves is of particular importance for *all* women, and particularly Christian women. This has been one of their imaginative roles throughout their history, but now as they increase their efforts towards self- definition it becomes important for women to look at what they are doing and the responses that this generates.

Before looking at this present history there is an important qualification that has to be made. There are lots of sorts of nuns. Indeed, for the majority the word 'nun' is inaccurate. Most of the 'nuns' that we see on the street are not 'nuns' at all – they are 'sisters'. 'Nuns' are women living in solemn vows, normally contemplatives and usually 'enclosed' (confined to their convents and both protected and controlled by the rules of enclosure which owe their formulation more to the institutional authorities than to the desires of the convents themselves). 'Nuns' include the monastic orders, like the Benedictines, Carthusians and Cistercians. The 'sisters' orders, the active or as they prefer to call themselves the 'apostolic orders', did not at their inception envisage living an 'enclosed' life, but working in the word in various forms of service. The correct term which refers to both 'nuns' and 'sisters' is 'women religious'. Nonetheless I am using the word 'nun' in its popular inclusive sense, despite the fact that many of them will themselves properly disapprove. It is the common term. I, and an increasing number of nuns themselves, find the world 'religious' difficult in as much as it implies that lay women, following their different vocation, are somehow less religious, less holy, and that nuns have a 'better' vocation. Moreover, the word 'sister' and the idea of sisterhood has taken on a new meaning with the growth of the Women's Movement and is used by me in this book in a specific value-laden sense. There is a particular danger of confusion if the word 'sister' is used to describe nuns precisely because so many of them demonstrate that quality of 'sisterhood' that I have already described.

None the less the difference between the 'contemplative' orders and the 'apostolic' ones is important. The problems which they have confronted and their possible futures are not the same; their political standing, their idea of mission and indeed their whole history are so profoundly separate that it is important to see how the two are distinguished. Contemplatives see their primary vocation as that of praising God and redeeming the world through prayer. They can only be seen as separate or cut off from the world by those who do not share their belief in the power of prayer and the community of Christians in the world. Thus they pray and adore for those who do not have the time, the inclination or the means to do it for themselves. This is their principal end, and their starting point: everything is subordinate to this. The original Benedictine rule insisted on a balance between prayer, study and physical labour – but the latter two were to enable the order and the individuals within it to pray *better*. The original purpose of enclosure was not to keep the nuns in, but to keep the distractions of the world out. More recently some orders have seen the need to take the model of contemplation and adoration out into the world – to make it visible to those who were deprived of the knowledge of prayer. So, the Little Sisters of Jesus, for example, who live in tiny groups, in ordinary houses and work in secular jobs still regard themselves as contemplatives, because their life-style and structures are essentially focussed around the business of prayer, of oneness with the adoration of God.

The apostolic orders, on the other hand, although they would see prayer as the essential fuel of their selves and of their work, were formed in order to serve God in the world: to serve Jesus' sisters and brothers in whatever needs they might have. Most apostolic orders were founded with some specific charitable end: educating, healing, converting, for instance. The list of founders' intentions is long; and the sort of work undertaken by apostolic orders has developed still further since the Second Vatican Council, but the basic drive is to active service.

From this very cursory outline the difficulties that the orders encounter may begin to emerge. The contemplative orders have, to a greater or lesser extent, always had the approval of the Roman

Catholic Hierarchy, although they were anathema to the Protestant Reformers because enclosed contemplation can only make sense when it occurs in a denomination with a universalist ecclesiology. If salvation is seen in terms of predestined virtues, and as an individual achievement, then the life of contemplation (especially the forms in which it appeared in the pre-Reformation era) has little value. Moreover the idea of being 'set apart' is antithetical to the original Protestant ethic which stresses family life, hard work and active will. In Catholicism, however, whether Roman, Orthodox or (since the nineteenth century) Anglican, contemplative orders have enjoyed a marked degree of respect. The power and authority of the women's monasteries and the individual women within them has indeed created something of a double bind for women within Catholicism. The great monastic orders undeniably provided a place of learning, autonomy and power for women as well as providing a 'respectable alternative' to marriage for those who wanted such. Individual women have been able to profit from this power base: neither Catherine of Siena nor Teresa of Avila came from a class background which would have allowed them any political, intellectual or administrative standing but for the religious orders. The political influence of Hilda of Whitby far outclassed that of any other woman of her period, and so on. But the threat that this sort of authority might have posed the establishment was vitiated by the extreme asceticism and denial of sexuality that the religious houses practised. In addition, the monastic houses identified their interests with those of the clerical caste rather than with those of other women. The model of the virtuous women with which they provided the Church was anti-sexual, anti-domestic and detached from the world. Women who did not want or were not able to enjoy this position were probably undermined by its very success. The contemplative and virginal life was presented as the best, and at times the only, way for women to achieve holiness and respect within the Christian community; and from this women's own sexuality was devalued and with it the work and calling of the majority of women.

The origins of women's contemplative communities were ancient and the benefits of them, in terms of service to the Church, so clear; they fitted naturally into the mainstream of theology and practice; they represented clearly a fitting image of women. Not surprisingly they presented the hierarchy with little conflict most of the time. Of course they were hemmed around with rules and regulations not of their own choosing, their standing diminished after the end of the Middle Ages, and their lives were by no means easy, but on the whole they were allowed and encouraged to flourish.

The apostolic orders on the other hand presented a greater threat to the Church's masculine-dominated ideology. Women should not be out on the streets alone, visible to everyone and active on their own behalf. Christian women should not be visibly self-ruling, self-determining and choosing their own work without proper reference to the natural higher authority. Above all 'nuns' should be set apart from the world in cloistered holiness – did not Jesus himself say that 'Mary had chosen the better part' while Martha was bustling about trying to be good and getting in the way of the Lord's work? The male hierarchy was continually unhappy about the appearance of apostolic orders and moved quickly to make them as nearly like the contemplatives as possible. This pattern was so consistently repeated that when Louise de Marillac wanted to found an order to work among the poor in the 1630s, whose 'convent is the sickroom, their chapel the parish church, their cloister the city streets' her friend and colleague Vincent de Paul advised her strongly against even trying to claim official church recognition for her Daughters of Charity, as this would bring them immediately under the disciplines of the Church and would make it virtually impossible for them to do the sort of work for which they were being created.

Throughout the nineteenth century, however, the apostolic orders gained a great deal more autonomy and authority. The limited choices for middle-class women was probably one of the factors involved – the apostolic orders grew at an amazing rate throughout the nineteenth century. In the USA for example there were 1,375 nuns in 1850 but by 1900 the number had grown to almost 40,000.[4] But it was not just their numbers which led to their new independence. As important was the increasing respect they gained. The visible and degrading poverty of the new, industrial poor was startling and horrific to the middle-class society that profited from it. Nuns were conspicuous for both the dedication and the competence of their service here, and again in the numerous wars of the century. Florence Nightingale, for example, was immensely impressed not just by the willingness of nuns, but by their excellent training and the opportunities open to them:

No man can tell what [the Catholic Church] is to women, their training, their discipline, their hopes, their home . . . for what training is there compared to that of the Catholic nun? . . . I have seen something of different kinds of nun, am no longer young and do not speak from enthusiasm but from experience. There is nothing like the training in these days which the Sacred Heart or the Order of St. Vincent gives to women.[5]

Well trained and freed from many of the Victorian notions of propriety, the nineteenth-century nuns inevitably attracted praise. A Protestant hospital matron in the American Civil War made the contrast clear:

A very nice lady, a member of the Methodist Church, told me that she would go into the hospital if she had in it a brother, a surgeon. I wonder if the Sisters of Charity have brothers, surgeons, in the hospitals where they go? *It seems strange that they can do with honour what is wrong for Christian women to do.* Well I cannot but pity those who have such a false notion of propriety.[6]

The Anglican orders were able to establish themselves in England, despite strong anti-papalist feeling, principally because of their service during the cholera epidemics and in the Crimean War.

This increased general respect was important but the decisive factor in their self-development was the vast emigration from Roman Catholic countries (Ireland and Italy conspicuously) to the new countries like the Americas, Australia and Canada. Here the European Catholics arrived in an unsettled society which was dominated by a Protestant establishment. It was vital that Catholic communities were held together and their Catholic identity maintained, that they were educated and socially supported by the Roman Catholic Church. Nuns met this need. Initially organised and funded by the mother communities in Europe, they ran the schools, hospitals, parishes, missions and orphanages. They provided the social base for the new communities. They were far away and isolated by distance, slow communications and social difference from their Mother Houses and from the strict hierarchy of southern Europe. They had to make decisions for themselves; they had to alter the rules under which they had lived in the more stable Old World and they had to undertake new types of work as the new needs presented themselves. Both individual women and new orders took a level of autonomous responsibility that had never been experienced before, and this new self-awareness fed back to the countries from which they originally came.

Moreover, the expansion of the nuns' normal world-view was taking place at exactly the same time as the great struggle between conservatives and 'modernists' with the Roman Catholic Church. Modernists wanted the structures and laws of the Roman Catholic Church to take more account of the social and scientific developments going on around them. The political upheavals of the nineteenth century and the growth of democracy and socialism damaged some of the central imagery of the Roman Catholic Church and deeply divided those who were excited by the possibilities and those who were frightened at the changes. The work of the apostolic nuns, busy and independent, must have seemed one more threat to the conservative elements of the church – on their guard already against the dangerous phenomenon of 'Women's Rights'. In the first decade of the twentieth century the conservatives won what appeared to be a decisive political victory. In 1908 modernism was declared to be heretical – anyone who taught, defended or published 'modernist' material was outside the Roman Catholic Truth and could be disciplined, punished and excommunicated. But this was only one part of the consolidation of power within the Vatican that the conservatives wanted. Rome, in two official documents, *Conditae a Christo* in 1900 and the *Normae* of 1901, laid down a rigid and uniform system for granting official approval to the constitutions of religious orders. New orders found recognition harder to obtain and the older orders had to present their constitutions for re-approval and vetting. The triumphant papalist faction pressed ahead with another key scheme: the revision of canon law – the legal code of the Roman Catholic Church – which was codified in 1917 for the first time in 600 years. Earlier the situation of nuns had been radically different and the apostolic orders as they now existed had hardly been imagined. In the intervening time they had developed spontaneously in response to particular circumstances; but the new canon law took no account of these differences and the laws applied equally to every type of active order. Specifically, regulations governing cloister (enclosure) became obligatory, which meant that even on the most active orders a degree of enclosure was imposed. This was supervised by means of a five-yearly questionnaire which the heads of congregations were required to submit to Rome and which measured in meticulous detail the degree to which the rules were being kept. This made the apostolic orders less able to respond to the needs of the world. Not only were they less able to observe the need, but some needs obviously could not be met by the large institutions living under a detailed rule book. The new rules cut nuns off in another sense: it became very hard to develop the warm and supportive relationships between nuns and other individuals (parish priests, bishops and even lay people) which had done so much to inform and enrich the nuns' lives before the canons were imposed.

But enclosure was not the only restriction that the nuns now experienced: canonical hours laid down a detailed prescription for the manner and content of prayer. There was a detailed supervision of the sorts of apostolates that women's orders were allowed to undertake which seemed more influenced by Victorian notions of propriety than by the commands of the gospel: among the tasks now considered unsuitable for nuns were the care of babies, the nursing of maternity cases and the staffing of co-educational schools.

Although the number of women entering convents did not immediately suffer, there was an inevitable ossifying of the tradition. The habit (official costume) of each order became absolutely fixed: most of the habits of the apostolic orders had been created as something suitable, inconspicuous and cheap, suited to local custom – but what might have been perfectly appropriate in fifteenth-century Germany might well not only look silly in twentieth-century Africa, but also be inconvenient, unhealthy and alienating to the people the nuns wishes to serve. Orders could no longer change their apostolic work without the gravest difficulty: teaching orders in England, formed in the nineteenth century to teach the daughters of Roman Catholic converts, were stuck in the 1960s with large private schools which many of the nuns could not help but feel were neither works of charity, nor even very appropriate educational establishments.

Underlying the precise provisions of the canonical code was a new stress on centralism, rigid hierarchy and distinct channels of obedience. The conservatives in the Vatican felt that free-thinking and localised authority led to chaos; countries like America had demonstrated that, left to themselves, they could too easily absorb notions of independence, self-development and individualism. The decree against 'modernism' outlined and condemned a specific form of the spiritual disease which was called 'Americanism' and meant that tendency to assert individual authority over the collective uniformity of the Church. The nuns were only one group affected by this stress but they were affected very seriously because the new centralism was coupled with a presupposed infantility on the part of women and the need to eradicate all their natural impulses. The easy association of women and children in the eyes of the all-male Roman Catholic authorities was a reflection of Victorian social thinking. Nuns who had escaped the Victorian feminine stereotype because the hierarchy needed them were now afflicted with it at precisely the point when it was becoming a defunct social model.

One consequence of this was the further elevation of the Mother Superior. Nuns were now more cut off than ever from parish priests and doctors, for example, and had less chance of any relationship with them. That comradeship was replaced by the authority of the Mother Superior, who was herself by training and law absolutely obedient to *her* superior, the local bishop or other designated leader. Her nuns, seeing her as Christ in the convent, bowing to the floor when she passed, privileged to sit at her feet during the periods of free-association (some nuns today remember when 'free-association' meant sitting round Mother while she selected topics of conversation)[7] were less consciously aware of how the male authorities dominated their lives. Mary Daly, in *Gyn/ecology*[8] makes the interesting point that sexist authority very often uses women themselves as the instrument of male oppression. Because certain women exercise authority over other women in a limited context, the victims do not experience this as sexist oppression but rather are drawn closer to men as detached and rational, while their suppressed feelings of anger are directed only at other women. Moreover, the women they see as disciplinarians are women of power; the idea that womanpower is dangerous is instilled, and women are further separated from each other, 'divided and conquered'. Mary Daly does not use the example of Mother Superiors and Novice Mistresses, but instead analyses how women (usually mothers) are the agents of foot-binding in China, genital mutilation and infibulation in Africa, and sexual conditioning in the West. Certainly this idea should not be pressed too far because there were clearly Mother Superiors of real insight, creativity and love, under whose care individual nuns developed mature and rich personalities; but it is worth considering because one of the emphases that many orders made was on a new model of internal authority – a different understanding of obedience to a domestic superior. This is one of the changes least understood and most resisted by the hierarchy, and is not parallelled in the men's orders.

I have given considerable attention to the way in which the nuns were in the first half of this century increasingly brought into and under the control of the Roman Catholic institutional structures because I believe that it has had a major effect on the way that their contemporary history has developed. Present books about nuns, by ignoring this factor and treating nuns as though they were isolated and genuinely autonomous, give a rather distorted picture of what has taken place; and in particular diminishes the immense courage and determination of nuns who have sought their own liberation. I am sure that it is only by seeing nuns as part of a highly clerical, pyramidical, male-dominated establishment that it is possible to understand what has happened to nuns and to appreciate both the tensions and the successes of the rapid changes in the 1960s and 1970s.

The parallels, including the chronological ones, between the incorporation of the nuns and of the women's missionary societies seem clear. Both groups developed independence and power throughout the nineteenth century and both groups were taken seriously enough by the relevant establishment. They were forcibly integrated and reduced to service organisations in the first quarter of the twentieth century. Like the missionary societies, nuns did not necessarily perceive this as a negative development: they had gained a high level of recognition and interest from the hierarchy; they were properly acknowledged within the structures of Roman Catholicism and their role was made clear. The vowed, conventual life was given a renewed standing as the highest vocation for women. This ideal was given an added emphasis by the popularity of two contemporary saints. Thérèse of Lisieux died in 1897; her spiritual autobiography *The Story of a Soul* was published soon after her death to instant international popularity. A contemplative who died at twenty-four, she became the 'greatest missionary of our age'. This ordinary young women living, in silence, a daily round of prayer and work, with faults of pride and obstinacy to be overcome, a certain moodiness to be fought, inward and outward trials to be faced, managed to save more souls and work more miracles than any of her more outwardly heroic contemporaries. The genuine toughness of Thérèse's mind (including the fact that she always longed to become a priest) was concealed under her own flowery sweet imagery; her original manuscript was heavily edited so that the sweeter qualities were emphasised. She did more, probably, to confirm the new model of the nun, and new model of *female* holiness than Canon Law could possibly have accomplished. Another saint who upheld the same ideals was Maria Goretti, a pious Italian twelve-year-old who preferred death by stabbing to loss of virginity by rape. She was murdered in 1902 and adopted by many Catholics as a model of a true virgin martyr. The instant popularity of Maria Goretti and the model of femininity that she offered was certainly more destructive to women's self-image than that of Thérèse of Lisieux, but in the short term her death led to a cult of 'heroic virginity' which made the life of a nun appear very attractive.[9]

For all these reasons (and probably others like the heavy male death toll throughout Europe of the First World War) numbers were not adversely effected by the canons of 1917 and the general disciplining of the nuns. On the contrary, in the 1930s and 1940s the religious orders reached new peaks in terms of entrants, stability and status within Catholicism. Although fewer new Roman Catholic orders were founded, those that existed consolidated themselves, and much encouragement could be drawn from the fact that religious orders within the Anglican Church, now more acceptable, were flourishing. It was not until the 1950s that the number of women seeking entrance to the religious orders began to drop. This did not lead to a quick reduction in overall numbers, because life-expectation was still rising, but it did generate a first feeling of uneasiness which was a cause for the self-examination and self-criticism which emerged in the late 1950s.

But there were other, more important, reasons for the unease. The suppression of liberal thinking at the beginning of the century had not been completely successful. With the improved media communications of the post-war era the changes and developments in theology were more readily available to all. The liberal cause was gaining strength for all kinds of reasons, along them growth in ecumenical thinking that the Protestant churches were developing, the renewed popularity of progressive theology and the emergence of new independent nation states. As the empires of the West collapsed – either graciously or bloodily – and the 'white man's burden' was laid down, the imperial and patronising model of the Roman Catholic Church carried less conviction. Moreover women could now, without the heroic difficulties of the nineteenth century, enter all sorts of professional fields which had previously been confined to nuns. The 1950s was the decade of family life: suddenly being a mother was not a second-class vocation as compared to being a virgin – on the contrary mothers were now seen as the stabilising force in society, the real teachers of the faith to the next generation and a particular model of holiness and self-sacrifice.

However, there were two particular developments which are worth looking at in a little more detail. Although they were apparently 'secular' changes, the effect they had on nuns was enormous. The underlying ideas about education and childhood underwent a reversal; and the popularisation of Freud and other psychoanalytical work expanded rapidly.

The understanding of children and the role of education which had developed in the nineteenth century was that the child, if not 'bad', was at least 'uncivilised', dangerous and unruly. The purpose of education was to discipline – by punishment, reward, or a judicious combination of both – and control the child and teach it the ways of adult life, particularly by an example of cool, calm self-control. 'Spoiling the child' was the ultimately damaging act (hence the rigid four-hour feeding schedules and early potty training which were demanded of mothers of the tiniest infants in the 1940s and 1950s). These views were given an added emphasis towards the end of the nineteenth century by the shift down the social scale of compulsory education. This meant that middle-class educators, teaching working-class children, saw themselves as 'civilising' the whole of 'the poor'. In the colonies the same pattern was repeated – the natives could be brought out of their primitive poverty by absorbing European civilising education. (It is not just women who suffer from the analogy with children; black people are the victims of this process too.) The Roman Catholic Church, combining pragmatic need with its ideas about femininity, had managed to direct a disproportionate number of nuns into the field of education, particularly in the New World. This preponderance of teaching orders meant that any change in the basic theory of teaching had a much larger effect on the apostolic orders than it would have done in the mid-nineteenth century.

Although Froebel developed his radical educational theories in the nineteenth century it naturally took a long time for these to percolate through the system and arrive at the level of classroom practice.

Froebel, and increasingly others, too, had a very different idea about what the child was – naturally intelligent, eager to learn, unrepressed, good (a return to the romantic model of the child as innocent without the romantic understanding that he was best left in this perfect innocence). Children, modern educators now maintained, were capable of self-discipline and must only be loved and feel secure and provided with the equipment and teachers which would foster their curiosity and creativity. By the 1960s these understandings were not only well known, but were taught as standard in teachers' training colleges and had also affected the childhood educational experience of at least a number of women now considering entering the religious orders. The rigidity of the rules in the convents made it nearly impossible for this new understanding to be absorbed into the convent life-style. Nuns were carefully taught to break their own wills by the strict 'guardianship of the senses' – which meant in some cases never raising the eyes and walking in a specified manner – by giving up one's will completely to another, by disciplining one's body through mortifications and penances. The new educational theories went precisely against their own training, which could not be changed because of the canons. Moreover there were the practical difficulties: hard to teach free eurythmics, and finger painting, and self-expression, or go on field trips in a medieval habit; harder still to associate freely and affectionately with the children, to spend time with their parents or even to arrange the 'open-ended lessons' of the modern type when one's life was governed absolutely by the ringing of bells for prayer time and by inflexible time-tables which governed every minute of the day and were supposed to have priority over the practical work.

These difficulties were not confined to teaching orders – work with children dominated the apostolates of nuns. Those, for example, running orphanges were forced to consider, in the light of the new understanding, if the large highly organised institutions to which they were committed were in fact the best way to bring up children already deprived of that new ideal, 'the natural home'.

Moreover the doubts that applied to the work that the nuns were doing inevitably must have spilled over into their own lives and formation. If children did not need to have every impulse expunged, did adult women? The growth of popular psychoanalytic understanding about the nature of the individual was repeating at the personal level the lesson of the educationalist. The work of Freud particularly raised important questions in the areas of sexuality and authority – attacking the basis of at least two of the vows made by nuns – chastity and obedience. The whole area of sexuality particularly was immensely problematic for nuns: twenty years on many have come to cheerful and open terms with this central problem but when the issue was first raised in the middle 1950s it was tearingly painful. The nuns' self-concepts depended on the idea that in renouncing *sex* (as opposed perhaps to maternity) they were renouncing something bad in favour of something good. Now psychiatry was arguing that it was impossible to renounce sexuality, and that repression was damaging to the wholeness of a personality. Perhaps chastity was not a simple question of avoiding a series of named carnal acts as a means of perfection, but something far more complex? Perhaps simple and absolute obedience to the Church in the person of Mother Superior was not proper humility, and the abandoning of all responsibility and autonomy into the power of a written rule was not virtuous, but only self-indulgent infantile dependence? These ideas were unsettling to nuns and the whole structure of conventual life depended on stability. They were not helped in working out this crucial area of their life by the extreme reluctance that Christianity as a whole, and the Roman Catholic Church in particular, displayed in dealing at all with psychology and psychiatry – believing that confession and penance would cope with guilt, and discipline and the sacraments with every other problem.

These difficulties were reflected in the 1950s not just by a decline in those seeking entrance to the religious orders. More alarmingly the first trickle of nuns began leaving their orders. For a nun who has made her final vows to leave without excommunication she has to seek a dispensation. This was then a rare and scandalous event – much like divorce. She could expect nothing from her community and probably little support from her family if they were Catholics themselves. In the 1950s the number of nuns leaving their orders was tiny compared to what it was to become, but it was a new phenomenon and a worrying one. It would probably have caused far more concern than it did if the various congregations had not been so isolated from each other: but although the 1917 canons had imposed a sort of uniformity on the orders it had also cut them off from each other. 'We didn't even know, before the reforms, of orders that existed on the next street,' one nun told me.

The Second Vatican Council probably happened at precisely the right time for the nuns. Despite the difficulties that they have experienced in the years since the Council, for them it seems to have been a movement whose time had come. Earlier the self-doubts might not have developed strongly enough for them to have taken full advantage of the latitude allowed them and later the level of disillusion and despair might have made the enthusiastic and thoroughgoing reforms impossible. The Council did not in fact turn its attention to the religious orders until 1965, when its document *Perfectae Caritatis* was published. *Perfectae Caritatis* was not directed specifically at nuns but at all those living under religious vows, which included, of course, the men's orders too: but it is important to remember that nuns outnumber monks by more than 5 to 1.[10] The document urged renewal upon all congregations and religious orders: it urged in loving terms, never calling into question the need that the Church had for its religious orders, but it also commanded. The religious orders were to examine themselves in the light of the theology promulgated in the conciliar documents, particularly *Lumen Gentium* – the document dealing with the constitution of the Church – and *Gaudium et Spes* which dealt with the relationship of the Roman Catholic Church to the world. It is only in relation to the theology behind these decrees that the renewal among nuns makes any sense. Both are major theological statements and it is impossible to do justice to them in this context, but they revealed a direction that must be understood. They declared that the Church herself, which for centuries had been perceived as an isolated island of holiness in an evil world, was to understand her role rather differently. The Church was now to be seen by Catholics more in the nature of a sign, or sacrament, of God to God's own created order. Members of the Church were collectively a 'pilgrim people' seeking the Kingdom promised by Christ, rather than a specially favoured group already in receipt of those promises. The sanctification and salvation of the whole world was now a collective duty – individual sanctification became less of a priority to make way for a more corporate understanding of Grace. Because the image of the Church as 'set apart' lost ground to a new image of the Church as the 'leaven in the lump', the value of vocations 'in the world' – particularly in marriage and family life – was enhanced. No one state of life was to be held as naturally holier than any other, but all carried a responsibility, and each was vitally necessary to the wholeness of 'the Body of Christ'.

In the light of this theology *Perfectae Caritatis* directed the renewal of religious life. It recognised the ossification and the need for change; it took seriously the reality in which nuns lived and worked:

> The manner of life, of prayer and of work should be in harmony with the present-day physical and psychological condition of the members. It should also be in harmony with the needs of the apostolate, with the requirements of culture and with social and economic circumstances. This should be the case everywhere, but especially in mission territories.[11]

The directives especially urged that nuns should participate more in the decisions that affected them, both so that the renewal could go deeper and so that the individual responsibility, which was a watchword of the conciliar documents, was made a reality:

> Effective renewal and right adaptation cannot be achieved save with the co-operation of all the members of an institute. . . . Superiors, in matters which concern the destiny of the entire institute should find appropriate ways of consulting their subjects and should listen to them.[12]

This participation should also extend beyond the boundaries of the congregations themselves and religious should see themselves as part of a whole with shared and mutual interests:

> Conference or Councils of major superiors, erected by the Holy See, are to be welcomed. . . . Institutes and independent monastries should form federations if they belong in some measure to the same religious family . . . or they should form associations if they have the same or similar apostolates.[13]

Norms were laid down to guide the orders in their search for renewal. They were to be free to develop new life-styles and new areas of work based on three criteria (a) The gospel values which their way of life should express (this emphasis on gospel values over the structured values of the tradition was one of the marks of the Council, and one which created more confusion perhaps than any other) (b) the *Spirit* of the intention of the founder of the particular congregation (it seems likely that if the Bishops had had any idea of the extraordinary and unconventional women who had founded many of the apparently 'respectable' orders known to them they might have hesitated; as so often happens research into women's history has revealed to the nuns and to the world the astonishing diversity, autonomy and power of many 'invisible' women); and (c) the needs of the world (again the ways in which women were to perceive 'needs' changed very quickly in the 1960s and 1970s and the members of the Council probably had little expectation that orders like the Maryknoll Sisters would see combatting 'machismo' in Mexico by feminist consciousness-raising as responding to a real need).[14] The norms also laid down that 'It is the institutes themselves which have the main responsibility for renewal and adaptation'.[15] This too gave encouragement to the nuns who were determined to renew a strong position against conservative interference from the hierarchy although the document, one hopes without intended irony, points out that, 'The Bishops in their pastoral solicitude will give their kind help'.[16] All the congregations were commanded to hold general chapters within a maximum of three years from the publication of the instruction to examine their life and its renewal and that such chapters, 'Must arrange by some suitable means for an ample and free consultation of all the subjects'.[17]

But undoubtedly the most important provision was the 'temporary' suspension of both the canonical restrictions and the constitutions of the individual orders for the purposes of experimentation. Although they were meant to produce new constitutions, the approval of which were 'reserved to the competent authority', this suspension of discipline meant that nuns had a chance to work out what they wanted to do with their community lives without having to fight against the deeply internalised rules and structures of canonical obedience.[18] It does seem that without these provisions it would have been impossible – at a psychological level – for many of the congregations to go as far as they have done in self-examination and exploration. It is now demonstrated that women have a particular difficulty in asserting their own needs over the demands of a constituted authority and particularly if that authority is in any way beloved, or a traditional mediator of accepted authority. This was still more the case for nuns who were trained ideologically and practically in the habit of absolute obedience and a distrust of personal preference or inclination.

There were, of course, inevitable limitations in *Perfectae Caritatis*. One was the sexism which it continually displayed: despite the preponderance of women in religious orders the entire language is geared towards a male readership and whenever women are mentioned specifically it always in terms of a limitation or restriction:

'Papal Cloister is to be maintained' states *Perfectae Caritatis*,[19] with no sense that this imposes a real constriction on women's contemplative orders which does not permit them the rich 'combined' life that most male contemplative orders enjoy. There are cloistered men's orders, in fact, but here this is chosen by the monks themselves and is internally disciplined. The fate of the women Dominicans who have been split into two quite separate congregations by this instruction, while male Dominicans can continue to use the benefits of a mixed life-style, is a case in point.

Another problem which was not clarified by the conciliar documents was the role of authority within the experiments; while the nuns felt that they had been given sufficient autonomy by the Council to develop their own renewal programme more or less autonomously, this was by no means the understanding of their traditional superiors, the Bishops. Whether the criticism has been that the nuns were moving ahead too fast or not taking sufficient steps forward, there have always been Bishops who have felt it their duty to direct and control the experiments, and to inform the nuns concerned that they have not got it right.

On the one hand there is the now famous story of the nuns of The Immaculate Heart of Mary.[20] They were a large order of nuns whose Mother House was under the jurisdiction of the Bishop of California. Their main apostolate was teaching in parochial schools, but they also had some women of remarkable individual talent. They increasingly found that their rule made teaching well nigh impossible to perform properly. They wanted to make some, originally fairly minor, alterations to their rule – to shorten the length of their habits and to allow sisters to visit the homes of pupils unaccompanied, were two examples. They were resisted at every turn by their Bishop. As his intransigence became clearer the resistance to him mounted among many of the nuns, who were after all intelligent and highly qualified adults. Nuns started leaving the order in increasing numbers, either because they were so frustrated by the Bishop's interference or because they felt that the wrangling with the Bishop was in conflict with their idea of the religious life. Finally the Bishop informed the order that they could obey his directives or cease to exist. The remaining nuns took the latter option: the entire order was compulsorly returned to lay status. They now exist as an open, non-canonical community admitting not just celibate women, but men, couples and families to their experiment in Christian community life. It is too soon to say whether the new model will offer the Church a contribution so valuable that the collapse of a large and important established order was worth while. However, a recognised body was destroyed not so much by the ecclesial conservatism of the Bishop, but by his complete inability to recognise that a group of adult women had some right to control the minor details of their own lives. Clearly there were faults on both sides, but the fact remains that the IHM nuns were treated as children and the hierarchy were surprised when they acted as such.

It is important, however, to realise that the patronage is not one-sided – it is not just a question of radical nuns being opposed by a conservative hierarchy; the reverse is also the case – there are clerics who consider that nuns are a bunch of silly old women who cannot perceive the right course of renewal for themselves, without divine (masculine) direction from the Bishops. A French Bishop has written:

> Our colleagues in the episcopate consider that they have made very little or no progress in the way of adapting themselves or making things more humane. The Bishops are right. But they do not always realise how heavy the machinery is nor how hard it is to set it in motion. During the frequent congresses which the nuns are always glad to attend they hear lectures and exhortations which they receive with enthusiastic applause but in practice scarcely any progress can be observed . . . all the nuns mean well and many see what needs to be done, but none of them dare make a beginning.

This passage makes no mention of the fact that nuns were driven into their supposed lack of humaneness by a canon imposed on them in exactly the same spirit as this Bishop wants to impose renewal. It also ignores the very idea that nuns might, for themselves, be able to decide at what pace they will take their development. Most seriously it ignores the undeniable fact that if there is one group which has responded with wholesale active commitment to change – both in practice and in image – to the demands of the Second Vatican Council, it is not the episcopacy; it is not really until very recently the laity; it is certainly not the average parish priest; it is not even the monks; it is the nuns. Not all their changes have perhaps been for the good, and certainly the price paid for them has been alarmingly high, but unlike any other distinct group within the Roman Catholic

Church, after fifteen years of renewal nuns are often scarcely recognisable:

> Oh dear, of course we've changed. It's unimaginable.
> Everything. From medieval habits to a style that owes more to
> Marks and Spencers than to the traditions of Rome. From big
> houses to little. From isolation to public. From private holiness
> to political activism. From being nuns to, I hope, being women.
> You know, women whose job it is to be a nun. [21]

Although nuns who are committed to renewal will tell you that 'we have hardly scratched the surface' and that great areas remain almost untouched, the outside observer finds the difference enormous. Nuns are everywhere, doing things that thirty years ago would have seemed impossible.

Sr Briege O'Hare OSC has been commissioned by her order to 'respond to the leadings of the Spirit in seeking new forms of religious life and ministry'. She is the only Catholic living in a mixed ecumenical group – married, single, lay and clerical – in Kirkby, Liverpool, trying to build a 'spiritual community' for and with the people there.

Sr Mary George O'Reilly SHJC is Director of Administration for the Archdiocese of Newark, New Jersey. She sees administrative work as a ministry, and one suitable to an order whose primary work is teaching: 'I see an administrator as one who enables other people to fulfill their own plans and dedication.' Her appointment is seen by her Archbishop as being in line with his policy of 'fleshing out the vision of Vatican II'. [22]

Sr Janet Marie Peterworth OSO is working in Morgan Town, West Virginia, on an experiment to find out if it is possible to create a parish, 'to form the people of God into a loving, serving local church', without any priests. [23] Meanwhile in South America at least 150 nuns have been given the authority to run parishes in every way except the sacramental ones, because of the serious shortage of priests.

Sr Frances Tobin SL is the Field Education Director at St John's Provincial Seminary, in Michigan. Ninety-eight per cent of the students are male.

> Because I am there, day after day, I can say a lot of things to my
> brothers. 'Hey wait a minute. Doesn't this tradition belong
> equally to men and to women?' How credible are we as

Christians that we get so selective that we are down to white, middle-class and male? Change is slow and power is certainly one of *the* issues.[24]

Sr Eleanor Anstey SHM ran for the Iowa state senate on a Democratic ticket in 1972. She lost, but wanted to stay in politics. 'So many decisions, affecting the lives of thousands of people are made in the Legislature. . . . I saw so much apathy in government. I think we've got to have more people that care.'[25]

Sr Patricia Drydyk, by no means alone among nuns, is working in Southern California organising the fruit and vegetable boycott with the National Union of Farmworkers.

Sr Cecilia Wilms lives a life of solitude as a hermit in Spokane, Washington, USA. She describes her calling in a poem entitled *The Woman – Face of God:*

> I am woman . . .
> Called by the Lord
> To be for many people . . .
> Creative space
> Nurturing womb
> Channel of God's loving mercy
> And so reveal to them
> The woman face of God.[26]

Sr Yolana Rarango, Director of Youth Ministry in El Paso Texas, was one of the co-ordinators for the Women for Dialogue Conference, a feminist counter-conference held while the Pope and his Bishops were holding the third CELAM conference at Pueblo, Mexico, in 1979. They described the oppression of women as 'a very grave affair' and that while 'the women's cause' had to be placed 'within the world-wide process of liberation' it was still absolutely 'crucial for the changing of structures'.[27]

In Calcutta the Missionary Sisters of Charity, the fastest growing order in the world, bathe the lips of dying Buddhists with water from the Sacred Ganges.[28]

Sr Jano Maria Lueck OSB, who teaches English Literature at Oklahoma State University, is one of a large number of nuns in the USA who is actively engaged in the campaign to ratify the Equal Rights Amendment in the required number of states. (Nuns have a particular commitment, incidentally, in Louisiana because they feel that the Roman Catholic lobby there has so far prevented ratification.)[29]

This list is not meant to be either extreme or conclusive. Political activism is more common in the USA than in Europe. Even Dutch nuns, who have more totally abolished the habit than any other nationality, do not have the same involvement in institutional politics as nuns do in the USA – this may be because the USA still has a faith in institutional capitalism, or it may be due to the very broad liberal base of women's politics there. But even to the more traditional areas of teaching, nursing and parish work nuns are bringing a new understanding and new dynamic. One of the consequences of the last twenty years is that nuns are well educated and qualified, both theologically and professionally. Perhaps the conciliar injunction which, in first instance, received the most external observation was the one which said:

> The up-to-date renewal of the institutes depends very much on the training of the members. Their religious, apostolic, doctrinal and technical training should be continued to suitable establishments. They should also acquire whatever degrees they need.[30]

But this education, like the more general education of women in the nineteenth century, had inevitable ramifications. If you educate people to equal standard you must not be surprised if they demand equal responsibility at the end of it. Corpus Christi College was set up in 1965 in Bayswater, London, to provide a sound theological education for all Roman Catholics; 75 per cent of the students turned out to be nuns, responding to the conciliar requirement that they should be better educated. In 1972 the entire staff resigned after prolonged disputes with Cardinal Heenan. There were a number of difficulties, but perhaps the most revealing was the Cardinal's objection to priests getting the same theological education as 'untrained nuns and laymen'. Nuns had understood that the Second Vatican Council wanted them to be professionals in the service of the Church; that was their only justification. The closing of Corpus Christi College to them was yet another example of the discrimination against them. Not surprisingly many of them interpreted this discrimination as discrimination against them as women. They have been hampered continually by paternalism and lack of autonomy:

What we do particularly want is to be consulted, to be admitted into partnership with the clergy. To be recognised as respected and not just be the washers-up. Our particular congregation is 'out for women'; we do want to try and urge and encourage women to stand up for their rights. Not in an aggressive way but just insist on them; not just be 'yes father', and 'no father'.[31]

The sweeping changes have not just affected the professional work of nuns. They have gone much deeper than that. In many cases the entire life-style has changed. Some of these changes have been forced on nuns. Once they accepted the brutal reality of galloping inflation, declining vocations and a long period of instability they were obliged also to examine the ways in which they lived. But it is equally true that the old life-style no longer reflected the theology of community under which nuns wanted to live and grow. While the apostolate of any congregation was both institutional and uniform – every nun engaged in the same work and living exactly the same precise rule – the large institutions made a great deal of sense. With the multiplication of jobs the institutions came, more nearly, to replicate a family. The move into smaller and less structured groups was an inevitable progress from recognising this fact and accepting that the old institutions had not necessarily been the most healthy places for individual development (of course while individual development had a low priority this had not been important):

When you live in a smaller community you are much more aware of other people; you rub shoulders with them and have your corners knocked off by them. I think this is a very healthy change and makes for a holier quality of life altogether and it does not get away from the ideal of obedience, whatever they say, because everyone is here for a mission.[32]

As the change in apostolates promoted the smaller living groups, then these in their turn produced new questions about authority. (These changes must not of course be seen in a crudely chronological way; some congregations started off from the other end beginning with authority problems and working towards renewed work patterns. The circles overlap and enhance the richness of discovery.) The problems of authority fall into two categories. First there are the questions of internal authority: how one understands the vow of obedience in regard to the women who is 'the superior'. Second there is the question of external authority, a problem shared increasingly by other Roman Catholics and indeed by all Christians. What is the authority of 'the Church' in relation to the conscience of the individual? This was a harder question, perhaps, for Roman Catholics than for the more Protestant denominations, because the authority was actualised and incarnate for them – not a vague and speculative Jesus and the Gospels, but a forceful actuality in the persons of the hierarchy. Nuns were excluded from this hierarchy; despite the domestic power of the Superiors they were never understood as part of the official hierarchy; in the long run this was actually probably useful to them in their renewal. Because their power did not have the vested authority they were freer to examine and criticise it. But the problem of how they related to that external authority still remains a difficult issue.

The internal issue of authority was closely related to the vow of obedience. The tradition taught that Mother Superior was the direct representative of Christ and should be obeyed as Christ himself would be obeyed. But having these feelings about a distant and seldom directly encountered woman was rather different from sharing a kitchen with that woman, knowing intimately that there were marked differences between her and the Christ whom one worshipped. Moreover, a legitimate challenge to this model of absolute, unthinking obedience could be made on the basis of the conciliar instruction to examine the way of life in relation to the gospel: what sort of obedience would the Jesus of the New Testament have wanted and expected? The growth of liberation theology and of psychological understanding suggested strongly to nuns that Christ had never meant to demand an obedience that inflicted dependence, lack of self-motivation and masochistic guilt on his followers. Rather, he clearly wanted to lead them nearer to his own maturity by loving them into independence and growth. In addition, whatever the model of Superior as Christ might mean, the post-conciliar theology was stressing that in baptism every Christian became to some degree a Christ-in-the-world by their own spirit-filled authority. The idea that superiors should not only consult every nun in their orders but actually listen to them was just one indication of this change of mood.

In the light of this theological understanding many congregations changed their whole idea of leadership. In some even the name 'Mother Superior' has disappeared – to the confusion of everyone from salesmen to Bishops. Houses may have sister-in-charge, but they often see themselves as administrators and enablers rather than as Christ figures to their 'subjects'. Even in orders where the title has been kept, the model is usually far more collegial than the term implies, and the superior does not see her authority as over-riding the wishes of her counsellors, but as expressing it. This collegial model is one that in theory the Second Vatican Council inclined towards, but nuns have taken it further than other areas of the church seem to have done. The change in internal authority patterns is one of the aspects of renewal that the hierarchy find it most difficult to deal with or to respond to. Recently, deeming the period of experimentation to be over, the Vatican proposed a new canon to govern the life of the nuns. In the USA this proposed canon was submitted to a survey among nuns to glean an idea of its acceptability. In the whole the new canons were not well received, but the proposals about the role of superiors came in for some savagely negative criticism, and the editors of the survey report summed up the position emphatically:

> The treatment of the vows reflects neither the lived experience of many women religious today nor the developments in theology and praxis since Vatican II. The Canon on Obedience fails to provide for personal and communal discernment and participation and tends to negate an active responsible obedience. The idea of submission to a moderator is incompatible to the present theology of religious life as well as with experience. The action of God is evident within the entire community, in the events of the times and the responses of human beings to those events; yet the canon *identifies a single person as taking the place of God*. The present treatment of vows excludes other options . . . what sign or symbol is appropriate depends heavily on the charism of the institution, its mission and the sign of the times; legislation in universal law *should not only respect but encourage this diversity*.[33]

As almost all superiors are currently, in one way or another, elected, the nuns seem to be saying here what the women's groups discussed in the previous chapter are also saying: the democratic process is not a perfect one; it short-cuts the progress towards consensus which is more important than efficiency as commonly understood.

However, many nuns feel that they might have been able to work out their own internal authority difficulties if it were not for the continuous interference from outside. As I have indicated, the women's religious communities suffered throughout their history from regulation by external authorities. Some of this intrusion into their domestic affairs was justified by their own belief that they were a part, and a crucial part, of something larger – the Universal Church. But the 'protective custody' in which they found themselves was a frustration to their development as independent and free Christian adults. The difficulties emerged in every direction: at the parish level the priests found it difficult to respond to the renewed parish sister, who no longer wanted to wash up and pray on Father's behalf:

> Poor things, they will feel so threatened. It is part of the reality that many sisters are now more qualified than their priests because priests have just had the seminary training and haven't followed it up with any university degree or anything like that. I mean this must make them feel vulnerable.[34]

Added to this is the real problem of misogyny: the training for the priesthood is often achieved at a very high price, which can amount to sexual aversion therapy. Obviously this does not apply to every Roman Catholic priest – celibacy is a charism and a vocation and, with grace, can be nurtured for love and power. None the less many priests are, at a young age, cut off from the reality of women and taught to see them as a threat to their vocations. The canons governing house-keepers still state that, where possible, they should be ugly. In exchange for giving up this particular form of evil priests are subliminally promised an authority, a knowledge, and a power that exceed anything offered to lay people. It is not surprising that they are reduced, often, to authoritarian despotism, coupled with incomprehension and fear when confronted with active and intelligent women who are not only as celibate and 'pure' as they themselves are; but who also through their study of theology are better trained and who also regard themselves as Father's equal in holiness, dedication, knowledge and worth.

Further up the hierarchy the problems continue. Not only are nuns not properly represented within the Vatican bureaucracy, they also have to experience interference and discrimination from their 'local ordinaries', whether these are the Bishops or the heads of parallel men's orders. Nuns feel that the treatment they receive is not just a problem of clericism but also specifically of sexism. The survey mentioned above asked respondents to state on what grounds they objected to the proposed new canons. The number of times that sexual inequality and discrimination was mentioned, particularly in reference to nuns' relations with external authority, was noticeable. The survey concluded:

> The separate treatment of nuns and monks violates the principles of equality. Papal cloister is required for nuns but not for monks; the latter are given a greater scope for the apostolate than nuns. Nuns should not be required to receive spiritual care from the institutes of men with whom they are associated but permitted to seek it according to their own determination. Moreover if mutuality is taken seriously the institutes of men should derive assistance from the women's branches. There is discrimination between an Abbot and a Prioress in terms of authority and jurisdiction.[35]

Nuns still feel that their contribution to the Church is not properly recognised and that they are still treated as inferior, specifically as women. In 1970 the National Coalition of American Nuns – a self-declared feminist organisation came out with a sweeping demand for the 'complete autonomy of our religious institutes' and demanded that all 'clerics and clerical groups, both in Rome and in local jurisdictions, allow religious women to control the dynamics of their internal renewal processes and to open wider ministries to women'. Sr Margaret Ellan Traxler, the founder of the National Coalition, is clear:

> I love the Church, but it is my church, not their church. I will not let them drive me out of my Church; if they cannot take the pace we are setting then they can leave.[36]

The tension between nuns engage in their own renewal and the church authorities has in fact reached a pitch where the Vatican itself has felt obliged to take a note of it. In 1978 a document called *Mutuationes Relationes* was published, which urged steps to improve relations between the two parties. It was described to me as 'a very very good work, absolutely a step in the right direction and very much approved'.[37] Among other things the document recommends the setting up of diocesan councils which would include, as of right, representatives of the women's orders.

The problem is partly that nuns know, as an historical fact, that they collectively have gone further with the pressing business of renewal than any other corporate body. They know what the secular Christian feminist organisations do not always seem to know: that they do not need to ask anything of the Church, but on the contrary have a great deal to give if only those with the power can accept it. Sr Mary Shanahan SHJ, an Australian nun, explains quite clearly what while nuns are:

> moving – albeit slowly and painfully – to an understanding of the Church as a *sororal community* where growth comes through intra-personal relations at all levels, where problems and insights are shared and where work is done together;

the Bishops and diocesan clergy do not have the personal experience of what this can mean:

> In justice to the Bishops and as a means of educating them, the hierarchy should be involved in some way in the process that religious are undergoing and not simply presented with solutions when they have not even understood the problem.[38]

This self-confidence when it comes to prophesying to the rest of the Church is probably the one thing that most gets the hierarchy on the raw. They could, it would seem, cope with nuns who do almost everything except teaching them their Christian duty: a role that women are more and more ready to undertake.[39] Nuns more and more see that their collective duty is to bear witness to the Church of the Church's own failure. The authorities do not like it. They like it less still when it is apparent that in fostering this role, nuns prefer to identify themselves with the laity, rather than with the interests of the clerical caste; or when nuns look not to properly constituted male-authority for advice but to each other. The amalgamations and federations of nuns which cross congregational boundaries are one of the leading marks of the renewal: from leadership conferences, recommended by the Vatican, to associations for 'senior religious', for Spanish-speaking nuns, and for all women who see the gospel of liberation in feminist terms. Nuns now seem to look to each other and to their identity with other women rather than to the traditional hierarchy for their sense of community and sisterhood.

Perhaps people would find it easier to tolerate the conviction of nuns that they have something to teach, if they realised the high price that nuns were prepared to pay for their renewal. The most visible part of that price has been in terms of numbers. It is not just that numbers of wouldbe entrants has declined sharply. Graver still has been the loss from within, a loss which did not manifest itself in real terms until after renewal was underway. The nuns that remain cannot blame that loss on conservatism: it has been inflicted directly by what they have tried to do. In the USA the number of nuns declined between 1965 and 1975 by about 41,000: 29 per cent of the total membership in ten years. Obviously some of this loss was through deaths not replaced by new members, but substantially it was from nuns seeking dispensation from their vows, or more seriously just drifting off without bothering about the formalities. In other countries the figures have not been so devastating, but there is nowhere that has not suffered; in France and Belgium the numbers amount to over 20 per cent, in Britain to somewhere between 12 and 18 per cent. Everywhere they have been dangerously high; dangerous in terms of the future and devastating in terms of personal loss. The nuns leaving were, moreover, precisely the most energetic, progressive and potentially skilled members of a community (skilled it must be said in worldly terms – obviously they were not especially skilled in the religious life).

The reasons for this mass exodus have been reviewed ad nauseam. Some of them have, I hope, emerged in the course of this chapter. Conservatives see the decline in terms of secularisation both of the society in general and of the nuns in particular. They claim that renewal itself destroyed the meaning of religious life, and draw attention to the fact that conservative orders have suffered less than progressive ones, which is undeniably true. They also point to orders like Mother Theresa of Calcutta's Missionaries of Charity, which is growing explosively and attracting candidates of markedly 'high' quality. The fact that the Missionaries of Charity have received a media coverage un-paralleled in both volume and enthusiasm is not irrelevant, but is also not the whole story. The Missionaries of Charity are spectacular example of a difficult truth: the 'old fashioned' nun has recently acquired a new status – while before she was sentimentalised and regarded as useless she is now waved under the noses of progressives as the only way forward.

Not only have nuns paid for renewal in terms of numbers; they have also given up their identity as 'specially holy' and sought identification with that which is ordinary and least admired in society – other women. One unusually honest nun told me that having fought to get rid of the habit she found that she 'hated going out, being looked at not as someone special, but as a dowdy, badly-dressed middle-aged frump. That was real poverty and *very* hard.' Progressive orders have opened themselves to the full consequences of female sexuality and paid the price for this boldness: a remarkable number of nuns have left their orders because they were 'in love', wanted to be married or could not cope with the self-denial involved with true celibacy, once they had recognised sexuality and sexual love as a good in itself. Others have left simply because of the conflicts. The Centre for the Applied Research in the Apostolate – a Washington DC based independent Roman Catholic research unit – did an investigation in 1978 among nuns who had left their canonical orders but had not left 'religious life': that is they had moved into new orders, either individually or as a group.[40] They were asked why they had left their orders and what was the purpose of their new groups (almost all of them non-canonical, that is without the official recognition of the Church, so that they would appear among the figures of those who had stopped 'being nuns'). Almost all those questioned said that their experience of religious life had fostered immaturity and left them with strong feelings of bitterness and anger. The stated purposes in forming the new groups, however, were extremely diverse and reflected more on the limitation of choices available than a failure in the ideals of monastic commitment: reactions against the failure of their community to take renewal seriously; a desire for a new life-style; reaction against decisions to limit the apostolate; a desire to pursue wider types of spirituality.[41]

Among the nuns who have stayed the course, who have opened themselves fully to renewal and have found that their sense of direction was confirmed, there is a new spirit of confidence and security. They are decreasingly introspective and turning back to the world and its ever pressing problems:

I have spent ten years trying to work out how I was different from other women not in vows. Now I don't care: this is where I am, what am I going to do with it? That is the only question. You don't have to have answers all the time; you find the answers and the self-confidence by doing what you have to do.[42]

The sense that the worst is over is clear among many nuns. The price has been paid, now there is work to be done. The work seems very often to be defined in offering themselves to the Church and to

79

the outside world as a model of what will happen if the call to Christian renewal is taken seriously. Nuns now claim for themselves, and I believe with justification, a prophetic role. They describe this in different ways, but the sense that they have an important key and one that has been earned is evident, surprisingly often, under a real humility. They are offering a model of sisterhood and of a direction for the whole Church, a new understanding of authority based on mutuality, a new type of communication and personal openness. Sr Ruth Duckworth SC sums this new prophetic role up quite clearly:

> Perhaps the special vocation of religious life today is precisely to take risks so as to play out on its tiny stage the drama of the Church, gaining experience through taking risks, because the life of a few nuns can be put at risk, more than can the whole Church.

She goes on to describe the areas where the risks are and need to be taken. First there is unity understood as communion in diversity. Then exploring the relation to one's own history, which inevitably includes a certain iconoclasm. There are problems of structure and law and how far you can push these boundaries out before chaos comes. There is the complicated balance between authority and mutual dependence and service; this itself entails other questions of collegiality and co-responsibility. There are the inter-related matters of diversity of ministry, lived and shared poverty and spirituality. And finally there is what she describes as the 'problem of the mode of presence': how do we evangelise and prophesy? This she is convinced is the new prophetic vocation of nuns: and with a final, moving bravado, she concludes 'to work out within the boundaries of a miniature faith community the problems of the whole church calls for humility, detachment and courage.'[43]

Because nuns have been obliged to work their way through all this confusing material within a very rigid and formalised structure, they have been forced to examine many problems that women outside the system have been able to dodge or ignore. The tensions cannot be underestimated. They can, however, be seen as the painful but healthy birthpangs of a new understanding. The whole Roman Catholic Church, like the whole of Christianity itself, has been through, and is still enduring, an intensely difficult and chaotic period of growth. Those people who have most really grasped the need and meaning for change have inevitably been through the most difficulty and chaos. During this period all other women have also been through a social upheaval. Nuns are present in a real sense in the front-line of both upheavals – often from their own courageous choice, but also from a knowledge that the changes would have to be dealt with whether they consented or not. Despite the cost, their enthusiastic and active consent will probably prove in the long run to have served their own interests. They will certainly have served those of the wider Church. The areas of the greatest tension and difficulty will probably prove to be the areas of most value and service:

> Because the renewal in theology coincides in time with the new self-awareness of women, it is possible for theology to serve a unique function in empowering women to construct new models for interpreting themselves and for their role in society.[44]

Or, in other words, nuns now armed with a long period of self-analysis and excellent professional qualifications – their own, not those prescribed by a masculist institution – can now do the crucial work of bringing together the theory and practice of Christian women participating equally and specially in the divine truth.

Nuns have been sentimentalised and idealised before. I do not want to add to that burden by laying another burden of the same type upon them. There are lots and lots of cranky disagreeable nuns. It is to their history, rather than to their saintly personalities that I look and see a model of sisterhood engaged in struggle. They have set out on the difficult journey towards autonomy, freedom and love:

> I have been a member of a Roman Catholic religious community of international dimension for over forty years. The first twenty-five were happy active years, lived in the stable framework of a way of life that little change from day to day and seemed geared to remaining so for ever. The last fifteen years have seen changes so radical and so far reaching that those days seem to belong to another age. People who see our communities from the outside say that they have hardly recognised us: and truth to tell sometimes we have difficulty in recognising ourselves. And where are we going? We cannot know, nor do we need to know – but we believe that our movement has been in a good direction. We do not think that all is now done that

81

needs to be done. On the contrary we have a strong suspicion that change has come to stay. But we know that we are more alive, more vitally united, freer to love and serve; and we are content not to see the future, since not to know the future is something to do with what we call faith.[45]

CHAPTER 4

ORDINATION

Thou shalt lay thy hands upon her in the presence of the Presbyters, the Deacons and the Deaconesses, saying, 'Thou who didst fill Deborah, Hannah and Huldah with the Holy Spirit, thou who in the Temple didst appoint women to keep the holy door, Look upon thy servant chosen for the ministry, and give to her the Holy Spirit that she may worthily perform the office committed unto her.'[1]

If there is one area, more than any other, in which the conflict between nuns and their hierarchy is visible it is in the question of the admission of women to the 'orders' of the Roman Catholic Church. Nuns of course are not alone in making this demand, but in the USA they have been among the leaders of this campaign. Roman Catholics have developed a militant attitude to this demand very fast. Only twenty years ago the St Joan's Alliance submitted to the Second Vatican Council the modestly worded statement:

The St. Joan's Alliance re-affirms its loyalty and filial devotion and expresses its conviction that should the Church in her wisdom and her good time decide to extend to women the dignity of the priesthood, women would be willing and eager to respond.[2]

Within fourteen years Roman Catholic women had not only developed the impetus to organise a large-scale conference demanding the ordination of women but had obliged the Vatican to respond to the issue. In January 1977 the Vatican released its *Declaration on the Question of the Admission of Women to the Ministerial Priesthood*, in which it stated in absolute terms that the exclusion of women was founded on Christ's conscious will and is basic to the Church's understanding of priesthood and therefore cannot be altered. In any previous period of modern history so emphatically worded a statement would have closed the issue. This did not happen, and on the contrary Roman Catholic women have continued to articulate their demand with an ever-increasing determination. Because of their administrative experience nuns have been in the forefront of this debate, but it has never been a question of wanting their special role in the Church recognised through ordination, but rather of expressing their solidarity with other women.

Roman Catholics have thus joined the Protestant denominations in their active struggle to end discrimination in the professional structure of their churches. I have tried throughout the rest of this book to limit the discussion of denominational differences, as being irrelevant to the issues. But it is important when discussing the denominations' own official ministries to have some understanding of the divisions that exist. These differences affect understanding about ordination, different ministries and the relationship between the ministers, the individuals served by them and the institutional structures. The Anglican factional terms 'high church' and 'low church' can be usefully extended through the denominations here. They refer to the doctrines about the abstract concept of the Church. 'Low church' groups give a low value to the idea of a church as anything other than the sum of its parts. Some groups give such a low priority to this idea that they completely deny the existence of any such thing as a Universal Church: their congregations meet for the benefit of the members and as a convenient means of evangelisation. The relationship between one congregation and the next is of no spiritual significance, but a matter of convenience and charity. For example some Baptist congregations are not members of the Baptist Union; nor are congregations obliged to call their minister from the Union's list of accredited ministers, which is seen only as a pastoral aid: the authorisation of a minister comes solely from the individual congregation. 'High church' denominations, on the other hand, give a very high priority to the idea of the *Church*, which, existing not just in time but in eternity, also is greater than the sum of its parts and has an independent identity. The unity of separate congregations is not optional or convenient, it is essential and inescapable; all congregations are absolutely united in the Church and ecclesiastical authority comes not from the congregation but from the Church Herself, mediated through a hierarchic system. This means that individual members meet not just as a mutually beneficial support group, but because they are a part of something larger. This understanding lies behind the rule that Catholics should attend Mass every Sunday and on 'Holy Days of Obligation'. They participate in acts of worship which are meant to express their complete union with Christ – who is made present to them through material signs which guarantee Jesus' own actual presence. These are called sacraments. Because the sacraments belong not to the congregation, but to the whole Church, they only become 'valid signs' – the guarantee only applies – when the Church (in the persons of the Church's hierarchy) says that they are. One of these 'signs', and the present guarantee of the validity of the others, is the ordained ministries of the Church. These can be conferred on people by Bishops, who 'inherit' this right through the tradition from St Peter himself (this is what is meant by the Apostolic Succession), and once given cannot be taken away. A priest is a priest forever. Not because a congregation want to be ministered to, nor because of the priest's own virtues, but because the Church has declared that this is the case.

At one end of this spectrum are denominations like the Disciples of Christ and many Baptists who see ordination as a matter of practicality and not doctrine; working up the scale there are Congregationalist and Reformed Churches, Presbyterians, Methodists and Lutherans. The Lutherans, still a self-confidently Protestant denomination, see authorised ministry as 'a mediating agency for imparting of faith through the gospels and the sacraments'.[3] Above them on this scale are the Anglican Communion, the Roman Catholics and the Orthodox churches, all of whom hold that ordination is a sacrament in itself and the priest, in a specific way, is a representative of Christ, ontologically changed by indelible ordination.

Some of the Protestant denominations have never denied the possibility of women being ordained ministers. At different times in history there have been women Baptist, Methodist Episcopal, Methodist Protestant and Pentecostalist ministers leading congregations, but these were always individual women over-riding the difficulties set before them, rather than an organised movement to insist that women be ordained. After the beginning of the twentieth century a number of factors led to a rapid change and evolution among women's professional ministries in all the denominations. A consequence of the women's suffrage movement and the increase in professional openings and educational opportunities for women was that the various denominations had to offer women some stake in the official ministries or they would simply lose their labour. Moreover, as I said earlier, through the missionary societies women had demonstrated both their ability to act as evangelical ministers overseas, and their ability to organise and administrate at home. The incorporation of these organisations into the official structures meant that women who had previously had a separate channel for their energy and vocation now had to demand of the denominations themselves the right to serve and exercise ministry.

Another important factor was the 'professionalisation' of the Christian community. In the twentieth century there was an increasing awareness of educational and social professionalism: the old voluntary system was not good enough. One factor here was certainly the decline of servants whose presence had made it possible for middle-class women to give time and service outside the home for free. This pool of labour began to dry up after the First World War. But there were also changes in the ideas about what a local congregation was meant to be. Numbers of worshippers began to decline from their Victorian peaks and the congregations were smaller and less self-confident. The idea of the parochial church as 'the local centre of the community' began to emerge – influenced perhaps by the success that the Roman Catholics had made of this role in the new immigrant communities of the nineteenth century. For this to work there was a new need for paid and trained youth workers, parish assistants, social workers and catechists.

Under different titles all the denominations began to develop these roles, which were often attractive to women and corresponded with fairly traditional ideas of what women could properly be doing. The notion of the Deaconess – which had good Biblical tradition behind it – emerged with renewed emphasis. In 1910 the Kaiserworth Conference in Germany attracted over 20,000 Deaconesses from the Protestant denominations. The Anglican Communion also opened up this ministry. The Bishop of London had in fact 'ordered' a Deaconess in 1862 and they had developed throughout the Anglican communion in the late nineteenth century. But in the changed climate of the twentieth century the Anglican Deaconesses posed a problem: were they just 'authorised church workers', specially set apart, or were they 'in orders', members of the clergy? The Lambeth

Conference – the ten-yearly international meeting of Bishops 'in communion with the See of Canterbury' – tied itself in knots over this question, declaring in 1920 that Deaconesses were in Holy Orders, and in 1930 that they were not. This confusion revealed clearly the tensions around women's ministry within the institutional structures of the Church.

The numbers of ordained women in the denominations that did permit this began to rise; and the women concerned became more conscious of their position. An American Association of Women Preachers was founded in 1919 and in 1921 the Association began to publish a regular periodical, the *Women's Pulpit*. In 1920 the Congregational Harvard Theological Seminary declared, 'In view of the changed attitude towards the ordination of women, we no longer require women to state on entering the seminary that they do not expect to enter the ministry.'[5] By 1927 there were 100 women ministers in the American Congregationalist Church, as opposed to less than 40 in 1900.[6]

It would be wrong to suggest that women wanting to be ordained now found their path easy. One Congregationalist seminarian, Margaret Johnstone, was urged to become a pastor's assistant or a religious educator. When this failed she was told:

We are your friends. It is because we know so well the frustration awaiting any women in the ministry that we are urging you to enter related work. We are trying to protect you not only from heartbreak, but also ridicule. . . . And consider our obligation to protect the dignity of the profession.[7]

None the less the growth of women professional church workers, and the visibility of ordained women in some denominations, did affect those which still did not permit the ordination of women. Throughout the period between the two World Wars the position of women improved. Denominations began to admit women as elders, to give voting rights to lay women and to allow women to address synodical meetings. These were of course minute gains, but they laid the groundwork for rapid developments in the years after the Second World War. From 1950 onwards more and more of the Protestant denominations opened their ordained ministries to women. In 1970 the Lutheran churches in the USA voted to do so – they were the last main American Protestant church to do so. In 1974 the British Methodists followed. This meant that throughout the world the full authorised ministry of Protestant churches was open to women. The campaign had lasted little more than a century.

At first this seemed like a final victory. Once again it seemed that the way was open for a 'new era of co-operation between men and women':

> Yet women's victory has somehow been a hollow one. Equal access to the ordained ministry has not resulted in equal access to positions of leadership traditionally available to the clergy. Everywhere women ministers face longer period of unemployment, lower salaries, less opportunity to shoulder full responsibility and less likelihood of appointment or selection to leadership positions within ecclesiological structures. . . . Ordination, far from being the culmination of women's expanding participation, is another beginning point in a history of beginning points.[8]

One of the problems for ordained Protestant women has been their relative isolation. With the exception of the British Methodist Church which ordained simultaneously a group of over 100 women ministers in 1974, the approach has tended to be piecemeal. Each denomination has its own training seminaries and the women preparing themselves for the ministry were isolated in tiny numbers within these predominantly male establishments. In addition the evolution towards ordination was gradual and in many of the denominations was finally approved without a massive conscious-ness-raising campaign which involved lay women and created a tight network of support and sisterly concern. Women tended to be admitted one by one more on their own personal merits than as a point of theological principle.[9] Although this is consistent with Protestant theology of the ministry it has cut ordained women off from each other and from a sense of collectivity and identification with other women. In the USA and Europe where ecumenism is more highly developed, this is less marked than in Britain, but remains an important factor. The Rev. Ruth Matthews, a Baptist minister, was the only woman in her training college in Oxford in the 1960s. There was no Christian Women's Movement then, and she still finds it difficult to identify herself with the feminist caucus. None the less she felt the masculine bias of the training programme as oppressive:

I did feel terribly discriminated against. Everything was oriented to the fact that they were all men; in small ways, like the rule saying you could not be alone with a *woman* in college, with the door shut. Pastoral problems were always dealt with from that angle and when I said, 'And how am I expected to deal with *men*' all I ever got was a big laugh from everybody. If you are the only woman at anything they will always make jokes. And when we were away at Conferences or things, they always had prayers for wives and families. . . . And then I had the discrimination of not finding a job, when everyone else was going to find one easily. You were told you were a problem. 'We are going to have problems settling you, Miss Vincent.' You are always a 'problem'.[10]

Ruth Matthews's 'problems' increased when she wanted to get married. Although Baptists have no tradition of celibate pastors, and indeed react strongly against this, she was the first Baptist professional – including the Women Workers – in the English Baptist Union who had ever proposed staying on at work after getting married. After training she worked in a parish as the assistant minister; when she told her senior that she was planning to get married:

he said, 'I thought you had given up that sort of thing.' He found it difficult . . . because apparently he could only see me as a minister if I was some kind of sexless person, or at least de-sexed – some kind of 'set apart virgin female'.[11]

This kind of de-sexing of ordained women as a subtle form of sexual discrimination is very common. Ruth Matthews was once asked by an official Baptist panel if when she was in the pulpit she saw herself 'more as a woman or as a minister' when she preached, as though the two were incompatible and she had to make some sort of choice. On her marriage to another Baptist minister she was obliged to leave her denomination's pension scheme despite her declared commitment to continuing in the ministry.

When she and her husband were expecting their first child they took a job-sharing appointment with a congregation in Swindon, Wiltshire. The congregation there amalgamated in an ecumenical experiment with the local Methodist, United Reformed and Church of Christ congregations. One of the immediate advantages was that the combined congregations could afford a large ministerial team – so that Ruth Matthews ceased to be the only woman in the professional group. The team had a commitment to a greater balance and in 1978 the group consisted of three women and four men. The job-sharing arrangement, so enthusiastically greeted in the Women's Movement, seemed to her to be only a partial success:

> I don't favour it as a normal situation, it was only because of our having small children. I think it one way of not really having women ministers. It's been very nice and easy for us but it's often cheating really – because they have still got a man, a 'real' minister. People can still say, 'This is our minister's wife.' No one ever introduces John [her husband] as 'our minister's husband'. It's not that they ask John to do different things, it's just that they don't *have* to regard me as a minister while he's here.[12]

As soon as their children were both in school the Matthews gave up the job-sharing arrangement. Ruth Matthews took an 'ordinary' pastoral job – though still in an ecumenical parish – while her husband left the ministry to become a 'house-husband' and free-lance writer.

But despite the continuing difficulties Ruth Matthews has a profoundly theological commitment to the full ministry of women:

> I believe, strongly, that at least half or a third of all clergy should be women. Not because I come at it from any Women's Rights point of view, but because if you only have men you don't adequately represent the nature of God. The necessity for the ordination of women is clear to me. What is important is that people should in some sense find God and should be able to live and work in ways that open up the fullness of human life. The Christian Church should be the vehicle for this. . . .[13]
>
> Many biblical texts are difficult to interpret: the one which tells us that God made us in his image is notoriously so. However if you take it seriously you have to grapple with the fact that in this is included the other phrase, 'male and female created he them'. 'In his image . . . male and female.' . . .
>
> There are many who would agree that language is important but who want to stop there. It is my conviction that recovery or discovery is impossible if it is not seen as well as heard. . . . As

we represent God to one another, as we allow the image of God to be seen in the world, so we must represent him in his fullness as male and female.[14]

One of the problems, as she admits readily, with being a Baptist is that strategically there is not much that can be done. Because of the autonomy of individual Baptist congregations it is hard to organise any coherent campaign:

The advantage of a superstructure sort of Church is that if the Romans decide to ordain women, then that would be that. . . . We can't do it that way, and so there is no way that 'joining things' has ever been very relevant to me. There can never be any 'Baptist Movement to make it better' because there is really nothing you can do except let yourself be a token women, just so that people can get used to you.[15]

Part of the difficulty for Ruth Matthews is her determination to stay in the parochial ministry, where the sense of being able to do so little is pronounced. Many ordained women do not get pastoral jobs and often do not even look for them. A surprisingly high proportion of ordained women do not work within congregations; very few indeed have chief pastoral oversight. Some women argue that they do not want, or believe in, such a ministry. The criticism of the normal parish ministry may well be a sound one, but so long as team ministries are the only place in which women are pastorally visible it is hard for them not to be relegated, in line with accepted social custom, to help-and-support roles. It surely cannot be the job of ordained women to mediate between lay people and 'real' male ministers. It seems to me that they must either challenge the structure of ordained ministry radically from outside the privileged clerical caste, or they must be prepared to carry the image of God as female and male to the limits of pastoral understanding. At the moment there can hardly be much point in worrying that they might be presenting a distorted picture of women's authority to the local congregations. Ruth Matthews's commitment to a pastoral leadership ministry (and of course she is not the only example) is not going to lead to an easy life, but it does hold an integrity and a profound challenge.

In the meantime many women ordained in the Protestant denominations work outside the traditional ministerial areas. Apart from the motives suggested above there are two other important reasons for this. One is that women seem to have a looser attachment to denominational boundaries than men. I have discussed this phenomenon already, but in relation to the ordained ministry it is true that women often feel that working in ecumenical relationships, or working in areas where Christian institutions are reaching outwards to the rest of society, rather than within tight denominational congregations, more nearly corresponds to their ideal of Christian ministry. Many women developed their faith and vocation within the struggle for women's status in the churches and have received their own sense of ministry from being ministered to, not by the institutional church, but by looser and more flexible groupings of concerned people. All women who achieve ordination have experienced discrimination and sexism from their own denomination – sometimes even without being aware of it – and this alienation, if it has been healed at all, is most likely to have been healed within non-denominational, non-official groups, frequently with a radical critique of the institutional Church. Male clergy loyal to the institutional framework are more than likely to be affirmed by the praise and support of their denominations after they have been accepted for training. The ideal of ecumenism is also closely in line with much feminist theological thinking: the breaking down, by personal warmth, of socially imposed and 'rationally' defended barriers; the struggle against the determinism of history; the desire to use points of tension in human relationships creatively.

Moreover, it is not often that a congregation can afford a woman minister the space to work particularly on 'women's concerns'. At the national level or within the ecumenical and social work agencies there are more likely to be such specialised jobs. The experience of discrimination is likely to make this a focus of women's energies. Additionally so long as 'maleness' is regarded by society as both normal and ideal, with women as an adjunct or a problem in relation to this norm, then women do have to claim a special duty to minister to other women.

When this intellectual theory is allied to the experience of sisterhood that many women have and to the continued discrimination of congregations it is not surprising that many women do not choose to work with the traditional pastoral ministry, and particularly in the areas of creating new ministerial models based on feminist understandings. The Rev. Joan Martin, an ordained Presbyterian, for example, works for the Church and Society Division of the National

Council of Churches in their New York office. This department has six central areas of concern and Joan Martin is responsible for the Justice for Women Programme. As a black woman she has tried 'to give a special vitality to that part of the job description which demands a special focus on the relationship between racism and sexism. . . . The majority of white women refuse a holistic analysis.'[16] Like most ordained people, Joan Martin trained in a parish ministry and sees herself as a 'strongly pastoral type'. But compared to her present work she found that her real interests were not fully represented in parochial life, and that the work-style she has been able to develop at the National Council is more in tune with her own ideas of ministry. In particular her colleagues in the Church and Society Division have:

> desired a collective feminist style with the understanding that this is a racially diverse group – and that we bring different cultural styles as well as gender and bureaucratic styles. We are working on something collegial; we have a drive towards consensus. Because of the work we are doing together, women who felt isolated in their own denominations now feel together ecumenically; they now feel they can exert some power that they couldn't individually.
>
> My main constituency here is women who do work like me, so my constituency reflects my own interests.[17]

Joan Martin is clear that the problems are not solved by moving out of the pastoral ministry and into the national area:

> I do not believe that the National Council's response is as adequate as it could be. The staff person at the Women and Ministry Department is a quarter-time person. That reflects the extent to which the Churches do not want to admit there is a problem with professional women in ministry.[18]

None the less she at least is able to come to grips with the particular issues that underlie her own vocation and she is able to share her concerns with other women.

In a period of recession such as we are now entering there is a certain farcical element in speaking as though one could make real choices between one sort of job area and another. It is still early to say whether, given all the obstacles (including the increasing difficulty that younger middle-class women – precisely those who developed the women's professional ministries in the Church in the 1920s – are having with Christianity itself, let alone its institutional structures) the percentage of ordained women will increase to the point where congregations will be obliged to choose between having a woman pastor or having none at all. What difference this might make to the expectations that ordained pastors and their lay people have of each other, and how this would affect clerical status within the denominations and in society at large are speculative questions. What Protestant ordained women have conclusively proved, in a remarkably short time, is that they can work and are determined to work, within a range of Christian ministries to the benefit of God and society; but that this itself has not solved the problem of sexism within Christianity.

For the denominations that fall above the Lutheran Church in my listing the problems are somewhat different. For all of them there is a more substantial theological problem. Proclaiming that the priesthood is something other than a simple job or function, and that the priest *is* to the community the personal presence of Christ Jesus, there remains the difficulty of working out how this is so and what it means. Believing that the Church is 'more than the sum of its parts', is Christ's continuing incarnation in the world, and that the accumulated knowledge of her history is as certain a source of revelation as the Gospels, it is more important for them to maintain a plausible continuity with the tradition. The fact that the social evolution of the last one hundred and fifty years has proved that women can physically and psychologically perform all the acts of priesthood is not, theologically, any sort of proof that women can or should be ordained.

The Protestant denominations moved towards the ordination of women in some sort of concert. They were able to use each other's experience. Of the remaining denominations this is less true. Within the Orthodox communities the subject has hardly raised itself at any but the most speculative level. Of all the denominations the Orthodox churches have the most fundamentalist understanding of the tradition; they also have a more highly spiritualised understanding of the Church and the Christian community. Orthodox practice, moreover, places a much higher symbolic value on feminity and femaleness – this seldom leads to practical equality for women but it does lessen the sense that specifically female qualities are excluded from the Church. The word 'Eastern' that frequently precedes 'Orthodox' is of more than geographical significance. While women in the West are increasingly aware that public 'equality' has been bought at the expense of female values this is less true in the East. Women are held in a particular double bind when their rights as individuals in relation to the men around them are limited, but their abstract symbolic value as woman is high. It seems unlikely, therefore, that the ordination of women in the Orthodox churches will emerge into the realm of practical politics for a long time. The Orthodox communities in the West have a strong ethnic tendency, desiring to maintain the 'home' culture from which they feel themselves separated, while many of the indigenous Orthodox denominations are under serious pressure from external political forces – the opposition of the Soviet bloc to religion is well publicised, but the emergence of a powerful and militant Islamic revival and the political instability of countries like Greece also make many traditional strongholds of Orthodoxy naturally less than eager to engage in any internal dissension.

In the Roman Catholic Church the debate about the ordination of women to the priesthood is more developed. In the USA particularly there is increasingly militant pressure on the authorities, but, with women still formally excluded from so many of the other activities of that church, the discussion about ordination takes place in a far wider context. The universalism of Roman Catholicism creates additional problems. While opinion polls in the USA suggest that up to 60 per cent of Roman Catholics find the ordination of women acceptable,[19] this is certainly not the case in Italy, South America or many parts of Africa.

Within the Anglican Communion the situation is still more confusing because some of the participant national churches do ordain women to the priesthood – in Hong Kong, the USA, Canada and New Zealand – while the majority do not. The non-ordaining churches adopt a variety of approaches to the minority, to the women so ordained, and to the basic right of such churches to make the decision in the first place. In so far as the Anglican Communion is capable of taking a 'collegial position', the 1978 Lambeth Conference – the first to meet after member churches had started ordaining women – stated only that while no church was obliged to ordain women, all should respect the member churches who had so decided. Apart from a small group in the USA there has been no corporate schism from the Communion over the ordination of women – on either side. Some individuals have left, either because they could not accept the ordination, or because they could not tolerate the continuing refusal to ordain women.

Anglicanism is a peculiar form of Christian faith. It was formed from political necessity rather than theological conviction. It is of all denominations the most pragmatic and non-dogmatic: its principal dogma seems to be its own lack of dogmatism. It contains, usually quite comfortably, a vast range of theological opinions. There are Anglicans who cannot be distinguished from Methodists, Lutherans or Presbyterians along with Erastians – those who believe that the Church is 'the spiritual arm of the state' – and others who claim that nothing but some minor points of discipline separate their Church from Roman Catholicism. Because of the way that Anglicanism was exported from Britain to the colonies and beyond, there are not only differing individuals but whole member churches which take on a particular theological colouring according to who the original missionaries were and how political relations with Britain fared subsequently. These differences add enormously to the problems surrounding the ordination of women. Because it was the first major canonical change affecting all branches of the Anglican Communion the ordination of women has raised profound questions about the whole concept of Anglicanism: to what extent have the participant national churches the authority to act unilaterally? What effect does such a decision have on other members? These are not points of abstract theology: until the last few years any priest ordained in any of the member churches of the Anglican Communion was recognised by all other members. If a priest wanted to live in another country he would not have had to seek reordination, but only request his new Bishop to license him and this was a central sign of the 'Communion'; this focus of unity no longer exists. The decision of the Church of England Synod in 1977 not to license women priests from other provinces made manifest the unity problem which the women-ordaining provinces had created by their unilateral actions.

At the 1968 Lambeth Conference the ordination of women was discussed. The consensus of opinion was that there were no fundamental objections to the ordination of women within the context of Anglican theology. None the less because of the dissension and unhappiness of a very large number of people, the Conference requested that no individual province or national church should proceed to ordain women candidates at this time. This 'request' was differently understood by different Bishops. In 1971 the Bishop of Hong Kong ordained the Rev. Jane Hwang and the Rev. Joyce Bennet, Deaconesses, to the priesthood. The Diocese of Hong Kong is an anomaly. All other dioceses are grouped into provinces within which the Bishops form a college. For example in England there are two provinces – York and Canterbury each with its Archbishop. The Diocese of Hong Kong used to be one Diocese in the Province of South China; however, since the Chinese Revolution all the other dioceses have disappeared and Hong Kong remains as a sort of province of one. This gives the Bishop there both a powerful autonomy and an isolation not experienced by any other Anglican Bishop. The diocese of Hong Kong also enjoys a unique history in relation to women's ministry. As a missionary territory it had experienced women's leadership; but by population and culture its Anglicanism is emphatically Western. In 1944 the Bishop of Hong Kong, faced with a serious shortage of priests and a desperate pastoral need in the face of the Japanese invasion and the segregated concentration camps, ordained the Rev. Li Tim Oi to the priesthood with the permission of his local synod. Because of the wartime conditions she actually functioned as a priest for a short while, but Canterbury and York refused to accept the ordination and she voluntarily resigned her orders.

The Bishop of Hong Kong, drawing on both these traditions, declared that the isolation of his diocese, its particular needs and its experience of women's ministry made it the ideal place for a 'controlled experiment' with women priests. The fuss that has gathered round the ordination of women to the priesthood in other countries has rather obscured the significance of the 1971 ordinations. The very quietness and episcopal leadership in these ordinations made them both less conspicuous and more important. Although many people did not approve of these ordinations, they did not create the international protest that the wartime ordination had done; no diocese, province or national church declared the Diocese of Hong Kong to be excommunicate. The validity of the Hong Kong ordinations has never been officially challenged.

Since 1971 there have been women priests in the Anglican Communion. Whether they are licensed to officiate in different provinces is actually irrelevant. This is important as much of the higher-principled objection to the ordination of women comes from Catholic Anglicans who feel that this would imperil relationships with Rome. But these are precisely the same people who argue against national autonomy for member churches on the grounds that the Church is one and universal. Thus there is a deep and divisive lack of clarity on the part of those who continue to declare that they will leave the Church of England if women are ordained or licensed here, since their understanding of the Church is that these national boundaries are no more than administrative conveniences. The acceptance of the Hong Kong ordinations by the rest of the Anglican Communion changed the situation more completely than most people are willing to recognise.

Unfortunately the actions of the Bishop of Hong Kong did not clarify the situation. By describing his ordinations as 'experimental' and a response to an urgent pastoral need, he left open the question of whether women, like men, had the same right to offer themselves to the Church as candidates for ordination. This was the specific challenge taken up in the USA.

The ruling body of the Episcopal Church in the USA is the National Convention, a conference which meets every three years and consists of all Bishops and elected priests and lay people from each diocese. In 1970 Convention, while rejecting the priesthood of women, agreed that Episcopal Church Deaconesses were in Holy Orders, and moreover the same Holy Order as the male Deacons. In the Anglican Communion – as in the Roman Catholic and Orthodox Churches – it is necessary to be ordained a Deacon before one can be ordained to the priesthood. Clarifying the fact that women were members of the full diaconate was thus a necessary step before women could claim that they were properly and fully qualified to be priests. Some people thus saw the agreement about the diaconate as a move towards the ordination of women to the priesthood. From 1970 onwards there was a growing group of women who saw priesthood as their professional work in the Episcopal Church. The Rev. Jeanette Piccard, for example, had felt herself called to the priesthood since the age of eleven; in 1970 she was seventy-four. She had never wanted to become a Deaconess, 'Quite simply that was never my calling,' she told me. But now, despite being a retired educationalist, she entered seminary and trained as a Deacon. In 1965 she had been introduced to Suzanne Hiatt – then a recent seminary graduate – who openly affirmed her desire and determination to be ordained to the priesthood. Jeanette Piccard summed up the meeting: 'For over a half a century I had been forced to wonder if I was altogether sane. Meeting Sue Hiatt, hearing her say what I did not even like to think, changed my life.'[20]

The 1970 ruling on the Diaconate, followed by the Hong Kong ordinations in 1971, changed the climate in the USA. The determination to see women ordained as priests took on a new vitality. An odd chronological coincidence fostered the new feeling: under US law ministers of religion and those training for ordination were exempted from the military draft. In the late 1960s the number of seminarians had increased markedly in response to the heavy conscription for the Vietnam War; the seminaries, all of which are privately funded, had expanded gladly to receive these applicants. By the early 1970s, however, the threat of the draft was receding and enrolments falling. In order to keep up their student body Episcopalian seminaries were willing to accept more women students. There was therefore a large number of qualified, trained women to create a pressure group. The American media were sympathetic to the women's case and this allowed the arguments in favour of women's ordination to disseminate widely. The pro-ordination campaign – still a fairly loose network – approached the 1973 Convention in Louisville with considerable optimism. The Convention rejected the motion to change the canon and permit their ordination.

It is very hard to describe, or even at a distance fully to understand, the sense of shock and betrayal that women felt at this decision; but it was certainly very real. The feeling that the change had been defeated by a voting technicality[21] – since a majority of delegates had voted in favour – added to a conviction that the institutional church itself was acting Pharisaically – putting the letter of the Law above the will of God. Women not previously concerned with the issue felt that an injustice had been done which demanded their active involvement; the campaign developed a far wider base than it had had before and numerous groups and individuals began working almost immediately to have the decision reversed at the next Convention at Minneapolis in 1976. Simultaneously an increasing number of women felt that they were no longer bound by the unjust canonical process, and from this grew the determination to prevail upon some individual Bishop to ordain some qualified women, immediately and in defiance of the Convention. Particularly in New York, where a group of women Deacons had the support of their own parish communities and where the Bishop was broadly sympathetic to their situation, the pressure mounted. In December 1973 five of these Deacons presented themselves formally to be ordained in the Cathedral while the Bishop was ordaining five men. The Bishop's refusal, sensed by many people there as being a reluctant and last-moment resolution, was considered by these women as being the end of the search for 'legal' ordination. The question ceased to be whether they would seek uncanonical, irregular ordination, but when and where and at the hands of which Bishop. By the summer of 1974 these questions too were answered. An invitation to almost every women Deacon who had been in orders for the regulation minimum of six months was issued. On 29 July at the Church of the Advocate in Philadelphia, Bishops Daniel Corrigan, Robert de Witt and Edward Welles ordained to the sacred priesthood, before a congregation of over 2,000, Marrill Bittner, Alla Bozarth–Campbell, Alison Cheek, Emily Hewitt, Carter Heyward, Suzanne Hiatt, Marie Moorefield, Jeanette Piccard, Betty Scheiss, Katrina Swanson and Nancy Witting. In terms of the Catholic theology of the priesthood, upheld within the Anglican Communion in its official statements, these ordinations were outrageous. In terms of the theology commonly accepted in the USA and in terms of the conscientious conviction of the women concerned they were both courageous and prophetic.

The 'irregularity' of the ordinations was not seriously questioned by any of the participants. Only one of them was canonically resident in the diocese where the ordinations were performed. None of the women's own Bishops had delegated the ordaining Bishops to act for them. None of the ordained Bishops were Diocesans – they were unable to license the priests they had ordained. This illegality meant different things to different women. Carol Anderson, for example, who had been among the most active of the New York Deacons, decided that she personally could not be so ordained. She had sought ordination throughout solely as a means to a fuller pastoral ministry; and she recognised, as did all the women who were ordained, that this act would eliminate any possibility of being a 'normal' parish priest in the Episcopal Church.[22] At the other end of the scale Emily Hewitt saw the illegal nature of the ordinations in the same light. For her the willingness to be ordained at Philadelphia marked not the beginning but the end of a priestly ministry. She believed that at Philadelphia God was asking her to give up everything, including her own vocation. For her Philadelphia was a prophetic, final act. After making her final decision to be there she took the entrance examination for Law School: she knew there would be no future for her in the Church. She has never performed a priestly sacramental act.[23]

But to the fears and complaints that the illegal ordinations would set back the 'cause' of women in the Church it has to be pointed out that the Philadelphia ordinations – with the further ordination of three women in Washington the following winter – were effective. Despite the mounting fury, the declaration by the Bishops that the ordinations were 'invalid'[24] and the increasing unrest in the conservative sections of the Episcopal Church, the pro-ordination party went to Minneapolis in 1976 with the impasse broken. There were women priests, accepted by large section of the Episcopal Church, acting out priestly ministries wherever and whenever they could. Convention was obliged to recognise that women were no longer asking for a favour, but proclaiming their own reality.

It would be wrong, however, to suggest that the result was a foregone conclusion. The opposition party, which had influential support in high places – including the Presiding Bishop himself, who was to declare after the Convention that 'a woman can no more be a priest than she can be a husband or father' (in the light of which it seems extraordinary, if not unprincipled, that he should wish to continue to preside over a body capable of claiming such absurdities) – had also been organising itself since Louisville. Its strongest card was its commitment to leaving the Episcopal Church if the Ordination Canon was changed. Many people occupying the undecided middle ground must have felt they were being blackmailed by both sides – when they voted they were voting for a schism, their choice was only which one.

Moreover, the pro-ordination party was not as unified as it had been. One faction, holding out for respectability and a straightforward 'yes vote', had thoroughly compromised itself on feminist issues – and even proposed abandoning the fifteen 'irregular' women priests if that would facilitate the canonical change. There was also an extreme radical group which feared the inevitable watering down and co-option process that was likely to occur once women were legally accepted into the system. Alla Bozarth-Campbell has written about her feelings at the Convention:

When I say that I had some small amount of hope for the General Convention I don't mean that I thought legislation was necessary

. . . but there's no question about the healing value of a positive political act. The negative side of Convention's intervention in the issue was that it implied that political action was the necessary approval of the humanity and holiness of women. . . . We are strongly sensitive to the threat of being co-opted as women, into a sexist structure that would not allow us the expression of our femaleness as ministers (lay or ordained) but would attempt to absorb us into patriarchy . . . allowing a few token women into the sacred ranks of priesthood and episcopally . . . but maintaining its mysogynistic posture toward lay women.[25]

Despite the conflicts within and without, on Thursday 16 September 1976 the General Convention voted by a comfortable majority that women could be admitted to the priesthood of the Episcopal Church. The following Tuesday the Bishops (whose concern alone it was) decided not to require any further ordination of the fifteen priests whose standing was unaffected by Convention's vote.[26] They recommended that the women be regularised by means of some public service which should have reconciling elements both for the women and the people of their diocese.

At this point women in the Episcopal Church in the USA, along with their sisters in Hong Kong, Canada, and New Zealand, begin to share the same problems as the ordained women of the Protestant Churches. Because of the intensity of the struggle in the USA, some of the problems of appointments, of clericism and of continuing negative attitudes to women are exacerbated there. Moreover, because of the higher symbolic value of priesthood and the higher doctrine of the church, within Anglicanism people who feel passionately, on either side, cannot just persuade their congregations to employ, or not to employ, a woman and leave it at that.

As the struggle for ordination spreads into other member churches of the Anglican Communion and in the Roman Catholic Church too, it is important to look clearly at the history of other denominations and particularly those that have a shared understanding of ordination. Alla Bozarth-Campbell's fear that legalising ordination may amount to no more than 'jobs for the girls' and the speedy co-option of women of energy and ability into the clericised institution is not a baseless one. The system required of people who seek regular ordination is one easily adapted to the process of co-option.

The would-be ordinand has to pass through a veritable obstacle course of selection conferences, seminary experience, examinations and – in some countries – psychological tests. One has to prove oneself a suitable person, on terms set entirely by the institution. The aspirant to Holy Orders is restricted, if ordination is the goal, by the need to appear 'good enough' and is cut off from lay people and fixed within the clerical caste who alone can give the authority for ordination. In exchange for behaving well enough to be allowed to join the club, the ordained minister is given certain clerical privileges whose comfort and value no one would deny. Both Pauline Webb of the English Methodist Church in the early 1970s and more recently Dr Una Kroll, an Anglican, have decided that it was impossible both to fight for the right of women's ordination and expect to be ordained oneself. To get oneself ordained it is necessary, they both felt, to have a certain aura of respectability. In the prevailing political climate it is impossible to combine that acceptability with the prophetic, critical role necessary to force the denominations con-cerned into recognising the equal God-image in women. It is unlikely that the attitude of ordained women towards the ordaining authorities is going to be as critical as those of someone who is not seeking ordination. On the other hand, ordained women do have power and influence; and, moreover, provide an educative role-model for other women. This complicated balance of pros and cons makes it hard for women to determine where their efforts are best directed. In the light of the complexities many women retreat into an individualistic understanding of personal vocation which, far from solving anything, further confuses the issues.

The recent history of women in institutional Christianity proves only that ordination itself does not solve any problems. Its precise value is very hard to assess, even within denominations where there is no *theological* debate. On the one hand, the gradual increase of respect for women's contribution led directly to the ordination of women and from this it is possible to argue that a circular effect has been started – more women entering the ordained professional ministry may lead in its turn to an increased recognition of women within Christianity generally. Or, it may in a subtle way make it *harder* for other women to lay claim to their own vocation, because the most obvious charge of discrimination is eliminated. All institutions with histories as long as Christianity's are accomplished in the art of co-opting dissident factions. Women who have achieved clerical

status have to be particularly careful that they do not allow themselves to be used against women whose vocations are more individualistic, charismatic or structurally radical.[27] The clerical model
is a very old and very powerful one. By inviting some of the most
able and enthusiastic women into its power structures institutional
Christianity may be able to evade the more profound issues of
in-built sexism and dualism.

The danger has increased since the women now training for
ordination do not have to face the explicit discrimination that
women confronted up until the middle-1970s. A number of observers have noticed an increasing conservatism or at least quiescence
among women seminarians:

> Old Testament scholar Phyllis Trible notes a serious internal
> obstacle for the future. In the early 1970s she comments, there
> were few women teachers or students in the seminaries. Now,
> however, seminary doors are open – at Andover Newton where
> Trible taught until her move to Union this year, the student
> body is 50% female. Ironically because they have not suffered
> personally, many of the women now studying want nothing to
> do with the Women's Movement that made their entrance
> possible. They are willing to accept a traditionally male
> theological consciousness. If this trend continues women in the
> field of education will increasingly be serving up what Mary
> Daly calls 'male ideas in drag'.[28]

Even in the Episcopal Church in the USA where the struggle is
that much more recent and more bloody, the Rev. Sue Hiatt notes
the same problem.[29] In Britain, where feminist theology and perspectives have not really got off the ground yet, the danger is all the
greater.

This is not a spurious concern. Many interested people have noted
the increased respectability and clerical identification of many of the
ordained women. The middle-class and academic bias of the clerical
profession as a whole adds to the problem. Pauline Webb, with a
typical loving comprehension, comments that:

> I find it very difficult to pass any judgement on this, because I
> understand the vulnerability of women who are in the ministry.
> They have to prove themselves and on the whole do not want to
> get caught up in any controversy. They want to be accepted as

ministers in their own right and any emphasis put on them as *women ministers tends to make them nervous*.[30] I would have liked to see women developing a different style of ministry and not just fitting into the patterns demanded of them in the male ministry. But talking to women ministers I hear that there are still many sectors where they are not accepted as 'proper ministers'; and so I can understand why the women feel that they have to demonstrate that they are proper. But I do think it is a pity, because they need to be different and *we* need a different kind of ministry.[31]

Somewhere some of the women who have been ordained, and many who support them, do seem to have forgotten that the issue was originally raised because women felt that there was an aspect or image of God that was not being presented to the world. Some ordained women take the definition of 'proper ministry' not from their own spiritual experience nor from the theological fact of their ordination, but from precisely that male model in opposition to which women fought for ecclesiological authorisation. There are ordained women who accept a 'second-class priesthood' quite knowingly. One woman in the USA told me that she did not take her turn with her fellow priests in the parish – she never sang the principal Sunday Eucharist, nor (it being an Episcopal church of that tradition) was she on the rota for the confessional. Although she spoke of a gradual acceptance, it seems to me that it is *more* undermining for women's self-image to have an 'inferior' priest around than it would be to have no women priests at all.

None of this is meant to condemn the courage or faith of those women who have sought and fought for what they believed to be their own ministries. I raise it so that choices can be made in the future with more awareness. The Church of England in particular is at a point where it must decide (if the decision has not already been made by default) whether it wants a single victory of 'women's ordination now' – and is prepared to pay the price of that – or whether it is concerned for a wholeness of ministry. A holistic approach is harder and less likely to be marked by victories or consolations. It demands a radical analysis of the problems of institutional clericism, sexism, ministry, denominational and social division – all those dualisms of which the non-presence of women in the priesthood is but a minute and fragmentary example. To choose the more wide-based understanding does not of course eliminate demanding ordination as a tactical aim, but it does require tackling the question from a rather different perspective.

The development of the debate in the Church of England has been slower than in her sister church in the USA. This is partly because the penetration of feminist ideas into wider popular culture has been more limited; it is also a result of a wide range of other factors, ideological, practical and structural. First there is a stronger sense of unified ecclesiology in Britain than in the USA: Carol Anderson summed up this difference with the aphorism – 'In America we have no theology, in England you have no energy. Now when we get the two together . . . !'[32] This difference is apparent at all levels: the Bishops in England seem to have a stronger sense of collegiality than their counterparts across the Atlantic. But the women seeking ordination here too have a stronger sense of the Church's authority and are less likely to see ordination as no more than a legalistic affirmation of an internal spiritual condition. This difference is best illustrated by responses to the negative votes on women's ordination in the two countries. In 1973, as the Louisville Convention rejected the motion for change, a lay deputy, Donald Belcher, rose to his feet immediately and said:

> I rise on a point of personal privilege. There is a priest in the Diocese of Pennsyvania who has counselled many of us lovingly and wisely . . . two nights ago I sat alone and wondered what I could possibly say to that loving and wise priest . . . I decided I would say 'Thank you for your gifts so far. . . . Do not despair Suzanne Hiatt for in God's eyes you are a priest indeed.'[33]

In 1978 when the same events occurred in England the voting figures were received in silence by Synod and it was from the spectators' gallery that the protest came. Dr Una Kroll cried out, 'We asked for bread and you gave us a stone!' Both were interventions of passion and commitment but Dr Kroll saw ordination as the gift of the Church to her daughters; and her expression was Biblical. Donald Belcher spoke of a priesthood already possessed, and proven by 'love and wisdom'; his language was not Biblical but interpersonal and charismatic. The correct response to Donald Belcher's understanding was the Philadelphia ordinations a year later. But the equally consistent consequence of Una Kroll's understanding was her passionate and moving appeal *against* 'irregular ordination' which she spelled out the following week:

> To all I have said what I believe . . . that it would be idiotic for any of us to get ordained irregularly at the moment or to officiate at services invalidly. . . . Let me be absolutely clear. I am not proposing to leave the Church of England. I am not proposing the formation of an alternative Church. I am not going to encourage dissidents to abstain from the sacraments. . . . The Holy Spirit is saying to us that we must use our energies and love to build up strong groups of people who are willing to ask for and participate in acts of worship under the leadership of women. We will do more in the long run for the Church if we do this than if we immediately arrange for the ordination of a few women in order to prove our point.[34]

This theological difference is important, but it is not the only factor that has slowed down the development of a practical campaign in the Church of England. There is also a political element that must not be ignored. While the General Convention meets once every three years for two weeks and is re-elected afresh each time, the Synod of the Church of England meets three times a year and the delegates are elected every four years. It is thus much harder to elect candidates who see the Ordination as their single priority. The very structure of Synod, moreover, favours the candidacy of conservative and ecclesial individuals: the preponderance in Synod of the middle classes, the retired and those professionally connected with the Church does not simply reflect the membership of the Church of England – it also indicates who has the time to attend.[35] The members of Synod additionally have a stronger corporate feeling than the Convention delegates – they have to continue to work with each other for up to four years after any divisive issue which is bound to make them more cautious and more respectful of each other's opinions. This drive towards unity, or at least towards the avoidance of too much tension, is probably a British characteristic anyway, a consequence of living in a smaller country among people who meet regularly.

Furthermore Synod is marked by its party politics. Various groups actually 'run' candidates for Synod and, although there are many Independents, there is the increasing tendency towards party loyalty and block voting. As always women are finding that where they do not command a powerful political machine of their own their concerns do not tend to be given priority. While almost all the recognisable groups give a nominal recognition to the importance of women's roles in the Church they do not see this as a primary goal. Moreover their competence to deal with the issue is consistently open to question. What confidence can one repose in a group like the Open Synod Group whose Manifesto for the 1980 Synodical Elections puts the ordination of women as the second item on its platform, but then goes on to entitle its section on lay ministry as 'The *Man* in the Pew'.[36] The Church Union (whose well organised opposition to the ordination vote in 1978 was undeniably instrumental in its defeat) constantly claims that it cares about the proper ministry of women – and set out to demonstrate this in 1979 with a day conference on 'The Ministries of Men and Women in the Church'[37] which was notable mainly for its clericism (the male priesthood proclaimed as the highest possible vocation), its outrageous sexism (which took the form of the most simplistic and anachronistic acceptance of opinions about the inferiority of women, coupled with endless inane jokes about the supposed beliefs of 'women's libbers') and its suppression of all debate. It is groups like this that dominate the Synod and make it unlikely that any discussion of women's issues will emerge as anything other than a stick to beat the opposing parties with.

Faced with these structural difficulties and with the defeat of the 1978 motion, women who strongly favour the ordination of women are left with a series of not very appealing options. The obvious plan of importing women ordained elsewhere for the combined task of ministering to those who wanted this and raising the consciousness of a wider public was thwarted by Synod's decision in 1979 not to license any women ordained in other branches of the Anglican Communion. Although this decision was reversed in 1982, other approaches have been developed in the meantime.

The most obvious thing to do is to get the 1978 decision reversed, and to this end an organisation called the Movement to Ordain Women was formed in 1979. Interestingly the defeat of both the motion to ordain and the motion to license women from overseas helped many Christians to grow up rapidly. Before the voting in 1978 there had been widespread criticism of the anti-ordination party for their 'politicking' – the Catholic party ran an impressive political machine and their superior organisation was attacked by pro-ordination activists as somehow 'cheating'. A passionate article in the *Church Times*, for instance, referred to 'those devious little men in black' and the sinister rise of party politics within the Synod, as though, left in peace, the Holy Spirit would have acted otherwise. But the lesson was quickly learned: anyone who believes in demo-cratic Synodical government rather than the casting of lots or the consultation of entrails could see that the Catholic Party had made good their claim to have a better Incarnational understanding and practice. It did not take MOW long to adopt the methods and principles that they had denounced.

MOW is a single-issue, national campaigning group. Ordination by Synodical change of the canons is the only platform of the group. Seeking to be persuasive and attractive to likely Synodical voters, MOW is often markedly conservative in its approaches. Its national committee includes a Bishop and several priests and its projected image of ordained women is determinedly unthreatening, and uncri-tical of existing structures. However, there are attempts to subvert this model from within: some members of MOW made a modest protest at an ordination service in St Paul's Cathedral in 1980, standing up with banners during the liturgy, to draw attention to the exclusion of women. There are obvious tensions within the orga-nisation of MOW as to 'how far' it is proper to go, but the official line is, so far, rigidly reformist and mannerly: for the sake of ordination there remains an apparent willingness to court co-option and elimin-ate a more radical and feminist critique of the Church.

An alternative to constitutional reform which women are taking is 'going underground'. Some women leave the Church altogether. This painful invisible decision, discounted by the opposition, is one in which women are seldom properly supported by their sisters. Women often experience a spiritual agony of loneliness and the final steps are made in the realisation that even other women cannot or will not provide a Christian experience of accepting love:

> I was desolated. I kept saying, 'I cannot bear this, I cannot bear to go to Church, to work on anything any more.' And women I have worked with over the last couple of years began to look at me as though I had some infectious disease – they didn't want to be near me in case despair was catching. That was the end. Even my Christian women friends acted as though I had committed the Sin against the Holy Spirit – and of course I had.[38]

Sometimes rather than leaving Christianity women go underground in a different way: they retreat from the material, historical Church into a private 'church' of their own where they can act as though the problems did not exist. Often this church will be a women's group, ecumenical, limited in size and with support as its primary object. As I have made clear in the chapter on women's groups, I believe strongly in their radical potential. It is only when they become introverted and are used as a substitute for institutional involvement that they can be criticised.

One activity related to these groups which is becoming increasingly common is the 'private' service of Holy Communion, celebrated by women ordained elsewhere, usually from the USA. I am probably not the best person to comment on these services, because my own theological bent makes it impossible for me to see them as valid sacraments: an unlicensed priest celebrates without the authority of the local Bishop, and it is only that Bishop's authority which can validate any sacrament. It does seem to me, however, that these services are inevitably consolatory rather than challenging, since by their very nature they are domestic and the congregation is self-selecting. They are thus very different from mass public 'illegal' services like the Ecumenical Eucharist at Riverside Drive, New York, in 1975, which was as blatant, proclamatory and as public as possible, an act of protest as well as praise. As these services become more common their effect may well become increasingly reactionary: a refusal to live with and struggle against the actual historical reality of discrimination is unlikely to change much. On the other hand, it is undeniable that these services and the ministry of women priests from abroad have made it possible for many women not just to survive within the Christian faith, but to grow and deepen in their love and hope.

Out of this dilemma have come some creative solutions, which can in turn feed back into the wider Church. An *Open Door* programme on the BBC in September 1980 showed the East London Christian Feminist Group 'sacramentalising' a slightly different commandment of Jesus, also traditionally linked with the Last Supper: they were washing one another's hands (feet being neither accessible nor convenient in our culture). This ritual has considerable support among radical Christians and especially those who for one reason or another are unable to celebrate the Eucharist among themselves – ecumenical groups who find their conflicting Eucharistic understandings a barrier between them, for instance. But for women it seems to have a particular potency. It is a moving and intimate act, and also brings to mind many of the central intentions of the Eucharist which have been lost or institutionalised over the years. The real and vital desire of women to create a sacramental worship together, despite our exclusions, must not be allowed merely to reduplicate what the Church already has and has used as a method of exclusion. We have to create something more, something better than the good we already have. Such creative solutions may enable us to make god-sense and richness out of the nonsense and poverty which has been inflicted on us.

Another approach to this problem has been developed. In Oxford a group of women now celebrate a monthly 'women's Eucharist', in which, while women do every single part of the Mass which can possibly be construed as permissible, they invite an ordained priest to perform the canon of consecration. The argument is that this, while avoiding illegality and thus the difficulties that some women might experience in attending such a service, not only allows women the experience of creating and leading the Christian community in its most central act, it also exposes the ridiculous aspects of the ban on ordination itself. Such a service makes a strong and visible protest against the current state of affairs while it also enables women to create their own style of worship *within* the proper structures of the Church.

For me these sorts of choice seem better theologically and politically than discreet illegality. They combine creative imagination with an acceptance of and confrontation with the reality of sexual discrimination within the Church. They can also so strengthen women while offering a route back into the institutional church that we can return with gifts in our hands, empowered by the experience of the desert. The Church needs the creative and innovative power of women's worship, I believe, more than it needs a few more priests – of whatever sex – doing the things that priests have always done.

This way of looking at the problems of exclusion illuminates yet another option that is also open – to develop the line taken by Dr Una Kroll in her letter following the November 1978 Synodical vote, which I quoted earlier in this chapter. She expanded her opinion that irregular ordinations should not then take place:

For this reason . . . that did not obtain in America – *we* are not ready to receive the ministry of ordained women yet. . . . We do not really know what it is in women that is so lacking in the Church today.

As an urgent practical step she suggested that women

try to arrange services at which women alone will preside. . . . It would give women an opportunity to develop alternative styles of worship, to write their own hymns, begin to use a different language about God, begin to share their insights. . . . Please urge your local Bishops . . . and your churches to use women's gifts more effectively.[39]

What Dr Kroll is talking about here is a broadly based campaign of education at the most profound level. Unlike the USA where the commercial press took up feminist theology very seriously and the media adopted the issue of ordination supportively, Britain has been seriously short of both proper analytical feminist theory and widely disseminated spirituality and worship tools. When Dr Kroll was writing in 1978 this dearth was nearly absolute; in the four years since then the situation has begun to improve. Some American material has been published over here; certain bookshops – though on the whole those of the left and the Women's Movement rather than the traditional theological outlets – have begun to import more material on the subject, and more recently still British women have begun to produce their own work. In 1981 SCM press published the first real volume of British feminist theology to attract proper attention: *Dispossessed Daughters of Eve* by Susan Dowell and Linda Hurcombe. The two writers, both with roots firmly in both Church and Women's Movement, used a specifically feminist methodology to examine the impact of the Women's Movement on theology and on the Church.

It is not just the publishing world which has responded to the need for a wider educational approach outlined by Dr Kroll. The issue is now becoming quite fashionable. The religious programmers on the television and radio networks have also approached the issues quite widely, with documentaries, discussion shows, and news items. The serious national press has produced an increasing number of feature articles. The Christian Women's Movement itself, as well as writing and seeking publication, has also begun to explore other avenues. Conferences, panels, research programmes proliferate, and MOW has recently sponsored two shows written by Monica Furlong examining the relationship of women to Christianity more broadly than the simple ordination issue, which have been performed at a central London Church, St James, Piccadilly. In this sense Dr Kroll's analysis of what was needed has proved accurate; there is a much higher awareness about what the issues are, and a much greater openness to what women have to say and what they feel they need than there was even a few years ago. Whether or not this leads towards the ordination of women cannot yet be established. What it certainly does do is broaden out the whole debate so that ordination is placed in its proper perspective: just one of the issues that trouble Christian women when they look at the churches today. The education must continue over as broad as possible a front, and seems to be much more crucial than a direct attack on the single ordination canon.

One of the forms that this education must take is to do everything possible to drive home to those who would rather not know the very real pain and distress that women are feeling. In July 1980 women began to take militant action by protesting at the ordination services which excluded women, and distributing pamphlets to those who attended such services. It seems likely that this will continue, and despite widespread liberal fears that this might alienate potential supporters, history suggests that the reverse will be the case. Militancy has always been effective both for gaining publicity for a cause and for making clear the depth of feeling.[40] In the arena of democratic constitutional reform there have been no major changes without militancy: whether or not those who hold power in the Church will conform themselves to such a secular model of refusing to give an inch without being forced to do so remains to be seen.

Unfortunately the educational approach can only be meaningful if it is wide-reaching and genuinely open to its own arguments. Una Kroll made it clear in her letter that there is more to be gained by a grass-roots educational campaign than 'if we immediately arrange for the ordination of a few women in order to prove our point'. And yet strategically Una Kroll and the Christian Parity Group, which she founded, seem to have over-invested in ordination. Literally over-invested in the sense that they committed themselves in 1979 to spending a great deal of money to fund one woman, Kath Burn, to train at an American seminary and be ordained over there. This drain of money and resources means inevitably that there is that much less to spend for educational and publicist programmes which might do more to open up the fullness of 'women created in the image of God', which is what the struggle is meant to be about. With the deepest respect for the Christian Parity Group which has done more to bridge the gap between Christian feminists and the older reformist endeavours than might have been imagined possible, one cannot help but notice that despite their claims to a holistic approach they have organised actively around few other issues than ordination. For instance the same Synodical meeting that debated ordination in 1978 also put the final stamp of approval on the new prayer book, and there was no organised protest against the sexist language and imagery of that book. While a motion on ordination can be re-introduced into Synod at almost any time, the new Prayer Book – as I will discuss in Chapter 6 – will provide the Church of England's official worship for at least the rest of this century.

The real danger of the current state of play on the ordination issue in the Church of England now is that it can correctly be perceived as 'winnable'. There seems little doubt in my mind that with a well co-ordinated campaign which looks tactically at the political realities the Synodical change could be initiated within the next few years, if women are prepared to make the necessary compromises and sac-rifices; but it would not be a feminist ordination. There are already women in the USA who would argue that in abandoning a feminist perspective for the short-term victory of authorised ordination, women paid too high a price. If the long term objective is to change the bias against not individual women, but the status of femaleness itself, then the value of all isolated victories must be measured carefully against the compromises and costs of winning them.

In the Roman Catholic Church the chances of victory are so slim at the present time that the attitude of women who seek this goal remains uncompromising and very much more radical. There is little point in 'selling out' if no one wants to buy you in. The official Roman Catholic position on women in the ordained ministries is both absolutely clear (it is unlikely to admit women *even* to the Diaconate at this time) and extremely confused (in as much as their reasons for so refusing are based mainly on pre-conciliar theology which has *officially* ceased to apply in other areas).

In 1963 John XXIII published his encyclical *Pacem in Terris* which in many ways set the tone for the Second Vatican Council. In this document he reasserted the full humanity of women:

Since women are becoming ever more conscious of their human dignity they will . . . demand rights befitting a human person both in domestic and in public life. [41]

Having defined women as human, he then defined human rights:

Human beings have the right to choose freely the state of life which they prefer, and therefore to set up a family, with equal rights and duties for men and women, and also the right to follow a vocation to the priesthood or to the religious life. [42]

The documents of the Second Vatican Council, although vague on precise application, imply the same understanding. *Gaudium et Spes* affirms the aspirations of women:

But forms of social or cultural discrimination in basic personal rights on the grounds of sex, race, colour, social conditions, language or religion, must be curbed and eradicated as incompatible with God's design. It is regrettable that these basic personal rights are not yet being respected everywhere, as is the case with women who are denied the chance freely to choose a husband, or a state of life, or to have access to the same educational and cultural benefits as are available to men. [43]

But against these progressive abstractions stands the rather less promising reality. *Humanae Vitae*, the controversial encyclical condemning 'artificial' birth control, struck many Catholics, and not of course just women, as being in conflict with the ideas of self-determination and personal freedom expressed in the abstract ideals of the Council. [44] They also appeared to be a repudiation of the claims for sexual equality and a recognition of the goodness of sexuality itself. The different treatment of nuns and monks in their renewal instruction was another sign that the equality preached to the world was not going to be allowed to affect the Church itself. Other regulations were so petty as to be ridiculous: girls and women were still not officially allowed to be 'servers' at Mass (the symbolic significance of this is that it gives lay people an authorised role inside the sanctuary); [45] men were to be preferred to women, and nuns to lay women for other liturgical activities such as readers or cantors; the Diaconate was not to open to women, despite the fact that this would not be a major break with the tradition as there is substantial evidence for Deaconesses in the Pauline Epistles and the Early Church. [46] The continued discipline of celibacy for priests was interpreted at least in part as a continued assessment of sexuality, and women's sexuality in particular, as being in opposition to the service of God.

Into this already confused and contradictory situation another element has to be introduced. The arguments against the ordination of women fall into three main categories. First, there is the 'continuing tradition of the Church' which Christians are obliged to respect as representing the will of God. Second, there is the position that priests in their sacramental office literally become 'alter Christi' – other Christs – and that this representation is confused if they do not 'correspond to the image of Christ in his humanity' – in his maleness. Third, that priests among their people are the leaders, shepherds, overseers, and that this role cannot be performed by women without distorting their 'natural' role and symbolic function. However, because of the very serious shortage of priests in some parts of the world, women (to date exclusively nuns, but that is irrelevant) have been given official pastoral charge over their communities, by the Bishops. They are authorised to call together the people of God, to lead them in prayer, to teach the faith, to distribute the Eucharistic sacraments. That is to say there are women who, with full episcopal authority, are performing all the priestly functions except the sacramental ones: this must call into very serious question the traditional understanding of what priesthood is and indeed what the role of the sacraments is within a Christian community. If a women can represent the Bishop who represents Christ, in his authoritative, administrative, teaching and leading roles, not only is the 'natural role' argument against ordination completely undermined, but the question as to why she cannot represent that Bishop the one other priestly role – the sacramental one – demands a new answer. The present position suggests either that the sacraments themselves have no intimate, crucial connection with the community and that the priest is simply a magician *or* that not ordaining women is nothing but a bizarre and out-dated prejudice.

Out of all this visible confusion there has arisen a radical critique of the whole understanding of priesthood. In a detailed questionnaire survey of 100 women who felt a calling to the Roman Catholic priesthood in the USA *every* woman questioned was deeply critical of the existing model of priesthood and did not seek ordination in order to 'join' that priesthood, but rather to change it.[47] Although it should not be overlooked that at present even to admit to such a vocation requires a certain internal radicalism, since obedience and submission are still inculcated in women brought up in the Roman Catholic Church, the fact remains that the position of women in the Roman Catholic Church forces a radical analysis on any woman who starts out on a feminist path. The Women's Ordination Conference – the largest Roman Catholic pressure group in the USA – is so critical of the structure and use of priesthood in the contemporary Church that there were complaints from some people after their last National Conference that far from being a pro-ordination assembly, it had presented an anti-ordination platform.[48]

In this climate compromise offers no attractions. Canon Mary Michael Simpson, an American Episcopal priest, who is also herself a nun, suggested to me that the symbolic importance of the ordination of women in the Roman Catholic Church was so great that she felt such women would be well advised to work for the possible – the ordination of nuns.[49] Whenever I mentioned this suggestion to Roman Catholic women involved in the campaign, whether nuns or lay people, they repudiated it absolutely. One nun told me emphatically:

> We are not talking about the ordination of nuns to the priesthood. We are not talking about the ordination of me, or you, or any other group. We are talking about the ordination of women: nun women, single women, married women, divorced women. Black women, white women, Chicano women. Women with children, women without children. We are only talking about the ordination of women. Otherwise there is simply no point at all.[50]

It is only in the USA that the campaign has gained much momentum in terms of practical politics; but that should not suggest that there is not a growing support among women in other countries. Although at present it seems improbable that there is much chance of a swift 'success' in the area of Roman Catholic ordination, there is emerging from the conflict a deepening sense of the power of women united and a coherent critique of the structural problems and sexist formulations of the Roman Catholic Church.

It is important to realise that it is not that the Roman Catholic Church is more sexist than other denominations – it just has the unique and valuable talent for making visible what other denomina tions attempt to deny. The prejudices of Christianity are made plainest in the Roman Catholic Church. The logical and theological inconsistencies at the heart of their position are only a clear statement of what all the denominations actually practise. No denomination officially admits to questioning that women are created in the image of God, capable of receiving grace and salvation offered in Christ's incarnation and in her resurrected life through the Church. Women, all technically agree, are equally beloved of God, equally desired by God and equally capable of desiring and responding to God. If that is really the case there are only two possible conclusions. The humanity that women and men share is, despite differences of biological function, historical and cultural experience and social conditioning, essentially the same, in which case there can be no reason for *not* ordaining women to whatever priestly model a denomination may believe in. *Or* women and men both image God but image *different aspects* of God. If this is the case then a church in which women are not equally represented at every level of authority – possibly in different forms but none the less visibly, equally and powerfully – cannot pretend that it is representing God to the world, because it is wantonly excluding one of the images of God which is known to be incarnate in creation. What makes no sense at all is to do what all the denominations do, either formally or in practice: to say simultaneously that women cannot share the authority that men have, because they are not men, but that they do not need to have their own authoritative ministries because they are represented *by* men.

One of the most serious problems one encounters here is the failure of Christianity to develop any real theology of psychology, or theology of anthropology. All the donominations struggle to decide both questions of ordination and, more worryingly, questions of sexual morality without any basic material on the subject. While anti-ordination factions continue to demonstrate their underlying and profound sexism and misogyny, pro-ordination people treat with contempt the theological insights offered by some theologians from sources such as primitive mythology, Jungian schools of psychology, the material reality of gender biology, and the ancient traditions of the female prophecy and the female nature of the Holy Spirit, because these insights do not fit in with their very natural desire, for immediate affirmative action now.[51]

I have tried in this chapter to present the ordination issue, but I have difficulties. In fairness to myself I want to explain those difficulties. In the eyes of a large number of people, both those involved and those who observe from outside, ordination is seen as *the Issue*. It is not my issue. I think that women who want to offer the Church a richer way forward are over-engaged – in relation to the probable usefulness – on ordination. I think such engagement is a tactical error carrying its own dangers which are considerable. I am not 'opposed' to the ordination of women on any of the normally raised theological grounds. If any denomination decides to ordain women to whatever its understanding of the ordained ministry is, there is nothing innate in women to stop them. On the contrary there are many reasons why women, from their immediate historical experience, would be very good both symbolically and functionally at the job.

My disinvolvement with the issue stems from a different and quite complicated position. This is a combination of a radical political position on feminism and ministry and a 'conservative' ecclesiology (my understanding of what the Church is). From the former position I find myself in agreement with Mary Daly's statement that:

> For women to seek ordination in the Christian Church is as destructive as it would be for black people to seek to become leaders in the Klu Klux Klan.[52]

I hope I have made clear by now that I do not perceive the sexism in Christianity as an isolated phenomenon, but as one aspect of an all-pervasive rejection and projection of the otherness. What is Other has been labelled as Bad and Outside. Racism, classism and the abuse of nature are other modes of the same projection. Clericism is also a sign of this dualism and one that is special to Christianity. In order to achieve ordination by legal means, it is necessary to persuade those who hold power to share it with you. They are unlikely (to put it mildly) to do so unless and until they believe that this will not threaten their defensive structures too dangerously – less dangerously certainly than not granting this access would do. The very act of obtaining constitutional ordination is an inevitable act of co-option into the clerical caste. It is possible, and many would argue this case, that the co-option involved is worth it: the admission of some women to this symbolic height will inevitably prove beneficial to women's self-esteem and to their status in the community at large. There is some truth in this. The question is whether the likely gains are worth the enormous and painful efforts required. This is a political decision, but, as women, we must guard against our own masochism and martyr complexes. If there are easier ways to substantial victories in the areas where we want them, then it is our duty as Christians to use them. A woman in the Christian Gay Movement said to me that she felt the pro-ordination people had got the whole thing back-to-front. If we tackled the issue of women's sexuality head-on, not only would the questions about ordination fall simply into place eventually, but there would be a broader base to fight from as the fight would then include gay people of both sexes. Here my conservative ecclesiology comes in. I am forced to beg on the issue of ordination, because I *cannot* militantly take. I do not believe that priesthood is a private business between me and God. Many ministries that the Church stands in need of are, I think, charismatic – unalienable gifts from God to an individual; they are personal vocations. Priesthood, however, belongs to the Church. An individual may have a vocation to offer herself to the Church to be considered for ordination: she does not have, in that sense, a vocation to be ordained. Priesthood (like the episcopacy and the Diaconate) is a tripartite deal between the individual, God and the institutional Church. Many people do not agree with this. Alla Bozarth-Campbell, for example, expressed:

> A firm conviction that she had come to Philadelphia in order for an Episcopal body of the faithful to recognise and confirm what is already an ontological reality: her participation in the priesthood of Christ. [Bishop] Dan Corrigan . . . smiled, 'Yes in the ways of God ontologically – you are already priests; you have always been priests; and you will always be priests.'[53]

Another of the Philadelphia ordinands expressed the same conviction in a sermon she gave at the ordination of a fellow Deacon:

> I do not believe that you are being 'zapped' tonight. I do not believe your ontological, your essential mode of being, will be changed . . . you will in fact be no more priest than you are right now.[54]

I do accept that these convictions are held in sincerity. Women who held them and felt that this was their condition had an absolute duty to seek ordination by any possible means. God had made them priests and they had an obligation to make the Church recognise this

God–act. But I do not believe that their understanding of priesthood was right.

I believe that the moment of ordination is the moment at which the person becomes a priest, because priesthood has no meaning without the Church, and it is the Church's to dispense. The meaning of priesthood is the bringing from the Bishop (who brings it from the whole universal and eternal Church) the presence of that universal to the particular congregation, or individual. Of course the congregation is a vital part of the whole Church so that there is circularity and co-responsibility at all times in this relationship. The visible circularity has been lost since the denominations destroyed the traditional custom whereby the people *elected* and proclaimed their Bishops. The 'oversight' claimed by priests as the justification of their leadership should not be understood as a power-wielding activity: a priest's presence is necessary at the celebration of the sacraments because since the Incarnation and Resurrection two paradoxical elements have been brought into synthesis – the mystical presence of eternity and the material presence of time/place/person. The priest – through no personal merit, but as the delegate of the whole Church personified in the Bishop – represents this universal element.

I believe that this understanding is not only correct in theological terms, but would also if more widely understood be effective in cutting down on clericism, whereas the view that a person is called directly by God, without any external supervision, to exercise a leadership ministry in the Church actually encourages clerical dominance. If the priest is understood only as a servant of the whole Church and strictly answerable to a Bishop, and in no way an autonomous leader, the cult of priest power will have difficulty establishing itself. It is interesting, for instance, that Carter Heyward, with her individualistic understanding of Holy Orders, in the same sermon that I have quoted above expresses a very clericised understanding of ministry. As her text for the sermon – which she affirmed with 'even greater gusto' after her own ordination – she took, 'The harvest is plentiful but the laborers are few; pray therefore the Lord of the harvest to send out laborers into his harvest', and interpreted 'laborers' as *priests* – Christians for whom 'the commitment to priesthood is central to their vocation, their profession, their life'.[55] As a lay person I rather resent the implication that God requires only priestly labourers for the harvest.

From this I draw two conclusions about the position of women.

As a representative of the universal Church – an apostle, one who is sent – the priest has an obligation to 'represent' the Church verbally, to preach and teach for the church the authorised faith of the Church. The rights of individual conscience which apply to lay people in all denominations must to some extent be curtailed in the case of a priest. It cannot be part of the function of a priest to preach anything that is not 'orthodox'. In this sense I find it hard to understand why anyone who was opposed to the sexist ideology of institutional Christianity, to its imagery, dualism, and misogynistic tradition, would want to be a priest now when there is a clear opportunity for prophetic witness.

The second point is sadder and more perplexing. In as much as priesthood belongs to the whole, indivisible Church only that Church can change the conditions of entry. That Church no longer has an incarnate form; the denominational divisions within Christianity are a deep sin against God and a wound in the flesh of the Body of Christ. Until the Church is reunited with herself there is no group which has the authority to open the priesthood to women. Denominational division and hatred is one more symptom of the same dualism, it is a symptom, as I have suggested, that women are specially able to heal. Our lack of ordination is therefore both a prophetic sign of that sin *and* a source of energy to heal that wound.

CHAPTER 5

WOMEN IN THE BUREAUCRACIES

◆◆◆

I'm a kept woman in the Bureaucracy
And, boy, do I earn my keep.[1]

The real danger of clericism and its vital connection with women becomes clearer when one looks directly at the way in which most of the 'professional' Christians are in fact employed. This is not parochially, pastorally or sacramentally: it is in administrating the institutional machinery of the denominational churches, and maintaining and servicing those administrators. It is here that the structural problems of dualism take on their most concrete forms – of hierarchy, clericism, sexism, racism and other injustices. It is here that the most radical challenges can be made, and the greatest gains achieved.

In the last twenty years there has been an enormous increase in the size and power of the Christian bureaucracies. Much of this has arisen for essentially healthy reasons. One of the consequences of the self-examination and renewal that the churches have all been undertaking since the 1950s has been a genuine attempt to broaden the power base and (to a greater or lesser extent) to 'democratise' all the denominations. Simultaneously there has been a growth in communication between the denominations in response to the ecumenical enthusiasm which renewal generated. Imagine the organisational skills necessary even to get the Second Vatican Council started – an international conference designed to last for several years, at which the agreed common language was one that no one really spoke, and at which the members were governed by a medieval protocol but observed by twentieth-century mass media – and then realise that on

a less dramatic scale the problems are repeated in every denominational church, at every level, from the international to the parochial,
and then ecumenically as well.

It is clear that modern theological concepts like collegiality,
Synodical government, lay participation and consultative procedures, though good in themselves, have massively increased the
bureaucracy of Christianity. Secular pressures of twentieth-century
life – investment, taxation, communication to name but a few – have
further added to that administrative load. Even those denominations
like the Baptist churches which theoretically operate on an entirely
congregational base have national pension schemes, recognised
training programmes and ecumenical committees all of which have
to be run by someone.

In 1975, for example, the Church of England spent £1,413,170 on its
central government. The Roman Catholic Church in England –
which makes no claim to being a central power and has much of its
administration run from Rome, spent over £150,000 and would like
to have more to spend.[2] Committees, commissions and central
programmes proliferate; and ecclesial civil services expand yearly.
Increasingly the real power shifts from the Princes of the Church in
their Cathedrals – which at least look conspicuously different from
the headquarters of other multi-national corporations – to office
blocks which do not, whether they come in the shape of the
ultra-modern sky-scraper on Riverside Drive, New York, which
houses the USA National Council of Churches, or the gracious
dignity of 1 Millbank, London, with its leather chairs and carved
staircases where, under the shadow of the Houses of Parliament, the
Church Commissioners – the managing directors of the Church of
England – run the central office of a business with an annual income
of £126,300,000.

Christians do not like to think of themselves as members of a large
business corporation. Although there has been a fashion for discussing decision-making processes almost endlessly, there is much less
willingness to talk about the background administration and finance
which keeps the whole thing going. This delicacy of feeling is not
seriously challenged by those who are on the inside of the bureaucracy who, it appears, like the element of secrecy. The result of the
reluctance to tackle head-on the Christian understanding of administration means that there is a dearth of anything that could be
described as 'institutional theology': what it means to be an institu-

tion engaged in the work of the gospel. What must it cost in terms of individuality and freedom to run a 'good machine'? Which ways of running such a machine most closely correspond to our Christian calling to love and justice and to the specific understanding of the theology of Christian community on which the different denominations ground themselves?

The document of the Second Vatican Council on the constitution of the Roman Catholic Church, *Lumen Gentium*, for example, starts off boldly enough:

> Since the Church, in Christ, is the nature of a sacrament – a sign and instrument . . . she here purposes to set forth as clearly as possible her own nature. . . . The one Mediator, Christ, has established and ever sustains here on earth his Holy Church, the community of Faith, Hope and Charity as a visible organisation through which he communicates truth and grace to all men. But the society structured with hierarchical organs and the mystical body of Christ, the visible society and the spiritual community, the earthly Church and the Church endowed with heavenly riches are not to be thought of as two realities. On the contrary they form one complex reality which comes together from a human and a divine element.[3]

But after this really splendid start *Lumen Gentium* manages to evade almost all the issues which it has here raised: it never mentions money (apart from the 'heavenly riches' there is the little matter of the 'earthly riches' which the Church founded by one who claimed that the poor were blessed has none the less accumulated). It does not discuss how the community of Faith, Hope and Charity is going to work out salary levels. It ignores the question of where in the 'hierarchical organs', the Christian ministries of accountancy, office management and audio-typing are going to fit. Finally it never once takes seriously the problem of how it has come about that if these 'two churches form one complex reality' Catholicism has managed, on its own admission, to be at different times and in different ways the instrument of oppression and injustice within and without. It does not examine how this might be changed.

And yet it is an undeniable fact that how an institution is run is closely, intimately, related to what that institution really is – and not just symbolically. The hand that prepares the budget rules the world in a very particular way; not only because of the very real importance of money, but also because money has become a measure of power and authority. Money is only the tip of the iceberg of control that is wielded by the behind-the-scenes agenda-preparers, appointment-makers, translators, and commission secretaries. The well known resistance of the Curial bureaucracy to the increased participation of even the Roman Catholic Diocesan Bishops in the internal affairs of the Vatican shows that they at least know where the power lies. Power is a very nice thing to have: it is seldom, if ever, given up voluntarily.

Someone who has done some initial work on institutional theology, Anne Scheibner – a business school graduate and activist in the Episcopal Church in the USA – sums up the problem:

> Ever since Constantine converted to Christianity in the 4th century . . . the Church in its institutional form has reflected the dominant social and political structures and attitudes of society. The Roman Catholic form still proclaims a feudal consciousness complete with Princes of the Church and a Lord to whom homage is paid. American Protestant Denominations to-day reflect the corporate model: secretaries make the coffee, type the correspondence and make airline reservations for executives whose corner offices, salaries and bureaucratic duties increase proportionately as they rise in the hierarchy. . . . In short the Church has never had an institutional form related to the Gospel. What does the Church's incarnation as a temporal institution mean for Christians?[4]

The question has always been important, indeed crucial, for Christianity, but it has become more central in recent times. We live, increasingly, in an institutional world, from the nuclear family to the multi-national corporation. It is now more than ever impossible to pretend that one can live alone: even hermits are dependent on the electrical power-works doing their job. Although Christianity still appears to seek to deny the fact, it is too late for us to be redeemed by the private and personal virtue of individuals. This is not to acquit individuals of the need for personal holiness, but to recognise that the holiness of previous generations has to take on a political aspect which has too often been ignored. It is not the duty of Christianity to deny this contemporary reality, but to show rather how the power of the Holy Spirit, the power of love, can transform and make holy this historical present:

The Church itself is a multi-national corporation of sorts with scattered jurisdiction linked by modern communication systems. The chief distinction institutionally however is that the Corporation has a quantifiable yearly summary of its performance, namely its net profit. . . . The Church has no such impediment.

The Church itself is therefore in a unique position to reverse its historical pattern of reflecting the society and to model a new form of institution which has neither its own perpetuation nor the accumulation of wealth as its goal.

No institution in history has ever voluntarily surrendered its power. . . . Individuals have surrendered power. . . . But if stewardship is to mean anything to-day it must be in institutional terms – not in terms of individual commitment.[5]

Christianity has always made a unique claim for itself. It is not just the individual members who are made Christ-like, but the institution itself is Christ, is the incarnation of Godhead. If this claim is to have any significance in the twentieth century then the institution itself, corporately, must follow that example of the voluntary renunciation of power, the willingness to die that others may live, of total self-sacrifice, and of living an example of loving justice. Love is a word that Christians use a good deal, but we have let it go soft on us: it is not enough to treat other people with an indulgent affection – Jesus' love included hard judgments, not just of those who opposed him, but of his own friends. 'Get thee behind me Satan,' he said to Peter[6] while he offered not only forgiveness but even excuses for those who killed him. His judgment extended to his own history and cultural tradition.

This is of course a problem for the whole Christian community. It is not at first sight specifically a women's issue. But the whole argument of the Women's Liberation Movement rests on the claim that sexist discrimination is not a question of individual women being deprived of individual privileges, but of a deep-rooted structural, institutional injustice which cannot be rectified by the promotion of a few token women to important jobs. The institutional models of our society are dependent on sexual discrimination. Women are particularly discriminated against within bureaucratic structures, but without being totally excluded from them: this puts them in a unique position to prophesy to the institution. The traditional

~~prophet has always been someone who belongs within a system~~ and pronounces judgment from that position of belonging.

Women therefore have a particular role to play in the transformation of institutional Christianity today. At various times in Christian history there have been brave attempts to subvert the Church from its slavish adherence to contemporary secular models, and to replace these paternalistic structures with others, more gospel-based: the Franciscan movement, Genevan Calvinism, the Leveller, Anabaptist and Quaker initiatives, and primitive Methodism are all examples, in their different ways, of assaults on the ideology of institutional Christianity in their own time. However, they inevitably lacked a concrete material understanding of how oppression worked. The nineteenth and twentieth centuries have helped supply this understanding with a scientific approach to economics, anthropology, history, sociology and psychology.

The Women's Movement, at its best, ignores no part of this analysis. Indeed, critical of most given dogma, it has been able to unify and expand many elements of it. Sisterhood, as an intellectual concept as well as a personal experience, can reclaim for Christianity – especially in the West which is where the institutional model was formed and from whence it was exported as a part of imperialism – its original identification with the oppressed and therefore the means of ending that oppression. Christian women can, if we can make institutional Christianity listen to us, make a special contribution to the evolution of Christian structures precisely because of our experience of being outside – less important, less rewarded and the recipients of the ungodly projections and exclusions of which we are all corporately guilty. The concept of mutual ministry outlined earlier is not just a matter of good will flowing between individuals. It can equally be applied to the administrative machinery as well, so that the contribution of each and every individual is understood as equally important to the well-being of the whole. This is what Paul was saying with his 'Church as the Body of Christ' imagery. The question is not really about 'better jobs for the girls' – although this may be one important way of raising the issue of discrimination. It is about ministry and service: who ministers to whom? How does the institutional church minister to the woman who cleans the office ashtrays? How does it accept and affirm her ministry? If one looks around modern offices – the home of contemporary institutions – it is inevitably women who form the majority of those employed in 'service jobs' – secretaries, catering and cleaning staff, receptionists. The denominational churches all claim to be institutions whose *raison d'être* is service. Jesus was quite clear about that. Women are thus specially placed, both theoretically and practically, within the Christian bureaucracies to take up the Christian challenge – to create institutional forms which can and do mediate God to God's world, and provide a model of justice for other corporations.

Before going on to show some of the ways in which women have responded to this challenge it is important to grasp the depth of the problem. It is neither the tradition nor the true teaching of Christianity to ignore its own structures. Most of the divisions and schisms within Christianity have been about the nature of authority: who had the right to govern, control and lead and how that right should be exercised. Until comparatively recently these questions have been adequately framed in 'theological' language. Now technological and institutional developments have outstripped the language that Christianity is comfortable using. The power and authority of Bishops can be debated in the language of the early Church with direct reference to the Bible and the Church Fathers. The power, accountability and status of the international tax expert and the lady who makes the coffee cannot. The collective unwillingness to face up to this difficulty, which is sensed as being somehow 'not spiritual' because it cannot be expressed in acceptably spiritual language, compounds the problem.

The way in which the churches perceive and use their administrative personnel is, in fact, disgraceful. It is frequently contrary to the most basic demands of the gospel; it reflects the dualistic thinking of too many Christians and the problems that the churches have in relating to daily life. It is interesting that these problems are quite specifically located in the administration of the official denominational institutions. While these all seem genuinely interested in supporting and observing the development of quite radical organisational structures among groups with alliances to Christianity – religious communities, other communal groupings, charitable organisations and so forth – they apparently have no intention of using these experiences for instruction or self-reflection. There are of course courageous exceptions to the overall lack of self-consciousness; but these must be recognised for what they are – proof that the general failure to develop less alienating structures is cowardice and self-interest not impossibility. Christian witness will remain hampered, if not actually crippled, by the fact that we appear to be furthest from what we claim for ourselves – the instrument of God on earth – at the very centre of our own life. The continual accusations from outside that the churches are 'hypocritical' may be ill-informed and ridiculously simplistic at times, but they are so frequently repeated that we are obliged to ask ourselves whether they do not have some underlying justification.

The particular question of the employment of women within the various Christian institutions is governed by two, not unrelated, factors. The first is simple sexism. The second, more complicated, is clericism.

On the question of sexism in employment the churches have allowed themselves to mirror almost exactly the patterns of the outside world. There are some individual women holding positions of relative authority. One of the most senior executives in the Church of England, for instance, is Dame Betty Ridley, one of the three Estates Commissioners. Almost every denomination has its token women in high positions. They are a tiny minority in all areas. Their appointment is often announced with a fanfare of congratulation. The appointment, for example, of Sr Mary George O'Reilly SHCJ as director of Administration for the Archdiocess of Newark, New Jersey, USA, was claimed to show that, 'The Church Authorities are recognising that well-qualified women have a part to play in its administration.' This is indeed an appointment of genuine importance and does represent a breakthrough in the Roman Catholic Church:

> Hitherto women in decision making roles in the Church have been limited to fields of education and social work, so her appointment is a new development. The Newark Archdiocesan Office of Administration was established in 1976. Under it are the offices of finance, development, communications, archdiocesan cemeteries, general services, co-operative supply services and the archdiocesan news-paper. . . . This appointment makes Sr Mary George O'Reilly one of the highest placed administrators in the Church.[7]

But without wishing to denigrate in any way the achievements against almost insuperable odds of this nun, it is important to point out that she is a nun (always, though wrongly, regarded by the hierarchy as less 'female' than lay women). Moreover it is hard to feel thrilled that sixty years after women got the vote and legal access to the professions and fifteen years after the Second Vatican Council both opened the door for new developments in nuns' apostolates *and* declared that job discrimination on grounds of sex was contrary to God's intent[8] that there should be *one* senior woman Roman Catholic executive in the world.

As a further defence against charges of sexism the institutional churches often argue that there is a shortage of women in those professional areas from which they would want to recruit staff. Here they have some sort of case. While the 1971 Census revealed that women made up 38 per cent of the British work force, less than 5 per cent held managerial posts and much of that 5 per cent was limited to fields in which the denominations have few openings – hairdressing, and boarding-house management, for example. The shortage is particularly acute in those professions most likely to be valuable to denominational administration. Less than 2 per cent of chartered accountants, of bank managers and of chartered surveyors are female; 93 per cent of solicitors are male.[9] But having conceded the point it is also important to stress that in Britain at least most of the churches tend to 'buy in' trained executives rather than train up their own, predominantly female, junior staff. Moreover none of the denominations in England have declared themselves formally to be Equal Opportunity Employers – and in this respect compare very badly with, for example, local councils which have similar employment needs. One departmental executive in the Church of England, whom I asked about a commitment to anti-discrimination, looked at me aghast and said, 'We don't need to make a commitment, of course as Christians we wouldn't discriminate.' He was unable to see anything other than coincidence in the fact that there were so few women in executive positions and defended the fact that the Church of England models its employment structures on the Civil Service – a conspicuous all-male club in the higher echelons although women predominate there too in the lower ranks.

The Church of England is a good example of how this concealed sexism works. It has officially committed itself to matching Civil Service rates of pay and therefore argues that it operates an equal pay scheme. However, as few of the executives posts are filled by women the *average* pay for women who fill most of the lower-grade jobs is conspicuously lower than the average pay for men. For example, in one department, the Advisory Committee for the Churches' Ministry[10] – the twelve 'executives', nine men and three women, are paid equally; they are listed equally in the *Church of England Year Book*[11] and enjoy equal status. But they are invisibly 'serviced' by five unmentioned, nameless secretaries, all of whom are women and all of whom are paid at a substantially lower rate. The department is further maintained by a cleaning staff, all of whom are women, by the central switch-board operators (who have always been female on the many occasions when I have rung Church House) and by the catering staff of Church House. All these latter, because they service the whole of Church House, do not even appear in the domestic accounts of the department.

The Church of England's adoption of the Civil Service pay scales and job structures is a very good example of Anne Scheibner's point that the churches 'accept the dominant social and political structures and attitudes of society.' Naturally these work against women because the dominant structures and attitudes of society are sexist. But they also work against justice and charity in a wider sense. The Rev. Ruth Wintle, a Deaconess who works for the Church of England's Advisory Council on the Church's Ministry, remarks that the Civil Service is in fact different administratively from the Church of England and adopting their scales has meant failing to take into account some crucial factors. Many of these are simply practical differences in working styles between one Church of England department and another, as well as between Church House and Whitehall:

> For example in our ACCM department, because selection conferences and our other work are nationally based, we [the executives] are out of the office a lot. The secretaries here are not typists; they carry a real load of responsibility, for continuity, for the whole shape of the work, and that is not recognised in our pay scales.[12]

But more importantly Ruth Wintle felt that there was a theological point at issue. The differentials in pay and status between her and her secretarial staff were contrary to the standards that the Church claimed to represent:

> It is simply disgraceful and has nothing to do with Christianity and the Church. There has to be some better way of working these things out that reflects *our* realities more.[13]

Although the debate continues, in 1978 the General Synod resound-
ingly defeated a motion which proposed to level out differentials
both parochially and nationally in the pay structure of the Church.
Parity is regarded, by the bureaucracy, as an interesting idea, but an
economic and personnel management insanity. Despite the fact that
numerous radical groups have worked on parity, and although it is
accepted that parish priests will work for a 'pittance', it is apparently
unbelievable to senior executive personnel that lay people might
interpret their own ministry in this way – might choose to work
within the Church because it was a way of using their talents in God's
service; or because the benefits of working for an open, experimental, equality-oriented employer might be interesting
enough to justify taking a lower salary. Moreover the 'pittance' for
those who are currently the best paid would, in terms of parity, mean
a substantial rise for the secretarial, service and janitorial staff. The
Church of England has recently been advertising for a Finance
Officer at a proposed salary of around £22,000 p.a. The national and
religious newspapers have been full of protests from parochial clergy
about the difference between this offer and their own stipends, but I
have not seen one letter questioning the difference between this
salary and those received by the women who will staff this executive's office. Interestingly the *Church Times* carried an article defend-
ing the Civil Service pay scale which pointed out that individuals
were of course free – and many availed themselves of the freedom –
to give as much of their salary as they chose back to the Church, or to
charity, in terms of stewardship. But this solution obviously evades
the *institutional* stewardship which is crucial to the Christian mission.

Money is not of course the issue. It is the most obvious symptom
of a secular approach to ecclesiological problems. The lower rungs of
the ecclesial ladder are not regarded as part of the 'real' Christian
work. The people who type letters and wash tea cups are not
regarded as 'ministers', their work is not seen as part of the work of
the Church. While all executive personnel within the administration
are expected to be Christians, this does not apply to the secretarial
staff. Their religious affiliation is not considered relevant in their job
application.

The hierarchies of power and authority practised within the
churches thus affect women in two distinct but related ways. First
they are excluded from the 'best jobs', which are substantially
performed by men. Second the jobs they do perform, necessary and

important jobs, closely in line, in contemporary terms, with the foot-washing ministries so emphasised by Jesus, are not regarded as Christian ministries. Related to this is a problem that is mentioned with painful frequency; whether or not the employers are aware of it, many employees, particularly office staff within Christian institutions, feel that Christian claims to good will are used as an excuse for careless or unbusinesslike handling of personnel problems.'[14] 'They can stab you in the back *so nicely*,' was how Pat Vowles, who works in the accounts department of a national Christian Missionary Society, put it. For many Christians their worshipping community has been the place of comfort and advice if they ran into difficulties at work; if the Church itself is your employer there is no one to perform that task. In addition there is the sense of betrayal because of the naive feeling that the 'Church at least ought to have behaved better'. For all the claims of similarity there is one conspicuous way in which the Church of England's bureaucracy differs from the Civil Service: no Trade Union has recognition, let alone negotiating rights, at Church House.

But as well as buying wholesale a secular approach to 'professionalism' and therefore to the unequal employment of women, the denominational churches have also developed another characteristic which acts even more potently against the effective use of women in the bureaucracy. And this is clericism.

The Acts of the Apostles tells us about an important incident early in the life of the Christian community. Because of some bureaucratic difficulties that were being encountered it was decided that: 'It is not right that we [the apostles] should give up preaching the word of God to serve at tables . . . we will devote ourselves to prayer and the ministry of the Word,'[15] and so they elected Deacons to do the administrative work. None the less the present-day 'Apostles' – the Bishops, their representatives the priests and the Protestant clergy (all of whom claim their authority from the Biblical concept of the Apostles) – apparently do not find any difficulty whatever in involving themselves with administration, and have no intention of confining themselves to preaching, praying and breaking bread. This, of course, is not a new phenomenon: the secular authority of the Bishops increased steadily throughout the history of the Church. But the modern bureaucratisation of Christianity has made the problem more visible. The clerical domination of the administrative machine is clear evidence that the clergy want to keep their power absolute. This is not exclusively a feminist complaint: it is a view supported by numerous witnesses who have no special concern with the role of women. David Perman, for instance, is quite explicit:

> For the Roman Catholic rank and file the finances of their church remain an impenetrable mystery, known only to a few prelates, finance officers and God. . . . The hierarchies have traditionally viewed finances as something intimately connected with their own spiritual and disciplinary authority. It would be going far beyond the principle of co-responsibility outlined in Vatican II for the Diocesan Bishop and his advisors to throw open the books, even to the Senate of Priests, let alone to the people at large.[16]

The Bishops' advisers are usually priests themselves. The Archdiocese of Westminster has ten Vicars General – the Bishop's administrative delegates. Nine of them are ordained priests. One of them, Mgr David Norris, told me that 'really they would have to be priests', although he immediately commented that in the early Church 'of course they would have been the Deacons'.[17]

The Roman Catholic Church, which is perhaps the worst of all the denominations in this respect, has at least worked out a theology of hierarchy with which to justify its clericism. The same tendency, however, is just as clear in all the other denominations. Pauline Webb, herself until 1980 a highly placed executive in the English Methodist Church, sees what she calls 'this clerical thing' as the major obstacle to the proper progress of women within Christianity:

> We did once have a layperson as Chairman of the World Council of Churches and everyone thought we were rather brave and impressive; now we have Archbishop Scott. And in the Methodist Church we have several women vice-presidents but the reason why we have never had a woman president is because the president is always a minister – even though there is no reason why it should be.[18]

Clericism is not dangerous to the Church just because it stops women getting the best jobs: that is just one symptom of the more deep-rooted problem. Clericism undermines and corrupts the Christian understanding of service, of ministry and of wholeness, interdependence, and community. Clericism is based on a belief, seldom if ever acknowledged, that some vocations – practical responses to God's call to commitment of life, in line with one's talents or training, in the service of the Church and the world – are better than others; and that the best vocation of all (if not the *only* recognised vocation) is being a clergyman. In every denomination – whether the ordination of women is allowed or not – the vast majority of those in the clerical caste are men. This denigrates the ministry and the sense of holiness of all lay people, but particularly of women. Clericism really has very little to do with ordination – although the identification of ordination with power and privilege may have a lot to do with why the ordination of women is so passionately resisted in some quarters. Clericism is about relating all jobs and functions perceived as important to the clergy with little or no consideration as to how this fits into the theology of ordination held by the particular denomination. While the Catholic denominations are particularly guilty visually, the Protestant denominations have added an aural confusion by using the word 'minister' to apply to ordained professionals. A 'minister' is one who ministers to, or serves, other people: the very wording of the debate about 'lay ministry' demonstrates the depths of the problem.

The New Testament evidence is, for once, remarkably unambiguous. The job of the apostles is to teach, pray and break bread. It is not to administrate. The context makes clear that the Deacons were not a waitress service, but were intended to sort out specific property problems. Some people felt that the goods held in common by the Christian community in Jerusalem were not being fairly distributed. The whole group accepted that there was a need for some special administrative skills and that this amounted to a particular formal responsibility necessary for the common good and distinct from the apostolic skills. The original debate was about administration. The only denomination that approaches that model now is the Baptist Church which has elected Deacons and a clergyperson (chosen, paid and housed by the congregation) jointly administering the local Christian community. The other denominations have allowed the diaconate, in this Biblical sense, and originally open to women and men, to evaporate completely. This model allowed both the Christian community and the world beyond it to see that all types of skill and vocation were necessary to and recognised by the Church, and thus affirmed the service of many more people.

The complaint is not that modern-day apostles are lousy administrators, or even likely to be so (though training people for up to six years for one specific job and then using them for something different is an extremely dubious use of resources). The real problem is that by allowing the clergy to dominate the whole bureaucratic machine, and allocating lay people to provide the back-up services; by giving clerical ministries a particular distinction and privilege in relation to lay ministries, institutional Christianity distorts the fundamental truth which it ought to be proclaiming: that all talents are equal – equally important to the health of the whole, and equally sanctifying.[19]

A very clear example of how clericism undermines the ministry of non-ordained people, and of women in particular, was provided in the USA in 1976. The Episcopal Church there had employed two women – Maria Cueto and Raisa Nemikin – to work as executive director and secretary to its National Commission on Hispanic Affairs. Both women were subpoenaed to appear before a Grand Jury investigating terrorist activities allegedly connected with Puerto Rican independence. They refused to testify. They argued that – since no record of Grand Jury proceedings is kept, and since the Grand Jury system is regarded with grave suspicion in political cases in the USA – agreeing to testify would destroy their credibility, and the confidence of their constituents in their ministry. They claimed exemption from testifying on the grounds that they were 'lay ministers of religion'. The judge disagreed with this claim, ruling that they were only social workers and not 'lay ministers'. Both women were sent to prison for nine months for contempt of court. The judge's decision was not surprising in view of the fact that the Episcopal Church hierarchy refused to endorse the women's claim. Presented with a real opportunity to identify the Church's mission to the oppressed and to make a stand on its explicit commitment to develop a meaningful lay ministry, the official voice of the Episcopal Church refused the women any support. It transpired that Bishop Allin – the presiding Bishop – and Bishop Wood had in fact passed their responsibility for the work of the Hispanic Affairs Commission on to Cueto and Nemikin when the investigators had approached them, and were prepared to support the Grand Jury against their own employees' claims to be 'lay ministers'. The political implications of these events are complicated, but the Episcopal Church hierarchy demonstrated at least two things quite clearly: that its identification with the legal establishment far outweighed its ability to understand racial and cultural solidarity among its own staff; and that the Episcopal Church does not regard social work, work on behalf of oppressed minorities, or administrative work, as 'Christian ministry' – that privilege is reserved for those who are ordained. Lay administrative and service personnel need not expect the same support or recognition as those doing the same jobs who are members of the clerical casts.

Because of the constitutional questions and because the women involved did actually go to prison this case is an extreme example of clericism in action; but it is not an isolated one. All the denominations internationally and unanimously denounce the 'increasing secularisation of the modern world'. Pope John Paul II has made his spectacular world tours a vehicle for condemning the materialism and greed of contemporary society. All the denominations now have Justice Departments and Boards for Social Responsibility and Panels for Economic Development, all of which hand out excellent moral advice and considerable detailed research. But there seems to be no recognition that this alone is not enough: the advice will fall on deaf ears while our own house is in such appalling disorder.

The genuine discipline of life-style and great generosity of individual Christians is immaterial when set beside the institutional practice of the denominational structures. The central heating level at Church House alone makes one question everything the Church of England has to say about ecological waste, Third World hunger and the plight of the elderly in winter. The Roman Catholic Commission for the Laity (presided over, I need hardly add, by a Bishop) in February 1980 published a document calling for a 'fairer distribution of the nation's resources' and urging the whole Church to commit itself to this. There does seem to be a worrying gap between the Commission's very moving call for all Roman Catholics to resist the cuts in public spending, to organise 'protests', and to insist on 'justice first as employees, employers, shareholders'[20] and the reality of the fact that the investment portfolios of the Roman Catholic Church are not available to the ordinary lay people who might want to examine their own corporate justice.

I have spent a considerable amount of time laying out the problem because it is complicated and vitally important. In her paper on Institutional Theology, Anne Scheibner sums up the Church's dilemma: 'How then can the Church as the Body of Christ come to terms with its institutional form which represents the "power and principalities" from which we have been freed?'[21] I believe that it is in part by looking at how women have handled the question that some pointers for the future can be found by the rest of the institution. Because of their particular relationship to the bureaucracy women are able to challenge and to change it. Anne Scheibner proposes three possible answers to her own question – all of which have been taken up by women in recent years. Looking at these is a way of organising the very diverse challenges to the institutional structures that women have been making:

> One [option] would be to renounce the institution and all its works. This path . . . seems honest enough if one is then prepared to be a mystic or prophet in the wilderness. . . . [But] it provides no help for those still wrestling with their demons and angels within the institutional framework.
>
> The second option would be to ignore the dilemma . . . to understand the institution as an ongoing tradition which imposes certain costs . . . one does the best one can under the circumstances.
>
> The third option is to see the Churches' institutional form . . . as an opportunity for special witness and vocation in the closing decades of the twentieth century.[22]

The first part of the first option is taken daily by those women who cannot stand it any more and who simply leave Christianity and their denominational church. Most of the once active women who leave do not seem to do so over theological difficulties with particular points of dogma. The new theological or philosophical insights are frequently not discovered until women have stopped practising their old faith and find they need something else to fill the gap. The reason most usually given for the departure is a final despair at the institutional Church's inability to come to terms with an individual's own needs. This failure leads to a belief that it is impossible for the Church ever to be able to manifest the incarnate Christ. Once that hope is dead there is no possible reason to remain a Christian. For instance, many women who left the Roman Catholic Church during the 1960s gave *Humanae Vitae* (the encyclical on Birth Control) as the cause of their departure. However, the fact that many others, while in equally strong disagreement with this encyclical, were able to stay active within their denomination suggests that it was not so much the content of *Humanae Vitae* itself, but the proof that, despite the promises of the Second Vatican Council, the institutional Church was unable to open itself up to the genuine distress of many women and the real implications of lay, sexual, female reality.

Often this serious drainage takes place among women who have been the most active. Being a woman who is politically active within Christianity is a cruel business. It usually involves making a public stand on something that our society has taught us is even more personal and embarrassing than sex – our relationship with God. People do not often become militant until they perceive some real hope of change: it is the loss of that hope which creates the disillusion. Taking a stand in faith and hope and finding that one's church immediately withdraws its love is often unbearable. Too frequently women find more sisterhood and succour outside the Church and life within it becomes not worth the pain. I do not believe that enough Christians realise how large and serious this drop-out rate is – I know that I did not until, working on this book, I had the repeated experience of going to talk to someone who had been involved in something interesting only to find that she had given up on Christianity. There are many women, from all denominations, who have left, women who once cared passionately and have now withdrawn. They are women whom we, the Church, have badly damaged and we do not know or care enough.

However, these are not the women best placed to be the 'prophets in the wilderness', a necessary part of the withdrawal if it is to have any meaning. To judge and prophesy you have to be tough and you have to have some hope that Christianity can still save and be saved.

Sr Anne Patricia Ware SL made such a stand in February 1980 when she resigned her job as Associate Director of the National Council of Churches' Commission on Faith and Order. She was in a position to make clear what she was doing because her job was an important one. The Roman Catholic Church is not a member of the World Council of Churches, but they have observers in many of the departments and in the USA have officially joined the Faith and Order Commission. As an executive officer of this Commission Sr Pat Ware was a leading representative of the Roman Catholic ecumenical movement in the USA. In her resignation letter she made clear that she was not planning to leave the Church, nor her own religious order, but wanted to dissociate herself from the bureaucracy. She said that when she started working at the National Council she was able 'to interpret the Roman Catholic position as authentically based on the statements and visions of Vatican II. However in these later years I have become increasingly disappointed with some of the positions of my Church and find it impossible to be an enthusiastic exponent!' On matters concerning women particularly she found representing the Roman Catholic position was sometimes 'really embarrassing'. By emphasising her determination to remain within the Church she made it clear that it was the institution not its basic faith that embarrassed her, and which she no longer felt able to represent. However, she concluded that there were hopeful signs among some Christians and especially among women 'including a sense of humour. I think that's why I want to work with women', she told a newspaper reporter. In this statement Sr Pat Ware managed to criticise the bureaucracy and to escape from it. She named very precisely her discontent and an area of hopeful alternative growth.

Another, even more unambiguous, sign of radical disassociation from the institutional church was the symbolic Exodus which Mary Daly led from the Harvard Memorial Chapel in 1971. It was the first time that a woman had been invited to preach at the principal Sunday service but Mary Daly did not see this as a breakthrough for women. Her whole sermon was a savage attack on the sexist structures of institutional Christianity. In contrast she offered her audience a new model:

Sisterhood is both revolutionary and revelatory. . . . Sisterhood is functioning as Church, proclaiming dimensions of truth which organised religion fails to proclaim. . . . It is a charismatic community in which we experience prophecy and healing. . . . It is a community with a mission . . . based on the prophetic insight that the sisterhood of women opens out to universal horizons, pointing outward to the Sisterhood of man.[23]

Having stated earlier in the sermon that 'unless insight gives birth to externalised action it will die', Mary Daly finally moved from rhetoric to action:

Sisters: the sisterhood of man cannot happen without a real Exodus. We can this morning demonstrate our exodus from sexist religion . . . we cannot really belong to institutional religion as it exists. It isn't good enough. . . . Our time has come. Let us affirm our faith in ourselves and our will to transcendence by rising and walking out together.[24]

Descending from the pulpit Mary Daly then led a mass departure from the chapel. This Exodus, modelled on the Exodus from Egypt, the people of God leaving slavery for freedom, was experienced by many women as passionately important and moving. 'I had the feeling of being a whole person for the first time,' someone said afterwards.[25] But it must be noted that Mary Daly went so far out that she never came back again.[26] She really has become a mystic in the desert, which, as Anne Scheibner rightly points out, provides 'no help to those still wrestling with their demons and angels within the institutional framework'. The very existence of women's 'heretical' groups, from Mary Daly's 'post-Christian feminism' to witches, Mother-Goddess worship and various pantheistic nature cults is itself a demonstration that women feel radically disgusted by the Church. However, by withdrawing so far from the cultural and social centre of society many feminist heretics seem to cut themselves off both from active political reality as well as from an effective ministry to other women.

There is another sort of dissociation, however, which is potentially more helpful. This is to take up a corporate stand in which a whole group produces a visible alternative structure which by existing very publicly stands in judgment over other Christian institutions. For such a group to have any purpose they have to define themselves not just as Christian but as *more* obedient to the gospel, the authentic tradition, and to the Holy Spirit then any available historical institution. This of course was the position taken by the original Protestant churches, whose claim was never that they moved away from Christian truth but that they radically returned to it. The fastest growing denomination in the USA at the moment is the Metropolitan Community Church – the MCC – which also has an international dimension, including a congregation in London. The MCC is best known to the rest of the world as the 'Gay Church' and is often seen as a single-issue Church, a cosy home for homosexual Christians. Many MCC congregations have been bitterly accused of sexism as bad as that found elsewhere, and particularly of a Biblical fundamentalism about women which is particularly offensive as the Pauline injunctions against homosexuality are as clear as those against women's participation. But the MCC congregation in New York city, which employs a woman pastor, sees sexist and homophobic attitudes as one and the same. 'It's wrong to see MCC as a single-issue church. That is not a possibility for us.'[27] The creation of MCC, as opposed to gay support groups within established denominations, or even ecumenically, demonstrates that MCC members are aware of the importance of institutional structures and are prepared to withdraw from them into a social desert where they can stand in judgment. The MCC has a special relationship to the first-century Church in that the membership itself is based on an identification with the oppressed. Experience has made individual members very wary of oppressive structures and they lay claim to the Pauline notion that salvation comes not from the Law, but from love and grace alone.

It seems unlikely, at present, that it would be possible to form a *Christian* denomination that was exclusively female. Although some feminist Christians clearly do see their own women's group as 'their Church', this is more likely to be a place of support and succour than a structured alternative to the established churches. However, the MCC does illustrate a possibility of a corporate withdrawal from the bureaucracy in order to stand in judgment over it, and it is a route that should not be imaginatively excluded.

The second possibility that Anne Scheibner proposes as a solution to the bureaucratic dilemma is to ignore it. Institutional inhumanity can be seen as an inevitable part of human frailty and women should just do the best they can; extracting such gains as are possible without challenging the basic assumptions. The validity of this option for women depends on what one perceives to be the problem and how one understands social change as taking place.

If the position of women within institutional Christianity is understood as an individual civil rights issue – a series of unfortunate coincidences isolated from any other miscarriages of justice within the bureaucracy and rectifiable on their own terms – then accepting the existing structures and working for the best possible deal within them makes good sense. The struggle for women's jobs in the denominational churches, in this view, is analogous to the struggle for women's employment within other professional and industrial bodies, where the merits of the institution are irrelevant to women's legal right to be employed there as they choose. There is an illuminating parallel here with the current debate within various denominations about investment in South Africa or in armament manufacture. It is perfectly honest, given an acceptance of democratic capitalism, to argue that Christians should not invest in immoral trading *without* asking whether they should have any investment money in the first place. Accepting the institutional forms, while demanding that women be better represented within them, is identical to this.

This position is often coupled to a belief that major changes can be brought about by a gradualist or reformist approach, and that this is in fact the best way of generating change. Obviously the sort of victories that will seem significant depend on how one understands change as happening: whether it works its way down from the top of an organisation, or up from a mass revolt at the bottom, or from a combination of the two. Whether it is possible to trust the good will of those who have power to give it up voluntarily, through persuasion, conversion and education; or whether it has to be forcibly wrested from those who have it. (This is the key difference between Fabians and Marxists, for example.) These sorts of considerations affect whether one believes that 'symbolic' gains are worth the price of possible co-option, liberalism and tokenism. Women who work to get better jobs and influential positions for women in the church bureaucracy argue that having women visible in any organisation is instrumental in raising the expectations and hopes of other women to such an extent that it is worth making considerable sacrifices of principle to obtain these positions. Jill Tweedie offered a clear example of this line of thought in her *Guardian* column during the 1979 General Election campaign when she suggested that it would be more in their interests for women to vote for Margaret Thatcher, as a woman, however reactionary her attitudes, than to elect another man. The effects of seeing a woman Prime Minister would outweigh the danger of five years of reactionary politics. Along similar lines some women working within institutional Christianity argue that it is of such importance to have women in visible positions of leadership – as Bishops, chairing committees, or holding down the best-paid and most influential jobs – that it is worth making considerable sacrifices of principle. In order to obtain these positions it is necessary to play the institutional game, and be perceived by the establishment as respectable and unthreatening. Compromise and repudiation of more radical demands may be necessary to achieve these ends and this must be accepted. (Interestingly the demands most readily abandoned often seem to be those that would link women's oppression with other forms of oppression: the repudiation of homosexual women, of socialist economic and class analysis, of non-nuclear family life-styles, of 'shared poverty', ecological suggestions, and of militant peace movements. Too often 'reformist' approaches end up demanding little more than a bigger slice of a rather stale cake.)

However, there is a more historical way of looking at the choices implied by adopting Anne Scheibner's second option. Dame Betty Ridley, the third Estates Commissioner, has been throughout her life an activist in the movement for women in the Anglican Church. Her commitment to the Church of England as a living faith and as an institution is immense and enduring. She was born in 1909; her father was Bishop of Stepney; her mother before marriage was a worker at the Church's St Margaret's Settlement in the East End. At nineteen she married an Anglican Priest. Her parents, within the context of a wider Anglicanism, both had a special concern for the ministries of women:

> While I was still a child I was growing up in an atmosphere of hearing about all the great efforts to get women's church work on a better footing. I grew up knowing how they were paid pittances and had no status.[28]

She first became involved in national Anglican politics when she was invited to join the Central Committee for Women's Work:

> I think I got put on as they thought it would be good to have a very young woman and sort of radical and so they could feel that something was happening. And I was on that awful old-girls network.[29]

But despite the self-deprecation and humour, Betty Ridley has worked within the structures for long enough to know how things can be done. She has also had a wide enough base never to see women's issues in isolation. In the 1978 Synodical debate on the Ordination of Women, she, perhaps alone, tried to put the argument into the context of evangelism, saying that the Church's stupidity in not ordaining women was one more thing that served only to alienate people who might want and need Christianity in their lives. She sees women being employed within the institution as important for bringing about the gradual sort of change that she believes in and which over the years she has seen working:

> I like to think that by remaining within church structures and working quietly from within I may have made a tiny

contribution to the future of women's work, including the priesthood eventually. . . .

So personally I don't think that the extreme women's liberation methods are the right ones for the church. But it is too easy for us who have grown up in a different atmosphere to be critical of new methods. I would like us women to be more united, but there is going to be a difficulty between those of us who want to work constitutionally, quietly, persuasively and those who want a different emphasis. I tell myself that it is those others who are going to be there to see the results and therefore they must not be excluded or driven out.[30]

As the nineteenth-century secular women's movement demonstrated, there is a point up to which gradualism is not only useful but necessary. The problem is knowing, as the militant suffragettes seemed to have known very precisely, when that approach has exhausted its possibilities, and confrontation and radical challenge become both possible and vital. Clearly the position adopted by Betty Ridley, and numerous other women through the years when, as she puts it, even to talk about the ordination of women 'had a bad smell', has brought us to a point where a more radical analysis and direct challenge are possible. What is distressingly noticeable is that the women most likely to hold to a belief that there is nothing much wrong with the institutional Church that a few symbolic victories won't cure are those women who have, or are likely to have those token jobs: women already on the inside – middle-class, educated women who are capable of commanding the respect of the establishment precisely because they do not endanger it. Too many women in the religious civil service argue that there is no oppression within the structures because they themselves have obtained positions of nominal authority. Perhaps they should enter into 'educational dialogue' with the night-cleaners who wash out their ashtrays. They are the 'kept women of the bureaucracy' and their pursuit of and commitment to token jobs is at the expense, not just of other women, but of themselves as well.

The final option that Anne Scheibner raises in her paper, that of seeing 'the institutional form as an opportunity for special witness and vocation', remains as the most viable way forward. In relation to a proper theology of the Incarnation which puts responsibility for salvation in the hands of human history, it is theoretically sounder than either ignoring or consenting to existing institutions. It demands that the Christian bureaucracies live up to their own claims of showing how even institutions, like every other phenomenon of human history, can be instruments of salvation and sources of grace. Unless one has a very privatised understanding of salvation there is no possible theological problem in politicising, combining with other people to achieve agreed ends. The feeling that political organisation somehow impedes the work of the Holy Spirit is something that has cramped and endangered the new democratic processes of the denominations in the last twenty years: Christians who believe happily in political action in the 'outside world' still have to learn that the same rules can be brought inside without grace flying out the window. No other option can offer the same hope for transformation and growth; for allegiance, loyalty, radical change and sisterhood. It is, however, a difficult choice and one calling for constant self-reflection and clarity. It is too easy to topple either towards co-option and compromise on the one hand, or towards dramatic repudiations and escapes on the other. In the face of overwhelming difficulties I offer the bureaucratic feminist radicals a fine Biblical motto:

Behold I send you out as sheep among wolves; so be wise as serpents and innocent as doves. Beware of *men*, for they will deliver you up to committees.[31]

A lovely little example of how it is possible to challenge the religious bureaucracies from within was provided in the Southern Presbyterian Church of the USA in 1976. The denomination's offices in Atlanta, Georgia, were faced with the not-uncommon problem of financial short-fall. It was clear that cuts would have to be made and a plan was drawn up as to how these should be executed. At a meeting called to discuss the proposals, a group within the administration got permission to present a minority report. Carole Etzler, who works in the Educational Department, then produced a guitar and sang:

> You ask me why I'm angry,
> You tell me not to shout,
> You say there's lots of folk round here
> That we can do without.
> But when the heads start rolling,
> I've never seen it fail,

The neck that will escape the axe
Is the nice, white, middle-class male.

You say we'll cut the functions
It will all be fair and square;
We'll trim off those peripheral jobs
And keep the main ones there.
But it's women and minorities
Who'll suffer, don't you see,
'Cause we're the ones you've always kept
On the periphery.[32]

The song went on to recommend that all jobs should be maintained and the short-fall met by reducing the salaries of the best paid.

By refusing to play the bureaucratic game, to get involved in the correct procedures of expressing disagreement; by bringing music and singing – which directly reflect the experience of worship and community for all Protestants – into the heart of a business meeting; by being very personal and judgmental about sinful self-interest later in the song, but in a style that cannot be dismissed as either aggressive or hysterical; and above all by presenting the gospel demands with clarity and humour, this small act of institutional protest is perfect.

It is not always easy, however, to make stands of this kind without incurring the wrath and even punishment of the bureaucracy. The case of Maria Cueto and Raisa Nemikin was mentioned earlier in the chapter: their radical challenge in identifying themselves with those to whom they ministered, rather than with the interests of the Establishment, landed them in prison. This is an extreme example, but not a unique one. From 1972–9 Joan Clark, a Methodist Deaconess, was employed as an executive administrator in the USA Methodist Women's Division. Her specific responsibilities included developing women's leadership and education and consciousness-raising on feminist and political issues. In 1976 the Women's Division adopted a policy statement on human sexuality which called, inter alia, for the 'elimination of homophobia' – the hatred and fear of homosexuals. In 1978, after six years of apparently satisfactory service within the Division, Joan Clark was given a year's study leave to research and make recommendations to her department on the effects of homophobia in church and society and how these could be combatted by the Methodist Church, and the gay community better served. In 1979 she submitted the report required of all staff members who have been on study leave. She felt that the Women's Division was hampered in its attempt to eliminate homophobia because there had been no real effort 'to personalise the issue by identifying as Lesbians women whom division members and staff already knew, worked with and respected'. She also felt that it was a matter of personal integrity that she should not write about homosexuality 'objectively', because that merely helped to foster the lie that gay people were Other – not like us, not inside. She therefore made it an integral part of the report to 'come out', to state unambiguously that she was a lesbian. She was sacked.[33]

Joan Clark has now taken her courage, energy and skills not out of institutional Christianity, but to a radical organisation called the Ecumenical Women's Center, in Chicago. This group tries to make its institutional protest simply by existing: the idea here is to bring together women's issues inside and outside the traditional Christian areas of concern, uniting such disparate matters as non-sexist worship and anti-rape campaigns. But beyond this they endeavour, on a limited budget, to create new styles of working and organising which can be used as a dynamic critique of the bureaucratic structures of the denominational churches. In employing Joan Clark as their co-ordinator they are not only joining the protest against her dismissal, they are also demonstrating that it should be possible for Christians to combine personal solidarity with efficient administration.

Groups like the Ecumenical Women's Center are an important part of how women can work on Anne Scheibner's third option. They occupy a middle ground between the 'real' professional administrations and the totally withdrawn alternatives. Although the Center is ecumenical the individual workers maintain a denominational connection precisely so that they can speak with and to their own denominations.[34] They also try to employ a mixture of ordained and lay women so that they can demonstrate the equality and co-responsibility between the two.

The Quixote Center in Washington DC is another such organisation, this time Roman Catholic. As their name suggests, they see their role as one of 'tilting at windmills' – taking up corporate issues that the Roman Catholic hierarchy refuses to handle. The Quixote Center is not exclusively a women's organisation, although many of the issues that it takes up are women's concerns. It is staffed by an equal team consisting of a priest, lay women and nuns, and it makes its facilities very openly available to people who might want them. One of their principal functions is finding funding from *within* the Roman Catholic community for projects that the hierarchy has rejected: this frequently consists of research into justice issues inside the Catholic Church itself. For example, the Quixote Center initiated, facilitated and published Sr Fran Ferder FSPA's psychological analysis of women who believed themselves called to the Roman Catholic priesthood.[35] Hierarchy-baiting was a strong element in this study. In 1972 the National Council of Bishops had commissioned and published a psychological study of existing priests in the Roman Catholic Church in the USA.[36] Despite the myths and speculations current about women who announced their personal calling to the priesthood there was no willingness on the part of the Bishops' Council to extend this research to female aspirants. Sr Fran Ferder deliberately used the same testing procedures, employed the same consultants, and compared her findings on women to the Priest Study findings wherever possible – usually to detriment of the priests. Moreover the sponsors of her study were all Roman Catholic organisations. This was not just a useful research project, it was a brilliantly calculated protest at the lack of equality in concern and pastoral support of the bureaucracy and a demonstration that outside the bureaucracy there were many good Roman Catholic institutions who did care.

Organisations like these – commoner in the USA than in Britain, because of the wider spread of feminism and easier finance – which remain determinedly within the Church on the one hand but offer an alternative model of organisation on the other, are crucial additions to the stand of individuals who do remain within the bureaucracy, but they too are not exempt from danger. Fr William Callahan, a priest who works at the Quixote Center, has recently been reprimanded and disciplined by his Church for his work in running Priests for Equality – an international network of priests who support the Ordination of Women. It is far harder for the hierarchy to discipline other workers at the Quixote Center: one is a nun who has the approval of her community for her work, the others are lay women. Short of excommunicating them all (and it is unlikely that they would pay much attention to this even if it were done) there is little that the authorities can do. But the Center depends on funds from concerned religious organisations, and by reprimanding Bill

Callahan the bureaucracy may be able to scare off more timorous donors and starve the Center out of existence.

Even so there is a greater security and strength in groups for those who want to make this sort of challenge to the administrative structures for which they work. As this is realised women within the bureaucracy are starting to look to the creation of supportive counter-structures. According to different traditions women look in diverse places for their style of collective action. In Britain, attempts to unionise, and to extract union recognition and negotiating rights from the management is an obvious course. The suspicion with which the church institutional management regards trade unionism in their own offices is so strong that it makes the endeavour worthwhile in itself, despite the knowledge that most Trade Unions are as unconcerned for women's rights and radical reorganisation of administrative structures as the management itself. Because of the mutual dislike between Christian women radicals and the New Left, particularly the feminist movement at large, there has been too little contact between the groups. Many alternative administrative structures, especially co-responsibility openness and worker control, are practised here and there throughout radical organisations in Britain. The National Women's Aid Federation, for example, struggles with a national organisation which wants to be both efficient and genuinely corporate; here the relationship between voluntary and paid workers has interesting implications for the churches. *Spare Rib* magazine practises collectivity, parity and (for lack of funds) shared poverty as well. Christians ought to find in themselves a stronger motivation for radical transformation of alienating structures now – as opposed to 'after the revolution', that utopian parousia of the left, because of the theological concept of 'sufficient grace'.

Women have a particular role to play in changing these structures, first because they are the articulate oppressed of Western bureaucracy, near enough to the centre to make themselves heard, but still not members of that elite, second because many of the women who have become 'eligible' for ordination in the last two decades are those who have spent much of their life working as administrative, executive and support personnel with the Christian bureaucracies. Despite the emerging problem of clericism among ordained women themselves, there is also a sense in which these new clergy should understand and recognise the importance of these lay ministries, precisely because they have been there for so long. They should thus be able to do more than has been done to eliminate bureaucratic distinctions between lay and ordained Christians. This special group of women, those who have moved as adults and sometimes even quite unexpectedly from one caste to another, is not going to be with us for very long, which makes the last quarter of this century a particularly important time for tackling the questions of bureaucratic clericism and dualism.

Most importantly, however, women have a unique experience of working, living and organising in groups which are conscientiously structured very differently from modern bureaucratic institutions. 'Sisters,' to quote Mary Daly, 'we really cannot belong to institutional religion as it exists. It isn't good enough.' We do now know that there are other and better ways of administering, organising and working together. We have both the vision and the energy to demand and create changes.

CHAPTER 6

LANGUAGE AND SPIRITUALITY

- - - - - - - - - - - - ◆◆◆ - - - - - - - - - - - -

> By the waters of Babylon we sat down and wept
>   when we remembered you, O Zion.
> As for our harps, we hung them up
>   on the trees in the midst of that land.
> For those who led us away captive asked of us a song,
> and our oppressors called for mirth:
>   'Sing us one of the songs of Zion'.
> How can we sing our God's song
>   in an alien land?[1]

Dear God, are boys really better than girls? I know you are one, but try to be fair.[2]

So what, when it comes right down to it, is all this clamour, chaos, disruption and fuss really about? The answer is immense and simple: God. This chapter is about worship and spirituality – our closest direct experience with the infinite. It does come at the end of the book not because I think there is somehow a progression of merit through theoretical analysis and political action upwards towards prayer, nor because worship is a minor matter to be tacked on at the end but because I believe in an unbroken circle: I would like this chapter to take us round to the start again.

It is not easy to talk about God; it is both too enormous and too private. Moreover, I personally do not feel myself so well acquainted with God that I can speak with authority. Not long ago I was with a small group of women late one evening.[3] We were in a quiet, tired mood, but wanted to stay together rather than go off and read or sleep alone. We needed a bed-time story that was somehow our own. I said, 'Women really must re-discover an oral tradition', and my friend and sister Jo Garcia said, 'But we have one. We're always telling each other stories.' Anyone who has lived inside the Women's Movement knows that this is true. I shall begin with a story.

29 July 1979. A hot, heavy New York Sunday. Later on it is going to rain spectacularly. 29 July is the Feast Day of Martha and Mary. It is also the date of the Philadelphia Ordinations in 1974. The fifth anniversary of this event had the consideration to fall on a Sunday. One of the places where this birthday was celebrated was in the Episcopal parish of St John in the Village – a small, very modern, mercifully air-conditioned church. Here the commemoration took the form of a celebration of all women's ministries in the Church over the last five years. Not just the words of the service and the sex of the sanctuary-party were re-ordered but the whole building was reshaped in an attempt to express the transforming power of the new women's spirituality.

The original initiative for this celebration had come from a regular member of the St John's congregation – Anne Scheibner. A graduate from Wellesley with a MA in business studies, coming from a family with deep roots in the Episcopal Church, she has been involved in radical renewal and Christian feminism since discovering in 1973 that her church did not ordain women. She was the national organiser for the Episcopal Women's Caucus in the period leading up to Philadelphia and Minneapolis. More recently she worked as the executive director of the Newark Diocese Venture in Mission and has been a member of the Urban Coalition. She is also an artist. St John's church building was designed in the 1960s deliberately to allow maximum flexibility and community use. None the less it was laid out almost all of the time as a very traditional church building with rows of pews facing towards an altar on a raised dais. Anne Scheibner asked the parish to let her use the excellent facilities for a 'Feminist Liturgical Art Project'. As she wrote in the parish bulletin:

> My aim is to help create a liturgical environment as a thank offering. . . . It is appropriate that this year we reflect on the place of women – both lay and ordained – in the church as a whole today. . . . As we plan our service we will explore further our feelings and perceptions so that the service itself will be an effective and accurate witness to where we are now – our

brokenness, our rejoicing, our hope. Thereby we hope to call attention to the fact that our pilgrimage is not ended.[4]

The Feminist Liturgical Art Project set about the physical transformation of the available space and also the creation of specific symbols. The traditional linear design of Christian churches, with the laity at the bottom and the back and then, separated usually by a physical barrier and raised higher as well, the altar surrounded by specially sanctified, specially dressed, people has seemed to many people to express visually the hieratic ladder that is in conflict with the Christian declarations on community; traditional pews separate individuals from one another and kneeling in their protection emphasises a privacy within it in contrast to the claims of corporate unity. Feminists believe that these are symbols of male-dominated culture and the source, as well as the sign, of our human dividedness. Bearing all this in mind the pews at St John's were cleared away from the central area. While they were being moved someone discovered that they would balance upright on what would normally be their ends. This casual discovery was utilised: with a delicate irony the pews were up-ended and grouped together in such a way that they formed huge pillars which were then arranged to encircle the congregation – those very material objects which had served to separate Christians from each other were now used to symbolise their closeness. Because of the design of the pews it was also discovered that grouped thus in vertical fours they naturally formed frames, curved hollows – caves, or wombs, which were then filled with suspended cardboard doves. This use of provided materials was reflected in all the art work. Even the shortage of funding for the project became a part of its strength and wholeness; cardboard boxes collected on the local streets were the principal medium. The group increasingly theologised from their experience, as Anne Scheibner wrote a weekly report for the parish bulletin:

> What are the major characterisitics of the Feminist Liturgical Art
> Project? First is the use of materials – cardboard, paper,
> poster-paints, which are easy to experiment with, use and
> discard. We are in an age of impermanence . . . Our theological
> symbols tend to embody the idea of unchanging and eternal
> truths. Is it not however the *process* of love, creativity and
> struggle which is unchanging, and not the physical symbols? If
> so then it is appropriate for the Church to try and find new ways

of expressing a Christian understanding of the world in which we live, which embody this reality of physical change.[5]

But the theology was growing out of the experience and the work in a dynamic way.

The major single artefact was a huge cross made out of old cardboard boxes. (Some people even tried to draw humorous theological analogies with the contemporary church from its alarming instability.) Many of these boxes had by chance originally been containers for alcohol and were thus neatly partitioned into bottle-sized squares by cardboard dividers: again these were exploited rather than denied. They created a series of little frames held in unity first by the boxes themselves and then by the towering symbol of the cross in which all things were united. Each little frame contained its own image: some from the natural world – shells, rocks, flowers; some from the human skills – jewellery models; and some from the history of women in Christianity – pious women-saint pictures, photographs of women involved in Church politics over the last five years, women at Philadelphia, at National Convention, at the Riverside Drive Ecumenical Eucharist; photographs of Maria Cueto and Raisa Nemikin;[6] and pictures of women in struggle throughout the world.

But the most important thing about the project was the community and energy that it generated. The church building itself, the Holy of Holies, became the living and working and chatting and nurturing place for an increasing group of people throughout the weeks approaching the service. Although having the sanctuary filled with whisky crates and beer cans remained unacceptable to some members of the congregation, others quite slowly began to participate, bringing their own treasures for the box-frames, helping with the considerable work involved and increasingly contributing time and creative ideas. Women also started coming in from the outside just to see what was keeping a church building lit and busy late into week-day evenings. One of the sweetest fruits of the project ripened months later at the adult baptism of a woman who had simply come to see what these crazy women were doing and stayed to find a community of sisterhood, love and holiness. Much of the creative energy generated was the gift of the generosity and administrative talent of the co-ordinator; but as the details of the service itself were worked out women were offering their own special gifts to the

Church in a new and liberating way. Interestingly the stress was not on developing new symbols but on transforming the old ones – doves, flames, crosses – which were being claimed by women as their own.

The form of service reflected this idea. A feminist Christian group, the Mother Thunder Mission – after the mother of the apostles James and John who 'were called the Sons of Thunder' – uses one of the rooms at St John's for their regular meeting. This group had devised a non-sexist liturgy which was used as the rite for the service.[7] The celebrant was the Rev. Carter Heyward – one of the Philadelphia-ordained priests. The Rev. Joan Martin, an ordained Presbyterian who works for the National Council of Churches in the Justice for Women section, read the Gospel. The Eucharist itself was an exciting event, the climax of a process started months before. But like the visual aspects of the scheme it used only traditional material. No new theology was claimed, the normally accepted necessary ingredients for a proper Holy Communion Service were all present; and yet they had been reclaimed, transformed and renewed by the women who had created both the environment and the rite and made the two inseparable. It was a new experience of worship – a women's experience, where men were welcome to participate and share (which they did), but where women, for once, set the terms.

Worship is a funny sort of business at the best of times. It lives at the heart of all religious experience. For Christians it is 'both our duty and our joy'.[8] Jesus' command that we pray – along with his command that we love one another – is one of the few instructions which has never been called into question. What he preached he clearly practised and found there the unification of his nature and the source of his power. So much is clear, and yet there remains a massive list of unanswered questions: not just about how to do it, but more fundamentally what it is and how it works. It is a subject on which every practitioner admits total inadequacy and yet, throughout Christian history, the tracts by the experts have poured out. Anyone on the outside wishing to find out more about this phenomenon will be overwhelmed by an enormous amount of conflicting data, advice, reports and methods.

One of the problems is that the words 'worship' and 'prayer' are used to describe a whole mass of activities which it would be easier – though dangerously wrong – to separate. There are two main areas, though they are so interconnected that this is hardly helpful: public and personal prayer. Public worship, the group or communal expression of faith (for which 'liturgy' is the technical term) may be more or less formalised, ritualised. Obviously the 'higher' a doctrine of the Church as a universal unity a denomination holds the more likely it is that the liturgy wll be uniform. The Roman Catholics and Orthodox maintain a central control over their rites which is, as far as possible, rigid. The person who participates at Mass or who prays the Breviary (the official non-sacramental prayer of the Church) believes herself united with the *whole Church* – not just on earth but in eternity also. The form of words and the ritual acts must reflect that unity. Whereas an extreme congregationalist denomination need not feel that, in finding a form of worship they feel comfortable with, they have a wider responsibility. All public prayer throughout Christian history seems to have contained certain elements whose function is twofold: educational (reading from sacred texts and preaching, for example) and consolidatory – unifying the individual members and corporately turning them towards God. Apart from the Holy Communion service itself, a powerful example of how this is done is singing together – which has been the practice not just of Christian communities but of almost all religious organisations throughout every culture. Indeed Christians, along with other spiritual disciplines have usually taken singing further into movement and dance – Western reticence about the body is a very isolated and historical phenomenon.

The other main area of prayer is personal: the individual alone with her God. The course and journey of prayer has been mapped over and over again. It is a strange adventure into a country with surprisingly few major landmarks and yet a plethora of roads: even the ultimate destination is not very clear. There are more contradictions than clarities, but the main purpose is 'knowing God' and 'living virtuously, harmoniously, well' and uniting these two into one whole. It is the duty – even in the denominations with the most corporate understandings – of every Christian to find an individual relationship with God and bring this back into social relationships.

In a perfectly unitative model there should not of course be any division between the two areas of prayer. The Benedictine rule, for example, tries hard to obliterate the boundary between liturgical and private (contemplative) prayer. It goes further and tries to close the gap between prayer and non-prayer altogether, so that all life is prayer – a unity and circularity is sought so that life can be holy and wholely lived. The Benedictine model is based on three pillars of liturgical prayer, mental study and physical labour; recognising the soul/mind/body divisions in humans, and by recognising them trying to weld them back together. Of course Benedictines are not the only group to work on this unity. I spent a weekend with other women trying to avoid making these separations: just being together (eating, dancing, swimming in the sea and being in silence) was itself worship and celebration and there was no need to designate special times as 'services'. But the Benedictines have been working on this project for 1,500 years in a structured and organised way so that their experience is of particular value. It is clear that although many people find that their contemplation and study and physical work deeply inform their liturgical prayer and that in its turn feeds and furnishes their work, the absolute unity of the two types of prayer is seldom if ever achieved.

Turning specifically to women it is important to realise that although they have had in the past little or no impact on the formal liturgical prayer of Christianity – partly because they were excluded from ordination and just as much because they were excluded from the formal study of theology – they have been important experts (if that is a permissible word) on personal prayer. The two women who have been named 'Doctors of the Church' by Roman Catholicism,[9] Teresa of Avila and Catherine of Siena, were no academic theologians but writers on contemplative spirituality and mystical prayer. They were both also important church reformers, but it is for their contribution to spirituality that they won the accolade of their church.

The history of Christianity from Mary's *Fiat* and her *Magnificat* onwards has seen the recognition of women as mystics. Dame Julian of Norwich – never canonised because her theology of sin and hell was in the eyes of the church authorities deficient (she believed that sin was useful and was not convinced that God could possibly damn anyone) – has proved an abiding spiritual resource.[10] Women have always shown a greater enthusiasm in terms of numbers, and indeed aptitude, for the contemplative life and being the recipients of mystical experience. The division – men as the liturgical public saints and women as mystical, magically holy, has not only made the union of the two more difficult, it has also worked to the disadvantage of women. Although obviously for those who do find that joyful and wordless union with God there is no greater blessing or vocation to seek for, this gift has been used against other women. I mentioned this in the earlier chapter about nuns and do not want to go over old ground, but the mystical experiences of women has been used to succour the image of women as being more simple and open to God, passive recipients, nearer to pre-lapsarian nature. Men in authority have exploited the gifts of women by allowing them to dictate that this is the best way, the only way, for women to be holy. The unitive joy of male mystics has always been a bit different: most male mystics have either been hermits – alone, adventurous and manly before God – or, because of the historical developments in monasticism, more engaged with other jobs – as priests, preachers or workers – and thus prayer has not been their only contact with the heart of the Church. While women have been obliged to choose between Martha and Mary roles, men have the option of combining the two.

But now women are emerging, theologically educated and increasingly determined to ignore the Pauline injunction to silence, into the arena of liturgical prayer. The fact that we, women and men together, have lived through a period of astonishing liturgical change which has corresponded to our own more social liberation, seems to have acted as an imaginative spur. While the church bureaucracies are leaning back exhausted, convinced that there has been enough change, many women feel that we have hardly started. Perhaps because we have been excluded onlookers for so many generations it is easier to see what needs doing. There are strong theological arguments for changing the very shape of most churches – whether it is the Catholic altar many miles away from the congregation who cannot, from their pews, look both at it and at the community; or the elevated Protestant pulpit from which the minister can thunder downwards representing the Deus ex machina appearing from on high. The new west-facing nave altars with the priest behind them completing a circle with the people are more historically authentic and more theologically sound: so it is not surprising that they accord more with a feminist vision, but, with old plant and conservative hearts, few churches dare to go far enough in this direction. The new liturgical fashion of receiving communion standing obliterates the need for the altar rail and that is visually an important symbol. So long as the division between the 'sanctuary party' – whether it is a robed choir or acolytes with candles – still exists it is vital that some of these should be women who are otherwise excluded not just symbolically but literally from the heart of the Christian Sacrifice (why conservative priests should be surprised at the lack of 'self-sacrifice' on the part of modern women – a complaint that is endlessly heard – when we are apparently not capable of performing the holy sacrifice itself is an interesting question). The incomprehension with which most women greet the reiteration that women are not to serve at Mass is best represented by a ten-year-old's letter to the Catholic Press:

> Why do you think we should not have girl servers? We should be a family. . . . Are there some of you who don't like girl servers? Please tell us why you don't like them? We can't think of any good reasons.[11]

But along with the desire that public worship should do more to express what we generally believe about community, equality and love there is one particular issue which is central to women's place in the Church. It is the question of 'inclusive' or 'non-sexist' liturgical language. Many of the changes that women are demanding in the language that the Church uses often look like little more than word games, but I believe there is something far more important at stake. It is not only the opposition who do not see the issue as one of importance: the Rev. Mary Levison for example, who was one of the leading campaigners for women's ordination in the Presbyterian Church of Scotland, feels that women who worry about the masculine bias of religious language are suffering from 'inferiority complexes and lack of confidence in their own potential holiness'.[12] For Christians, however, the whole business of language has a particular importance: the Jewish religion from which Christianity sprang and in which its own sacred texts are grounded, was a highly verbal faith – its cultic rules against 'graven images', visual representation, were strict and its non-verbal artistic culture thus very limited. God's revelation to the Hebrew people was a verbal one: the visible presence of God was always veiled from sight, and although natural and supernatural signs were recognised, the concept of visualising God was alien to Jewish understanding. Apart from Hagar, a foreigner, a woman and a slave, driven out of the camp by Abraham, no one in the Jewish tradition 'saw God and lived'. Yahweh was known by and in the Word of God. When God made the first covenant with the Jewish people this was understood as a verbal exchange: the tablets of the Law, which they should keep, were coupled with the gift of God's *name*, a sacred word, on which they could call and know they would be heard. Although Christianity quickly dropped the absolute prohibition on visual imagery we did maintain a very strong emphasis on words. 'In the beginning was the Word and the Word was God': Christ as that 'word incarnate', that which came from the mouth of God and took flesh: 'God' and 'God-speaking' are co-eternal and inseparable.[13] It is by words and by The Word that Christians claim to know God. All sacramentalists, of whatever political or denominational persuasion, share a conviction that in order to have a valid sacrament you do not only need the right materials and the right intention, you also need the right form of words. (This can be interpreted as traditionalism, magic, a search for unity or in a number of other ways: I am not speculating here on its meaning, but pointing it out.) Protestantism, in a different way, expresses the use convictions: by laying the stress of authority on the Biblical texts they assert that words have an absolute value. Christianity has laid great stress on verbal accuracy from the earliest time: the great Arian heresy which divided and nearly destroyed the early Church could also be seen, from a different perspective, as little more than a 'word game'.

It is also a fundamental Christian tradition (as well as common sense) that the words that Christianity chooses to use should as nearly as possible say what they are meant to mean, and be understood: mumbo jumbo, ritualistic incantation, and sounds are not enough. Paul, for example, stresses that people should not 'speak in tongues' publicly unless there is an interpreter available.[14] Both Latin and Greek, the languages which until comparatively recently were the languages of Christian theology, have a number of words which are missing in English. 'Homo' in Latin and 'anthropos' in Greek both mean 'a human being', while 'vir' and 'aner' mean 'a male human being', and that is what they *mean*. In English we have a curious situation in which the word 'man' is supposed to mean both an 'individual of the human species' *and* a 'male individual of the human species'. Grammarians argue that this is simply correct and anyway it does not matter because ninety-nine times out of a hundred it is perfectly obvious what is meant: 'Primitive *man* developed tools and language in response to *his* hunting needs' 'obviously' includes all human beings. 'Men' on a toilet door is 'obviously' not meant to imply that dogs, horses or goldfish should go elsewhere. However, there is a growing feeling that this does not tell the whole truth. In the first place it is not always 'obvious' which use of 'man' – and its gender pronouns – is meant. Here is a quotation from the Book of Common Prayer in which the use of the word shifts so confusingly that it has in fact thrown the whole Anglican Communion nearer to schism than at any time in its history:

> It is evident to all *men* diligently reading Holy Scripture and the ancient authors, that from the apostles' time there have been these orders of Ministers in Christ's Church: Bishops, Priests and Deacons. Which offices were evermore had in such reverent estimation that no *man* might presume to execute any of them except *he* were first called, tried, examined and known to have such qualities as are requisite for the same.[15]

Presumably the diligent 'men' of the first sentence includes women; but we know that the un-presuming 'man' of the second does not. Or does not in the case of Bishops and Priests, but does in the case of Deacons? Or does in some parts of the world? In this very passage the plot thickens when the instruction continues 'And the Bishop know-ing . . . any *Person* to be a *man* of virtuous conversation and without crime.'[16]

Another fine example of the floating meaning of the word 'man' is to be found in the Ten Commandments. It is reasonable to suppose that the people who are not to take God's name in vain, commit murder, theft, adultery or Sabbath-day work include women throughout. But unless the Hebrew community suffered from a wave of aggressive lesbianism unknown since early times we are forced to conclude that the 'man' who is forbidden to covet *his neighbour's wife* is a non-generic straightforward male man, because no one is proposing that 'wife' is a generic term inclusive of husbands.

But the real point here is not that confusion may arise, but – as is brought out in this example – the exclusively male use of the word ends up by subsuming the generic usage. So that, innocently think-ing they are using the word inclusively, writers go on to say things that cannot possibly apply to women. Finally, the image of women as an equal part of the species *homo sapiens* does indeed disappear. Elaine Morgan in her immensely charming and clever book *The Descent of Woman* has made clear how the double use of the word 'man' has clouded the minds of many evolutionary and behaviourist writers and actually distorted our understanding of the development of human culture.[17] Detailed sociological work leads to the same conclusions: whatever grammarians may say the confusion about the word 'man' exists at a conceptual level and is significantly instrumental in carrying forward and developing the notion that male persons are more important – culturally, historically and, in the last count, individually – than female persons.[18]

Moreover the word 'man' does not simply summon up, at the conceptual level, an undifferentiated person with male biological characteristics, but is actually value-laden in ways that Christians should think about very carefully. In 1972 two American sociologists tested 300 undergraduates by asking them to create, from newspaper and magazine pictures, collages illustrating certain themes. Half were assigned their theme using the word 'man': 'Industrial Man', 'Political Man', 'Social Man' and so forth. The other half were given the same concept differently expressed – 'Industrial Life', 'Political Behaviour', 'Society'. Not only did the group with the word 'man' in their titles show markedly fewer pictures of women or children – up to 30 per cent and 40 per cent in some cases. They also showed that the word 'man' induced images of power and dominance to a statistically significant degree. For example:

> 'Social Man' was portrayed as a sophisticated, white,
> party-going male (a half to two thirds of the pictures included the
> consumption of alcohol). . . . 'Society' involved scenes of social
> disruption and protest with a sub-theme of co-operation among
> people.
>   'Political Man' was portrayed by pictures of Nixon or other
> politicians making speeches. . . . 'Political Behaviour' was
> represented by prominent political figures also, but contained a
> secondary theme of people, including women and minority
> males, in political protest situations. . . . 'Economic Behaviour'
> appeared to elicit fewer pictures of bosses, corporate executives
> and capitalists than did the term 'Economic Man'.

Or in simpler language, the very word 'man' is not only *not* perceived as a generic and inclusive term, even by well educated subjects, but moreover the word itself is value-laden in a somewhat negative sense.[19] Each time a Christian congregation uses the word 'man' when it means 'all people' individuals should ask themselves whether the Christ-like human is a 'sophisticated white party-going male' or someone involved in social protest and 'co-operation among people'. While it is important not to put too much stress on one rather small bit of research, this bears out so precisely what an increasing number of women *feel* that it is worth drawing attention to.

There is a further and very important aspect to all this. The formal language of Christianity is not just a tool for expressing our faith; it should also be a means for teaching it. Not enough attention is given to the effects on small children of different genders in this linguistic 'game'. In the language that children learn in their early years considerable stress is put on the correct observation of gender identity. No 'inclusive generic uses' for the under-fives. When a toddler looks out the window and tells mummy that 'a man is coming to the door', mummy will correct her if it turns out to be a female man. Before school a child has to learn not only that gender identification is a necessary social skill, but also which gender she herself is. (The word really has to be is – you may *have* brown hair and black skin and a fat tummy, but you *are* female or male.) Later on in school the discovery for boys that 'man' can be an inclusive word is a natural part of what he is learning – that you can extend from the particular to the general, from yourself to the world; that what you perceive and know is a small but real part of a larger whole. For a girl discovery is rather different: what she is is less than the fullness of truth, she is unmentioned in the whole, the world is not a logical extension of her identity, but something else, different and alien. She is only a sub-species of the human whole.

This realisation and its implications were the initial impetus behind the request that the language of the churches give recognition to the sense of exclusion that women felt. It was essential that the Church respond even when the grammarians did not because there it was spiritually and psychologically vital that inclusiveness, membership, incorporation, equality and belonging be expressed. That was what the Christian faith was meant to be about. As soon as the issue was raised, however, it became clear that it was not simply a matter of working through every official text and changing the word 'man' to 'men and women' or 'people'. The linguistic exclusion of women had gone further than that. It may be grammatically 'correct' to say that 'man' can represent the whole human race, but it is preposterous to argue that 'brothers' includes sisters, or that 'sons' includes daughters. If in any social context I announced that I had three sons people would be legitimately surprised if two of them turned out to be female. When a priest says to a congregation consisting only of women (as often happens) 'Pray brethren . . .' or when the words of a hymn read 'O Brother man, fold to thy heart thy brother', it is well nigh impossible to feel a sense of incorporation. Hearing oneself addressed as a 'Son of Abraham' or of Israel not only excludes the hearer, it is also a blow to one's sense of the historical reality of women's experience. When we are included in that history it is not usually in a very attractive way. 'Daughters of Eve' is seldom meant as a compliment or even as a neutral way of describing women. The use of Adam and Eve is interesting all round: despite Adam's little ways, whenever he is liturgically recalled it is with a kind of compassionate pride – 'O happy fault, O necessary sin of Adam which won for us so great a redeemer.'[20] As descendants of Adam we claim an imaginative closeness to God, a personal interest in God's salvation. Eve, on the other hand, and her daughters by implication, summon up a much closer and more sinister connection with sin – often sexual in connotation – as well as being stupid, easily swayed and generally second-class. The idea that she too was made in God's image is carefully obscured.

Worse still, once one starts looking at language too closely we find that we have been committed to a whole range of images which do not only exclude us as women, they disgust us – politically, emotionally and theologically. Like many people I was welcomed into the Body of the Crucified Servant with a prayer that includes the earnest desire that 'I should 'Manfully fight under his banner and continue Christ's faithful soldier' throughout my life. With the exception of 'faithfully continuing', every image in this phrase must offend. I am a woman: 'Manfully', as the OED makes clear, means 'in a manly style' and 'manly' means 'having those qualities proper to a man as distinct from a woman or child'. But this obvious sexism is just the beginning: 'fighting' means acts of aggression, violence and killing; soldiers are the people paid to do this. The hero as warrior (officer-class from choice), and battle as glory are precisely contrary to Christ's injunctions that it was the peacemakers who were blessed, that we should love our enemies and turn the other cheek when someone hits us.[21] War, territorial aggression and the fear of violence seem to be the greatest sins of the world today: should we at the heart of the most central rite of our faith really be encouraging such images? Baptism could be the most 'female' of all the sacramental rituals of the church, and should be – it is a moment of birthing, when the new Christian passes from darkness through water into light. Even the traditional design of fonts underlie this woman-typology. We are received from the font/womb into the family, into the arms of 'Mother Church' – and our liturgy speaks to us of the male values of militarism.

The discovery of how deeply sexist and anti-Christian many of our liturgical materials were at least produced a creative problem for women. But the initial idea – that the language of the Christian community should not offend the sensibilities of some of its members without good cause – created another range of difficulties, which were more surprising. First, it is quite astonishingly hard to get anyone who does not personally feel the problem to take the idea seriously. It is hard to work out why this should be the case. When large numbers of men find themselves in a situation where for one reason or another the common usage prescribes *female* language, they rapidly develop the 'morbid sensibility' of which women are accused. A good example of this is primary school teaching. Until the middle of this century it was common to refer to the undifferentiated primary school teacher as 'she' – as almost all primary school teachers were in fact female. When men started entering the profession they found it insulting that they should be referred to in this way – bad grammar, bad politics, and bad for their egos. A young male teacher summed it up:

> The incorrect and improper use of the English language is a vestige of the nineteenth century image of the teacher and contrasts sharply with the vital image we attempt to set forth today. The interests of neither the men nor the women in our profession are served by grammatical usage which conjures up an anachronistic image of the nineteenth century school marm.[22]

If men can so easily perceive the damage done to their self-image by the simple pronoun 'she' it is curious that they do not understand why the reverse is also true. But when a Baptist Minister, the Rev. John Matthews, wrote to the Baptist Union complaining about their habit of addressing all circular letters to ordained ministers 'Dear Brother', the response made it clear he was simply being silly.

To counter those who claim that gendered language is unimportant and irrelevant, an old Christian maxim argues that, 'those without scruples should give way to those with scruples'. In charity, those who do not have strong feelings about this should let those who do have their own way. I suspect that if all language was changed, along these lines, to oblige those who feel excluded, people who maintain that it is a peripheral issue would find that their sensibilities were offended. This line was recently taken by the Roman Catholic Church in the USA. The National Conference of Bishops' Liturgy Secretariat produced two proposals for consideration. The first was simply to drop the word 'men' from the crucial sentence in the middle of the Eucharistic Prayer which proclaims that Christ's 'blood was shed for you and for all men' – which apart from being non-sexist would also be a more accurate translation of the Latin which reads 'pro multis' ('for many', as the Book of Common Prayer has). The second was to authorise the celebrant to 'substitute an inclusive word or phrase' in the liturgy 'wherever the generic term "man" or its equivalent is found'. The committee suggested 'men and women', 'the human family', 'the human race' or 'all people'. Sr Luanna Durst of the Secretariat explained their proposals:

> It is a fact that some members of our Eucharistic Assemblies feel excluded or alienated from the Prayer of the Church . . . even though this is not intended. What ever can be done to alleviate any hurt of feeling of alienation of a large segment of the assembly must be undertaken.[23]

She also mentioned that 'many many priests are doing this already' but without the authorisation that they would like. The Bishops' conference rejected both proposals. I suspect that this was not malicious, but stemmed from two causes – one already mentioned is the inability on the part of many people to realise that women really do care. The second reason, however, is a more profound problem and one to which Sr Luanna Durst also drew attention: the current authorised Roman Catholic Liturgy was translated from Latin into English in 1970, in response to the Vatican Council's instruction that the Mass should be celebrated in 'the language of the people. Unfortunately this was before the awareness of sexist implications in Language.'[24] This is not just true for the Roman Catholic Mass. The renewal in the denominations, with its creation of new liturgies and new translations, tends to have *just* preceded the sociological and linguistic work which feminism has generated, and which has awakened a new consciousness of the masculine bias of language and the serious implications that this has.

The NLC Roman Catholic Missal in Britain was published in 1973. The English translation of the Jerusalem Bible – the official modern Roman Catholic translation – was issued in 1966. The New English Bible – the most authoritative and scholarly of the modern English language translations – produced its New Testament in 1961 and the whole text in 1970. The new English Prayer Book has finally been authorised for use in 1981; the American Episcopal Prayer Book in 1979 – but the texts here have been in experimental use for some time. The new Breviary in English was promulgated 1974. For the Protestant churches the formal liturgy is not such an important issue, but throughout the 1960s and early 1970s the hymnals were all overhauled and many parishes invested heavily in new worship materials at that time. None of these changes have been easily received by large sections within all the denominations – some have been bitterly resisted. There is a sense of weariness, of a long job finally completed, which is not going to make the authorities concerned enthusiastic about returning to the task in order to satisfy a group whose feelings they really do not understand. Whether a denomination is committed to Biblical authority or to liturgical authority, this is a difficult historical moment to be raising the question of new translations and new texts.

As an additional problem, many people have a very strange idea about translation. Perhaps this is best exemplified by an article in the *Catholic Herald* in 1979: readers were invited to send their comments on a modernised version of the Lord's Prayer. One correspondent wrote in, 'No thank you. Jesus' own words are good enough for me.' As people believe as an unshakable fact that Mary wore blue and Jesus had a beard, they also believe that Jesus went round Galilee speaking in splendid late medieval English. The text that one has learned by heart, probably in infancy, is somehow the 'true' text and all modern language translations are less authentic. This feeling has made reception of the new liturgies and Biblical translations more difficult still. In addition they are often very ugly and sometimes even risible. There is also an important economic factor. The new Breviary costs over £40; but unless changes are forced through it will last a priest for life. My Concordance is for the Revised Standard Version: the one for the New English Bible will cost around £12 – it is easier to stick with the RSV. A Concordance for a non-sexist Bible would mean yet another outlay. In hard-pressed parishes introducing a new liturgy can be a major expense – not just new copies for everyone, but new music, new lectionary, modern hymnals. Most parishes have found that money once in the last fifteen years; they would be unwilling to find it again.

The US Episcopal Church made some glancing acknowledgment of the feminist argument in their new Prayer Book, but there is an overwhelming feeling that they hardly started on the job. In the Church of England it was never even raised as a serious issue although the same Synod that rejected women priests in November 1978 also took the final steps towards authorising the new liturgies. The gallery was packed for the ordination debate – by both parties – but the language of the Church, now fixed for at least this century, went unchallenged. Dr Una Kroll believes:

> There is much more resistance to this than there is to women's ordination. It has proved very hard to channel any of this understanding into the Church. . . . Of course it is vitally important but structurally it is proving very hard even to get these ideas into circulation. We have to feed much more of this kind of thinking into the Church. But how we are going to do that God knows, because the resistance is enormous.[25]

If the official denominational authorities have this level of resistance to 'inclusive language' to describe the people of God, it can easily be imagined how intense is the resistance to non-sexist language when it comes to talking about God.

The early Christian theologians were unanimous in their recognition that God was 'without qualities' – it was incorrect to ascribe to the Divine human qualities such as maleness. This has always been the orthodox teaching of Christianity. In seeking, however, to talk about God and trying to represent our identity with God it has always been permissible to use anthropomorphic imagery or analogies. Jesus himself spoke about God in terms of human relationships – usually that of father. As the language we use does inevitably determine the ideas we hold, an imbalance in favour of a masculine God has grown up. Una Kroll describes this as:

> A very theological issue for me, because it involves a whole heresy which has crept into a lot of what the Church has, by implication, taught. There has been a whole understanding of woman as taking her humanity from Adam rather than from God – and so it becomes through her relationship with a man

that she is saved. And that isn't in the Gospel at all. It is a matter of theology to correct this imbalance. The official doctrine of the Church hs been pretty clear on the fact of men and women's equality before the fact of God and the fact that they are both made in the image of God. It is just balance, not new theology that's needed: female aspects of God need to be emphasised not invented.[26]

Women have worked on this emphasis with zeal. The Rev. Kathryn Piccard, an Episcopalian priest, among others has combed the Bible to find female images of God, and worked on ways of feeding them into the liturgical life of the Church. She has a particular ministry as a consultant to parishes which wish to explore what is open to them and stresses that she wants to operate only within the 'authorised' rites of her Church. In the mass of baffled theory and anger there is something solid about her practical training course in non-sexist liturgy:

> The initial ways that a parish can move towards a non-sexist liturgy are by only using hymns that are OK – that's where my hymnal guide comes in handy – all hymns people know, no need to buy new materials. Then the preachers can clean up the sermons and their styles of illustration. They may come to realise that the lectionary itself is censored: if there are female images for God they have got in accidentally and they're not supported by the other lessons, so that becomes an area that needs attention. Then people make a surprised discovery. I and a number of other people who do this sort of consulting work can preach and teach and lead services and talk about God and do counselling and live our lives without using sexist language or imagery.[27]

Kathryn Piccard has prepared packs of materials: different Eucharistic rites, guidelines for hymns, readings and prayers. In America this sort of material is becoming increasingly available, from feminist sources and from within the Women's Departments of the different denominations. The Ecumenical Women's Center has published hymn books; the Methodist Church has issued authoritative guidelines. In Britain we are still underequipped in this respect: a group of women I was with recently really wanted to 'sing out God's song' together and we really did feel as though we were in that 'alien land' the Psalmist wrote of – we had practically no shared music that we felt was our own.

However, there is a completely different approach to the same problem: both a harder and far more radical one. The Mother Thunder Mission, whose liturgy was used at the St John's in the Village service I described at the beginning of the chapter, write in the introduction to their translation of the rite:

> How we talk about God is a question that is being answered in two quite different ways. . . . The first approach points out that masculine imagery and language have been disproportionately used of God and that we need to correct the imbalance by emphasising the feminine imagery which does not exist in our tradition. Proponents of this view usually argue the importance of God not becoming an 'IT' to us. . . .
>
> The other argument stresses that all our talk about God is metaphorical at best. To say that God is a person is not to say 'person as we are'. To use no gender nouns is not to make God an 'it', at least not in some Christians' experience.
>
> Two guidelines are followed in this Liturgy: whenever possible talk to God rather than about God, e.g. 'You have filled the hungry' rather than 'He has filled the hungry'. This seems entirely appropriate in a context of worship. Use 'God' to address God. (Think of 'God' as a kind of pronoun for the unspeakable referent.) Yes this does mean more repetition of 'God' than we are used to. It's worth it.[28]

The Rev. Martha Blacklock, one of the founding members of the Mother Thunder Mission and now Archdeacon for Women's Ministries in the Diocese of Newark, leans heavily to this second option and expands their rationale:

> Every once in a while someone comes up to Mother Thunder and complains bitterly that we're not saying God is She, or worshipping the Goddess. Frankly I don't find that much of an improvement. I just want to skip that stage. We're making a great mistake to say that God is capturable in our experience of other human beings. God is not like that. . . . Balancing imagery so that we find more of ourselves in worship may be some improvement, but I don't want to waste all that time on it – because it seems to be refurbishing God in *my* image. I would rather spend time encouraging people to experience God

directly: as 'you', not he or she.

That old sexist C.S. Lewis has someone say that there are really six genders, but on Earth they only know about two. I respond to that. Here we are talking about God in genders he/she, masculine/feminine, these attributes or those attributes – but to say, 'Well, actually, maybe there are 7 or 8 or 4011 genders' – and here we are parcelling God out just in terms of *us*.[29]

This approach which, because of imaginative and linguistic difficulties, is less common than the 'inclusive balance theory' has interesting repercussions. It is in fact more closely attuned to the earliest dogmatic teaching of the Church: it is more *traditional* as well as making more fundamental demands. At the same time it creates particular theological problems. First, the ineffable, un-nameable, indescribable God has to be brought into relationship with the first century Nazarene of whom we believe that 'the fullness of God was pleased to dwell'. The tension between God ineffable and God incarnate has always been the real issue for Christians. Questions of Christology do not go away. But the Women's Movement in the Church has raised the old question in new terms. It is hard to answer in traditional theological terms, because the terms do not admit the question. When we say, in the Creed and elsewhere, that 'god became man' the Latin uses the generic word 'homo' rather than the gender specific 'vir'. Most non-sexist liturgies translate this 'was born of the Virgin Mary and became human'.[30] This is the correct translation but it does not solve the problem. However many genders exist in the heart of God, becoming human means partaking fully of only one of these at any one time. Jesus' human gender was male. To suggest that it was not is to question the human reality of the Incarnation and without that foundation stone the whole edifice of Christianity collapses.

There are ways out of the dilemma. Sr Irene Benedict CSMV, among others, proposes that while Jesus was male in his historical Incarnation, in his Ascension he transcended gender.[31] But this just creates further, more serious, problems: Christians traditionally believe that not only did God become human, but that in death, resurrection and ascension Jesus carried our humanity back, as it were, to its divine source. He did not leave humanity with death in the tomb – and if he did then the resurrection has little or nothing to do with us. I want the whole of my humanity redeemed. Part of my humanity is my sexuality: it is not good enough to say, 'The important thing about the Incarnation was not that the Second Person of the Trinity became male – and white, of Jewish nationality, a carpenter, Aramaic-speaking, etc. – but human.'[32] What is humanity without sexuality, what is sexuality without gender?

That is only a single instance of the difficulties that liturgical language can raise. It is a question that goes to the heart of Christian theology and ideology. Many people are happy with some of the new Trinitarian formulae that are appearing: translating the older 'Father, Son and Holy Spirit' as 'Creator, Redeemer and Sanctifier' (the most popular of the non-sexist models) or 'God unbegotten, God incarnate, God among us'. But other people claim that Jesus' 'sonship' is a term of absolute meaning. Even people who do not want to say 'Father' may still want to express the closeness of Jesus' relationship to the ultimate Other, because through that relationship we have both the promise and the actuality of our own transcendence. This reveals another deficiency in the English language: there is no gender-neutral term for the parent/daughter-and-son relationship. 'Offspring' has no affectual content; 'child' not only implies infancy, it also need not imply intimacy; 'heir' refers to property and status relationships.

These are theological issues of intricate complexity. We grope around. I do not offer answers. I raise the questions only to show that the question of the language that the people of God use to talk about themselves and about their God are not just a matter of consolatory word games. Words themselves are a source of power, the language we have determines quite profoundly what we can think, imagine and create. Both the two approaches that women have begun to use have practical as well as theological limitations. The immediate limitation of the 'inclusive language theory' can be demonstrated by quoting a proposed Credal formulae:

> We believe in one God our Father and Mother, the
> Almighty. . . . One Lord Jesus Christ the only off-spring of
> God, eternally begotten and born of the mother/father.[33]

If you have to balance you have to repeat; if you have to repeat this often you end up with altogether too many words.

A practical limitation of the non-gender approach is that it cuts the use off from the history and development of the faith. It may be possible to balance the old male images with female ones: it is impossible to pretend that the Biblical writers, Jesus himself, and the women who have been before us on the road, did not use inter-personal terminology for their relationship with the ineffable. It grows increasingly hard for many women to share the prayer of the Christian community, in the Psalms for instance, because of its sexist, hierarchical and militaristic imagery. If we are going to deny ourselves personalised language as well we will become isolated from the historical reality of the Christian faith, as well as its whole expression.

None of this can diminish the importance of what has been done and is in the process of being done. The need to explore better ways of expressing our unity in Christ has not only revealed theological and linguistic bias, it has led to a creative upsurge of songs, prayers, liturgical settings[34] and an openness to experimentation which is exciting. At the same time there is a long way to go. Even as we try to decide how we want to talk about these things in public we have to go on an ever-deepening journey to discover more about who and what God is and who we are in relationship to that. The two languages are not and must not be separated, they must be brought into an ever closer relationship with one another, but in our divided, dualistic society they are still distinguishable.

So I move into the second area of prayer that I outlined at the beginning of the chapter – personal prayer. Here are many problems; and the first is that prayer has become a very intimate and private business. Women who will unblushingly discuss their orgasms, their psychiatrists and their labour-pains still are bashful about their relationship with God.

A more profound problem is the fact that those who go furthest on the prayer journey tend to have least to say. Many seemed to arrive at the place of profound silence; where there are no images and nothing to report except that it was a good place to be. (Although this place of unitative silence – the state of contemplation – is always represented as the apogee of Christian prayer, I have a strong sense that more people have been there than even know it. After slogging through the traditional Christian experts one would be nervous about claim-ing, even secretly such a privilege.) Thus when I was interviewing women for this book I nearly always asked them about their own spirituality and prayer-practice. The more obvious it was that the woman was a committed, happy and regular silent pray-er the less she seemed to have to say about it or about the God whom she encountered. None the less it is possible to say some things about the spirituality of Christian women today. This is partly because it is increasingly evolving as a group experience. The Charismatic Movement has opened afresh the possibility of corporate openness about prayer, while the Women's Movement small group has made it possible to share our once secret selves. Even among groups of Christian women who repudiate both movements they have had their effect. We are beginning to talk, to share, and to create something that is no longer private even though it is not public liturgical prayer either. The sense of joy, love and God-as-loving-movement-between-people is part of women's spirituality. Many of these aspects are discussed in the chapter on women's groups earlier in the book, but the affirmation of sisterhood informs so much of what women are doing more individually that it is important to remember how close the two are.

There is another reason why it is possible to talk about personal spirituality: the Christian community has always been graced with a supply of people with the very useful gift of talking about, finding images and symbols for and bringing back shapes of the unnameable Other: map-makers of the interior country. There are both the explicit spiritual writers – people who can describe their own experience in terms general enough to make sense to at least some of their audience – and artists. In recent centuries the Christian community has been better at giving recognition and support to the former than the latter, but both exist.

Every spiritual journey is a journey of a whole and unique person and consequently no two are ever the same. At the same time precisely because real prayer involves the whole of the person and a large part of that whole is socially formed there do seem to be discernible 'fashions' in prayer: groups of people, often very diverse, coming up with the same images and ideas. For example, very physical manifestations of mystical experience – levitation, trance states, super-natural fasting, stigmata and allied phenomena, and very genital-sexual psychic experiences – were apparently quite common in sixteenth-century Spain (Teresa of Avila is simply one of the better known); this is extremely rare today. So it is worth picking up on common images that women are finding and expressing individually, in the hope that they will tell us more about God

and about how we live God-lives and enrich the Christian community and the whole world.

First, of course, there is the overdue renewal of the spiritual
certainty that women – including each woman – were created by
God in God's image. You and I are in the image of God, partake of
holiness. The Rev. Alla Bozarth-Campbell, who is perhaps as near as
the Christian Feminist Movement gets to a traditional mystic of its
own, describes a process in her life which has been repeated for many
women:

> As I came to own and accept and celebrate my womanhood as a
> gift from God, bringing my own new value for the female side of
> life into prayer, I experienced a kind of inward leaping which
> was ecstatically physical as well as spiritual; an inward bodily
> leaping that made me feel God in my nerves and blood and deep
> down in my bone-marrow as well as in my emotions and
> intellect.
>
> I was not able to approach God with this kind of engagement
> until I began to open up my prayer life to the feminine aspects of
> God, and to celebrate my own femaleness in that aspect. And I
> didn't suspect the wholeness I missed until I began to experience
> it. . . . I don't suggest that this process is possible only for
> women. I only know that I came to it self-consciously as a
> woman, open to deeper discovery of my own nature through
> closer contact with the nature of God. . . . Reclaiming the
> feminine in worship helps me reclaim myself as a person created
> uniquely in the image of God, female. Now I know with my
> whole being that I am connected with God . . . and that the
> realisation of this connection is the reason for which I was born.[35]

Despite the frequent sneers, this is not the same thing as worshipping
'the Mother Goddess' (though why that should be, in itself, such a
risible thing to do is another question). One of the problems that
surrounds the whole area of identifying the female aspects in God
and in ourselves within the Christian framework is that the language
and cosmology of Christianity is based so extensively on Aquinas
(who based much of his work on Augustine). Along with all his
European contemporaries, Aquinas suffered from a serious biological misapprehension. He thought that the male role in biological
reproduction was the only active one; the male sperm contained,
complete but miniature, the new child and the woman provided only

a safe nurturing place for the microscopic infant to grow – the woman was the field where the man could sow his seed. This was not a metaphor or image: it was the scientific fact of the time. In considering the creative activity of God, producing life *ex nihilo*, the male role was inevitably dominant. By the time Western science was capable of a better understanding of human reproductive biology the split between theology and the natural sciences was well developed and Christian orthodox thinking never truly incorporated the facts of generation into its cosmological imagery.[36] It is partly because we have lived for so long now with the idea that science and spirituality are the polarised opposites (another fact of dualism) that we are unable to understand the enormous importance of this apparently small error. But the consequence of this misunderstanding was to add to the Christian denigration of women and also of nature itself. The man/woman division is very close to the spirit/material-nature one and the two fed each other during the formative period for Christian spiritual language and theology.

The attempt to reunite material reality with spirituality – an important and orthodox task for all Christians – has led particularly for women to a real need to reclaim, quite consciously, the holiness of femaleness itself.

This activity is not of course the exclusive prerogative of women; but inevitably it will be, at least for the time being, those who have the greatest need who are going to be the most willing to take the search for that holiness into the dangerous and dark corners of their lives. Only with this courage and openness will it be possible to come back again with the true images of the glorious and holy aspects of the nature of femaleness.

Sr Meinrad Craighead OSB is an enclosed contemplative. Before entering her order she was an artist of growing repute, and she has continued with her work since entering the enclosed life. She sees the work she now does as a direct consequence of her prayer life, and indeed as part of it:

All art is religious if it is about beauty, because beauty points beyond itself to the source. . . . Only contemplation can sustain this consecration because it directs the profoundest powers and keeps giving insight. . . . Prayer is the direction and renewal of the whole person . . . and this involves our bodies. Our bodies are channels to receive and give out this divine energy.[37]

In her most recent work, a book called *The Sign of the Tree*,[38] Meinrad Craighead takes 'the tree as an archetypal symbol which she uses to express the intensity and the wonder of the contemplative experience'.[39] From both her contemplative prayer and her physical labour in the convent garden she brings back a range of images which are dynamic and which incorporate (both explicitly in pictures like 'The Garden of the Mother' or 'The Primal Genatrix', and also at a much more profound level, in shapes which over and over again express women's bodies and genitalia) the God-ness and good-ness she finds in herself as woman. To an accusation that her work was 'too sensual' she responded:

> I think the sensual and spiritual mutually enlighten and inform each other . . . they are equal powers. For a Christian spiritual cannot mean non-material, nor is anything just material. . . . Perhaps my work is sensual *because* it is Christian.[40]

Another reason why the reclaiming of the mother in God is important now is that most people growing up in Western industrialised society have an appallingly limited experience of being fathered. Most of us did not experience fathering from our fathers in the terms that Jesus meant when he spoke of God as his 'Father' – cradled, fed, played with and taught. A recent survey on this indicated that less than 10 per cent of children now growing up had *ever* been alone with their fathers for sustained periods of their waking time. At the speculative level it is interesting that the growth of the idea of God the Father as judge (punisher) with Jesus as the friend and brother and Mary as the mother and mediator grew up as European literate society began to move away from an exclusively agricultural life-style (in which the father's role within the family is both more visible and more equal). When the science we teach even small children gives them the information that the mother plays an equal role in the creative, reproductive birth cycle (from the point of view of the child who sees pregnant women but never sees ejaculating men, women must appear to play a *more* important role) God as Father becomes an inadequate and distorting image, even without the exclusion of women-aspects. To some extent it is easier for a man to recognise the father usefully again, as he grows up trying to disidentify himself from the exclusively female adults with whom he has been obliged to associate as an infant. The father role perhaps becomes his sign of liberation and self-identity in the world. (Surely we must confuse small boys by insisting that they are male and then surrounding them with loving women whom they are not allowed to use as models?)[41]

The influence of psychoanalysis, and particularly of Jung, on women's emerging spirituality is certainly worth mentioning. Meinrad Craighead's art and her own commentary on it clearly reflect a debt to the archetypal imagery which he and his disciples delineated and expanded. Jungian typology can, and often is, used as a weapon against women's autonomy – particularly their practical and political participation – but for women engaged in spiritual journeying it can provide real insights and a validating licence to proceed. Sue Harris is a Christian writer who relies on these models in her attempt to express what is holy about being female:

> The feminine – as woman, as anima and as the body – is like
> Noah's Ark and the nativity stable: it receives and actively holds
> within itself whatever is poured in . . . it carries these embryos
> until they are transformed into something new and then releases
> them into life.[42]

Sue Harris argues that it is only through an understanding of the feminine – theologically, sacramentally, spiritually and physically – and recognising and accepting the differences that the breaches made by male-dominance can be healed and the Church liberated from misogyny and dualism.

However, it is important to realise that current trends in women's spirituality go far beyond an assertion that 'we are holy too', and it is only when this barrier is passed that it can become a creative contribution to the whole of life.

It is a truism that only the oppressed group can liberate not just itself but the oppressor also from the bonds of that oppression. White people are diminished by racism along with their victims; capitalists with workers; imperialist powers with their colonised people; men with women. But only the oppressed are in the position to recognise the gains of immediate action. At the foundations of all these divisions which diminish the possibilities of material transcendence for all humanity lie those patterns of thinking which are called dualism. Women, along with other oppressed groups, are on the underside of this divisive split. However much dualism may have been technically condemned by the Christian theologians it operates in their short-term interest: white, male, imperialist, bourgeois

Christians. It is not surprising, but it is delightful and important, that at the core of their spirituality women are discovering and proclaiming that oneness of body and soul, of spiritual and material, that unity which is the very opposite of dualism.

Deprived of access to the theological and intellectual debate, women over the centuries have been lumped with all the other things that distract 'spiritual man' from his escape from reality – historical, material process. As they struggle to declare themselves, despite the protestations, to be in 'the image of God' and full participants, as women, in salvation history women have begun to assert their identity with the 'lower orders'. Women, the early Church wrote and Western society maintains, are less spiritual than man because they are 'nearer to nature'. Christian women learning from the Black Power, the Gay Rights and the Women's Liberation Movements are beginning to reply, 'Yes. Nearer to nature, less spiritualised and therefore holier.' Nature, creation, bodies, blood, death and darkness are all part of God's plan and men's determination to deny them, escape from them and exploit them go some way to explaining the un-godly mess we are all in.

There is within Christian women's writing now a new note of nature mysticism – of expressing a corporate oneness with earth. It is easy to sentimentalise, and to escape from the violence, the savagery, the darkness, and the glory of nature. But because many of the expressions of this unity are less than perfect is not a good reason for backing away from truth. And some women are getting it right.

Meinrad Craighead says:

> One of my themes is our union with creation. Surely God means
> nature to sensitise us to other silences and rhythms. Nature
> refines and educates our senses and prepares us for the mystery of
> reality. All nature is a sign of the sacred in our midst. [43]

In *The Sign of the Tree* she goes further into this unity. One of her pictures called 'In the Garden of the Mother' carries this text:

> We worship God our Mother in solitude, seeking the secret
> places to be with her. . . . Everything in the garden magnifies
> her presence because everything pours from her source.
> Everything participates in her being. Everything is holy. . . .
> Searching for our mother we run through trees, lifting stones,
> kneeling at every pool and animal's hollow, looking into every
> cleft and beneath birds' wings. [44]

I believe despite the urban/rural differences that Meinrad Craighead is saying the same thing as Anne Scheibner was saying with her cardboard boxes. From all the sources the message is the same, whether they are 'radical feminist' or apparently totally orthodox and ecclesiological. Alla Bozarth-Campbell in poems like this

> Universal Body
> Worldflesh:
> My bones bones
> Of the old red stars.[45]

is saying precisely the same thing as Sr Maria Boulding OSB, an enclosed Benedictine nun, in her book on contemplative prayer. In a chapter called 'Towards Wholeness' she writes of a movement of growth away from the 'individualistic and ultra-spiritual' towards a place where:

> I may become more conscious of the great forces and movements which have shaped us: of creation and evolution . . . of the earth and the seasons, the stars, the sun, the moon . . . the megaliths and the ancient civilisations mean more to me.[46]

Helen Sands, a Roman Catholic lay woman from South London, works not just on expressing but on finding rituals and dances to incorporate this oneness. She works with ancient symbols – from Christian and other sources – and tries to refind them in nature. In the autumn of 1979 she led a 'pilgrimage' to the Kent sea-shore and there the group attempted to reconstruct mazes and spirals in the sand and follow their courses, inwards. It seemed afterwards an appropriate hilarity that they had forgotten to check the tide in advance and the patterns were carried away by a more efficient and ancient rhythm than their human one. One weekend I spent with Helen Sands and other women more recently we talked about the sea – as female, as rhythmical and as all-consuming. We ended up throwing beach pebbles into its embracing infinity, naming each throw with the sins we wanted drowned, cleansed and forgiven, and alternately our own power and love that we wanted to reunite with the sea. It was both religious ritual and play, but it was using nature as a symbol both of our unity with nature and our unity with each other.

Of the recognised major modern theologians, Teilhard de Chardin, perhaps comes nearest to a pantheistic nature mysticism. It is interesting to see that he was listed as the second most influential theological writer in Fran Ferder's study of Roman Catholic women who believe they have vocations to the priesthood.[47] He came above any women theologians and any writers on priesthood. Ferder's sample came from a wide geographical base and from a diversity of backgrounds (although they were rather well educated). The feeling that creation matters in a new and vital way to women is demonstrated by this finding.

In my own prayer life I have experienced this dimension. Two years ago I would have seen the ecology movement in human terms – identifying (though not I fear doing a lot about it) with the Christian Aid slogan 'Live simply that others may simply live'. 'Morally' I ought to eat less so that people in the Third World could eat more. I still believe that, but have now added a profounder theological aspect – respect and love for the created order reflects our true place in God's cosmos. Our claim to the right to 'name the beasts and have dominion over them' is contrary to the gospel, and if we are differentiated from the rest of nature in any real way it is in terms of consciousness and service. Not only do I feel that my dependence on and connectedness with creation is a fact, I also believe that it is good and holy. The matter around us and its process in time (history) is full of God, an equal source of revelation with the intellectual deposit of faith – the two are meaningless without each other. For me this interconnection is expressed gloriously in the Old Testament 'Song of the Three Children' or, as it is also called, 'The Canticle of Daniel' which Shadrach, Meshach and Abednego are supposed to have sung in the fiery furnace: 'All ye works of the Lord Bless ye the Lord, praise him and magnify him forever', which carefully works through the material world giving a voice to the praise of each member. (I have not yet found a non-sexist translation of this which has half the rhythm of the Prayer Book translation and will even tolerate the male-biased language in exchange for uniting myself with creation in that way.)

There are brave women who have taken this still further. It is not just nature (which has at least the cultural blessing of the Romantic Poets) with which women seek to reunite themselves. In a very moving series of articles in Lent 1980, Monica Furlong[48] wrote of re-claiming chaos and harrowing hell to bring back again everything that had been excluded. Christian theologians, although saying that God created *ex nihilo*, constantly imply that God is somehow a scientific organising principle whose main creative act was imposing

What we resist persists

order on chaos. Darkness, randomness, fear and craziness have been driven out and goodness was equated with order, discipline and control. Monica Furlong argued that this was precisely the wrong approach and that it was only by inviting the chaos back into our lives that we would have a realisation of the immensity of God, the goodness of ourselves, and the potential for unity, collaboration and human fullness. She went on to apply this theoretical position to many ethical problems, among them sexuality, church government and issues of international politics. Unless we recognise individually and collectively the strong forces that move us and in which we move as good we cannot use them creatively. While we label them as bad or sinful and then, unable to live with ourselves, project them on to others (women, black people, gay people) we will continue to live with social and personal disintegration, alienation and destruction.

Monica Furlong of course is not alone in this analysis, although she expressed it with a vivid clarity. Women do seem to be trying to open themselves up to their own darkness. It is easier for us than for men because we have been conditioned into believing that much of the darkness is us – once we discover our own holiness we can be less afraid, perhaps, of the dark than men, whose projections have been more complete. Helpful in this search has been much Oriental spirituality: the idea of Taoism, of living in harmony with everything around one. I have been surprised to discover how many Christian women throw the *I Ching*, for example, in their attempt to identify more and more with the largeness and complexity of the world. The Western-style 'hero' since the Reformation and Renaissance has been a solitary figure, in a noble but lonely struggle against forces which are always opposed to him but which he combats (whether triumphantly or to his tragic defeat) by will-power and assertion. Christ on the cross has been brought through much of Western art into conformity with this model. Women are proposing a new hero, who has not emerged yet in detail, but will somehow move with the forces of personality and nature, will be inseparably part of a larger community and rhythm. The medieval idea that all creation suffered with Christ in the crucifixion – the sun darkened, the earth trembled, even the Robin stained its breast trying to share that agony, his friends stayed as close as they could and afterwards took his body and tended to it – is more in tune with modern thinking, the suffering servant, rendered wordless and howling in desolation, rather than the warrior king stoical but noble, forgiving his enemies, making arrangements for his family and encouraging his companions.[49]

This darkness would be unbearable perhaps if it was not for another quality that illuminates women's spirituality, just as it sparkles in women's groups where unbearable anger and loss are articulated. When Alla Bozarth-Campbell was a small child she misheard the words of the traditional prayer 'Hail Mary', as children often do with much repeated texts. She grew up believing that the phrase which really says 'Holy Mary Mother of God pray for us sinners now and at the hour of our death', said, 'Holy Mary, Mother of God, *play with us* sinners. . . .' And from the glorious misapprehension she now writes:

> Play is also prayer. I still play with Mary; with my friends in the communion of saints and with God my mother. Play is the way into the real power of our creator.[50]

Elsewhere Alla Bozarth-Campbell speaks of a vision she once had. I confess I find this sort of vision rather uncomfortable, but I quote it because it expresses a sense of divine playfulness that feminist spirituality is developing. I expect that my own awkwardness is because I do not play enough with God. Teresa of Avila used to tease God and believe cheerfully that he teased her too, so Alla Bozarth-Campbell is keeping quite traditional company:

> I had long had a verbal communication with my angel, but never any visual image, so I invited my talky angel to put in an appearance. . . . I looked and couldn't believe what I saw! A stereotyped creature with golden hair, long white robe and wings, no less! I said 'O come on!' and Angel roared with laughter. The joke was on me. Angel said kindly but still laughing at me, 'Remember you are a product of your culture.'[51]

Although apparently not many women experience their holy play in quite this form (or else lack the nerve to tell us about it) the sense of play is real. In reclaiming feminine images of God many writers have looked at the Old Testament Wisdom Literature, identifying Wisdom (Sophia) with the Holy Spirit and correctly presenting this as a sustained image both of God-as-female and God-as-movement. Together with stressing the creative energy and deep knowledge of Sophia women writers return again and again to the playful elements. Sophia says of herself:

Then I was at his side each day
His darling and delight;
Playing in his presence continually,
Playing on the earth when it was made.[52]

Maria Boulding writes of play as something crucial to spiritual development. As we grow in prayer, she says:

There is a sense in which we grow younger, grow in the capacity to wonder and enjoy, and find in ourselves a new simplicity . . . we become free to play in God's presence. Play is not a means to an end, not utilitarian, but a human activity worth while in itself. Agility and grace, elegance and rhythm, the freedom of sheer enjoyment and easy control of movement, gesture, sound, word, colour – all these speak of the wholeness that God meant to exist in us. . . . The Myths speak of the *puer aeternus*, an eternal child or child-god who plays forever. The person who plays or dances participates in the dance of all creation. In laughter we touch an eternal order of rightness and sanity.[53]

The denominational structures might not recognise as prayer an evening I spent with women recently when we covered our faces with white clown make-up and danced. But the court jester was the one who spoke the truth. Shakespeare's Malvolio rejected the clown and was driven out of Paradise. It was prayer because we had come together to pray and that was how we chose, just then, to express it. Playfulness of course is not the exclusive domain of women. Just as Teilhard de Chardin spoke of unity with creation, so other orthodox male theologians – C. S. Lewis and Hugo Rahner, for example –[54] have spoken of play. But it seems easier for women to do it. Because society obliges women to carry the heavy share of child-care we also have access to the world of play. Sociologists have demonstrated over and over again that women lack 'competitive skills' (if that is a lack) and are frightened of success, and do not find the same pleasure in aggression and winning as men do. While these qualities may impede us in some places they are obvious advantages when it comes to playing in this way. God does not often seem to engage in competitive sports, but in true laughing playfulness. Anne Sexton the poet caught at the playfulness of God at the end of her sequence *The Awful Rowing toward God*:

'On with it!' He says and thus
We squat on the rocks by the sea
and play – can it be true –
a game of poker.
He calls me.
I win because I hold a royal straight flush.
He wins because he holds five aces.
A wild card has been announced
but I had not heard it
being in such a state of awe
when He took out the cards and dealt.
As he plunks down His five aces
and I sit grinning at my royal flush,
He starts to laugh,
the laughter rolling like a hoop out of His mouth
and into mine,
and such laughter that he doubles right over me
laughing a Rejoice-Chorus at our two triumphs.
Then I laugh, the fishy dock laughs
the sea laughs. The Island laughs.
The Absurd laughs.

Dearest Dealer,
I with my royal straight flush
love you so for your wild card,
that untameable, eternal, gut-drive ha-ha
and lucky love.[55]

There is little to add to something so perfect except that it is worth
remembering, as those with a good relationship with children know,
that it is not always that God plays (as adult) with us (as children).
God can reverse the game and be a child to our adult (our children
minister to us as much as we to them) or an equal, a lover – as the
moves and rhythms of the game demand. This playfulness not only
heals our wounds, it is a vital contribution to the wholeness of
Christ's body. Women seem ready both to explore it and offer it to
the world.

One final element of women's spirituality should be mentioned:
the re-exploration of mythology and history. Just as women have

needed to incorporate the physical creation into their spirituality afresh, so we have needed to range widely across the traditional terrain of myth and legend to find mirrors for our own aspirations. Male-dominated Western culture has not served women well; Sleeping Beauty does not reflect our spiritual longings very readily. Meinrad Craighead's search for images and stories on which she could pin her vision has taken her far outside the traditional Judaeo/Christian tradition: her tree images contain stories drawn from every mythological source – American Indian, Buddhist, Hellenic. Thetis Blacker, another Christian artist, finds monsters and hybrids that have little relationship to the acknowledged Christian zoo – at least as known in recent times: the medieval openness to all possibilities, as revealed in their gargoyle carving, is something that may be being returned to us. In these other mythologies we find there are other ways of describing both Immanuel, God-with-us, immanent, incarnate, *and* God transcendent, the nameless, unnameable source and sustainer of all things. Even in the re-working of traditional Christian images new ways and words are found. In confronting an idea or image of God not previously known to us, and accepting the possibility of that *too*, our own concept of God is stretched. The further it is stretched, the more inclusive it becomes, and so the more it corresponds to the Everything, Everywhere, All-inclusive that the Christian tradition claims is God. The idea that each person is created in God's image, unique and different, and therefore has the potential to reveal yet one more aspect of God, is deeply rooted in the Christian ideal of the Church. The totality of all the individuals creates something new; the absence of a single individual spoils the whole. So when women name the holy – not just in themselves, but in all those different elements that the historical fact of being female gives them a chance of confronting or understanding – they are not just making themselves feel better, they are giving the Christian community a God-gift.

Spirituality is both a personal journey and food for the body. It lives between these two points in a curious tension. Prayer is not finally about 'feeling good': it is about knowing God and loving and redeeming the world. It is not an alternative to life 'in the world', it is a point of entry into fullness of the world – politics, passion, thunderstorms, history and ticklish toes. Moreover all these things, and everything else, are the material for prayer, inalienable from it. We have to spin the circle faster and faster until the different spokes are indistinguishable and become one mass of movement.

God is ultimately Other, but the Beloved Other. God is the only activity that is outside the spinning circles; and God is the circle itself. There is a deep way in which it could be natural for men to seek God through female images and women to seek God through male language, because – if we abandoned the projection and denial game – that could become a natural expression of Otherness. This cannot happen while either side of the balanced difference is perceived at any level as being 'better than', 'superior to' or 'more holy than' the other.

CHAPTER 7

MOVING FORWARD – SOME CONCLUSIONS

❖❖❖

> Blessed are they whose strength is in thee: in
>   whose hearts are thy highways;
> Who going through the valley of misery use it for
>   a well and the pools are filled with water.
> They will go from strength to strength: and unto the
>   God of Gods appeareth every one of them in Zion.[1]

At the beginning of this book I spoke of cartography – map-making. I used this image quite consciously because I believe that women are exploring, discovering, opening up a New World, and that their adventures there are a source of inspiration and richness for us all. But there is another sense in which this is a happy image: the idea of the journey from the old known place into a new land is one of the most ancient and enduring icons of the spiritual life and of the Jewish Christian life in particular. The story is always the same: the Holy People are in a place where they become aware of their oppression, alienation and loss of freedom; with considerable effort they choose to free themselves, with great joy they set out for a new promised land (which always seems also to be a return to an old promised land). Pretty soon they find that they are not in the promised land but in the desert (literally in the desert in the case of Sarah and Abraham, of the Exodus community; spiritually in the desert with St John of the Cross's 'dark night of the soul'). They do not like it; the desert is a difficult place to be, usually they complain bitterly and who can blame them? Freedom is a hard and difficult road. Some members of the community, however, are enabled to keep faith through all the wanderings, keep in touch with the vision that set them out on this journey. Often it is not the same person all the time: Sarah and Abraham, for example, need each other to keep faith; in the Israelite community the burden of responsibility shifts around, no one is perfectly faithful – but the community maintains its faith. Eventually they arrive at what they believe to be the promised land. Only when they get there do they realise that it was in the desert, on the journey, while they were least secure, most vulnerable, that they learned who and what God was, who and what they themselves were. It is on the journey that things happen. On the journey Jacob sees the ladder between history and eternity; on the journey Naomi and Ruth discover the depths of love and sisterhood; on the road to Jerusalem and death his followers realise who Jesus is; on the road to Emmaeus the Resurrected word burns into human hearts; on the road to Damascus Paul meets Christ. You have to set out before you know what you are setting out for.

There is a new term to describe this phenomenon: Process Theology. 'We do not think ourselves into new ways of acting; we act ourselves into new ways of thinking.' We have to dare to set out. We can only dare to set out when we recognise how desperate the situation has become. Freedom and growth may extend to everyone but it is likely that only the victims, the oppressed, will actually recognise the true desperateness of the situation enough to act on that knowledge.

It is likely that by the time you read this book some of the precise details will be obsolete, or at least not the most up-to-date information. Even as I write this is true; women are no longer where they were when they spoke to me; those who have continued to travel adventurously have discovered new things that made what they told me no longer true. Even events have changed – the debate and organisation around the ordination of women in the Church of England, for example, has moved forward very fast in the second half of 1980. I suspect that this will accelerate. In that accelerating development new truths will be revealed, new people will emerge, new visions of the possible will form in our hearts which will lead to new journeys, new paths and a transformed map. This is inevitable so that I do not apologise for it; I point it out because it is important to realise that those women who have gone furthest into the new interior have the greatest realisation of how far there is to go. Mary Wollstonecraft believed that better education for women would solve most of the problems of their oppression. As soon as they started getting better education nineteenth-century feminists realised how little this was true – they had to extend their exploration into whole new areas of civil and economic rights. Once those goals were identified and women started out on the journey to win them it became apparent how deep the problems were; how ingrained and profound sexual privilege and sexual hostility were; how profoundly in the interests of the powerful sexual discrimination was; how damaging to the fabric of human history sexism was. Now we realise that brutally challenging mountain of suffrage has only opened up another enormous desert to be crossed. Keats caught at that painful reality when he described Cortez on his 'peak in Darien', silenced by the realisation that the journey had hardly begun, that the ground yet to be travelled was immense, apparently infinite. No matter with what enthusiasm and honesty the map-maker works the real explorers are in the act of rendering that work inaccurate, and obsolete.

Not, however, irrelevant. Travellers' tales and maps, even inaccurate ones, still have useful functions. They inspire other travellers to come out and join the exploration of the new land, to move into it, settle it and make it a home. And in doing this they not only cultivate the wilderness, they can also create a base from which new explorations can take place. In the early opening up of the Americas one of the greatest problems was the attenuated lines of support; when all new supplies and new settlers had to cross the whole Atlantic the new settlements were permanently imperilled. It was not until there were substantial settlements on the Atlantic coast that the opening up of the interior became a real possibility. The solitary visionary can only go on alone for so long: a community of support and love that is not too far away is important.

Another function of maps and reports from the frontier is to assist the explorers themselves. This is especially difficult and important for women:

> The entire history of women's struggle for self-determination has been muffled in silence over and over . . . each feminist work has tended to be received as if it emerged from nowhere; as if each of us had lived and thought and worked without any historical past or contextual present. This is one of the ways in which women's work and thinking has been made to seem sporadic, errant, orphaned of any tradition of its own. In fact we

do have a long feminist tradition, both oral and written, which
has built on itself over and over, recovering essential elements
even when those have been strangled or wiped out. . . . Each
contemporary feminist theorist [is] attacked or dismissed ad
feminam, as if her politics were simply an outburst of personal
bitterness or rage.[2]

(An example of this destruction of history is the apparent ignorance –
on both sides of the debate – that the issue of the ordination of
women to the priesthood was a living one in the early Church, and
has been under practical debate in the Church of England throughout
at least the last hundred years. If this were better known it would end
the tedious and distracting cry that the current round of this debate
was 'just a women's lib fad', an argument which continually inter-
rupts any serious discussion of the real issues.)

Because our history is destroyed and our present experience
belittled or treated on an individualistic or ad hoc basis we do not
have enough competent maps. We are cut off from the experiences of
each other and ourselves. We do not know where other women have
been or where they are. We have little idea of even the outlines of the
new world already opened up to us by the courage of earlier
explorers. We do not know how each little bit of new territory
relates to the other little bits. Not knowing, we blunder into old
traps which previous women thought they had identified and
learned to avoid. Not knowing, we disturb thoughtlessly the patient
work of other women. Not knowing, we waste time and repeat
errors. Not knowing, our vision is limited to what we can see for
ourselves alone. Not knowing, we too easily fall prey both to the
arrogance of believing that we are splendidly solitary and to the
threats that we are crazy. We need more maps.

There is a satirical version of the hymn 'Onward Christian
Soldiers' which reads:

> Like a mighty tortoise
> Moves the Church of God
> Brothers we are treading
> Where we've always trod.

Sisters, we know that this is true, and we also know that it is not
good enough. It is not enough any longer to recognise and bewail
our exclusion from the centres of power and holiness. It is not

enough, even, to demand and gain our re-entry into those centres. That would be like Moses organising a campaign to be the next Pharaoh. It is precisely as an oppressed group – and so identified with all other oppressed groups –that we have the authority to receive the vision and set out again on the next phase of the journey. The journey will lead again into the desert, through the valleys of misery, towards crucifixion. There is no other way, 'and freedom consists of . . . voices that have been broken and blood that has been shed; freedom tastes of pain.'³ We must always be on the point of setting out again.

In this book I have attempted to draw together some strands of contemporary events and tried to reveal some patterns in them. In the course of this I have met, and come to love and admire, a large number of women. I am absolutely convinced that the best way to express this loving admiration is not through veneration, imitation or exultation, but by recognition and thanksgiving and careful criticism. Because some particular group of women succeeded in some particular project that is not a reason to copy their methods. That is an insult to their adventurous spirit. Where they have been we do not need to go again – we need to use the base they have established to go further. Where they have been destroyed or mutilated we do not need to stand weeping: the blood of the martyrs fertilises the Church.

The current situation – both in the Church as microcosm, and in the macrocosm the world itself – is desperately serious. If anyone is going to survive we have to set out immediately. Jesus said that there was not even time to bury our dead. Keeping travelling has become not an ideal but a crude necessity.

What we can and must learn, however, from the women who have started the trail-blazing, is that feminism does offer a way forward, a way of healing our dangerous divisions and a way back to the Christian truth of service, equality, justice, and the renunciation of power through love. It is possible; it is only in a vision of that possibility that we can hope to have the courage to set out.

Over and over again I return to the courage of the women I have talked to in this book. It is not so difficult to engage in a struggle, even a struggle to the death, with something that is clearly the Enemy – named and known. The harder struggle is to engage seriously with something that is beloved. It is especially hard for women who are socialised in 'loving self-sacrifice' and in denying the validity and lovability of themselves and their own ideas. The women who struggle with institutional Christianity love the Faith — otherwise they would not be here: there are plenty of other options. Often to remain struggling with the Church women not only have to put up with its hostility and rejection but with the consistent mockery of other feminists who think they are either crazy or wasting everyone's time.

Carole Etzler in one of her songs describes this painful courage, and the vision that inspires it:

> Sometimes I wish my eyes hadn't been opened
> Just for an hour how sweet it would be
> Not to be struggling, not be striving
> But just sleep securely in our slavery.
>
> But now that I've seen with my eyes I can't close them
> Because deep inside me Somewhere I'd still know
> The road that my sisters and I have to travel
> And my heart would say 'yes' and my feet would say 'go'.[4]

The Christian religion, in conflict with its own vocation, offered people, and oddly enough women and other oppressed people particularly, a secure and loving sleep, in slavery. It is painful and difficult to wake up, and set out with 'no gold, nor silver nor copper in your belts, no bag for your journey, nor two tunics, nor sandals nor a staff'.[5] But women, driven by the vision of a promised land that they do not themselves probably even hope to enter, are doing just that.

> Who would true valour see
> Let them come hither;
> Some here will constant be
> Come wind come weather. . . .
>
> Hobgoblin nor foul fiend
> Shall her dispirit
> She knows she at the end
> Will life inherit.
> Then fancies flee away
> She'll fear not what men say;
> She'll labour night and day
> To be a pilgrim.[6]

NOTES

------------ ♦♦♦ ------------

CHAPTER 1   ROOTS AND BEGINNINGS

1 Kathleen Bliss, *The Service and Status of Women in the Churches* (SCM Press, 1948). A history of the Women's Desk, *A Voice for Women* by Susannah Herzel was published by the WCC in 1981.

2 The Mother Thunder *Liturgy of Eucharist*, and their *Order for Morning and Evening Prayer* is published privately. Obtainable from Mother Thunder Mission, P.O. Box 579, New York, NY 10011, USA.

3 The books that have explored this history are numerous. Among those that I have found most valuable, are: Jean Danielou SJ, *The Ministry of Women in the Early Church* (1960), trans. Rt Rev. Glyn Simon (Faith Press, 1974); R. Ruether and E. McLaughlin (eds), *Women of Spirit* (Simon & Schuster, 1979); E. Clark and H. Richardson (eds), *Women and Religion* (Harper & Row, 1977).

4 Both quotations taken from Marianne Katoppo, *Compassionate and Free* (World Council of Churches, 1979) which unfortunately does not contain detailed references to the original texts.

5 Looking at the contemporary position of women in the Church, I have confined myself, for practical reasons, to the Roman Catholic Church and denominations which are members of the World Council of Churches (WCC). This is not meant to denigrate the Society of Friends whose libertarian, anti-hierarchical tone offers something attractive to many contemporary women. But there is considerable debate within the Society itself as to 'how Christian' it actually is, and it is so structurally different from other denominations that it is hard to offer helpful comment. Also neglected are various other unaffiliated 'denominations' – charismatic, pentecostalist and 'free baptist' churches.

6 *The Passion of Saints Perpetua and Felicity*, trans. W. H. Shewring (Sheed & Ward, 1931).

7 Katherine Moore, *She For God* (Allison & Busby, 1978), p. 85 from Foxe's *Book of Martyrs*.

8 Betty Freidan, personal remark to Mary Daly, quoted in *Beyond God the Father* (Beacon Press, 1976).

9 Mary Daly, *The Church and the Second Sex* (Harper & Row, 1968).

10 Sarah Benton Doely, *Women's Liberation and the Church* (Association Press, 1970).

11 This particular image was presented to me by Rosemary Ruether during an interview with her at Garrett Evangelical Seminary, July 1979.

12 These are invented volumes; any similarity with books of such titles is accidental and no direct insult is intended.

13 Rosemary Radford Ruether, interview, July 1979. See note 10.

CHAPTER 2   WOMEN TOGETHER

1 I spent this weekend with the group in August 1979. It marked a turning point in my life, in that I discovered there that organised Christian feminism was something I wanted in my life – I would like to thank the whole group, and particularly Carole Etzler, who arranged for me to be there, for their love, warmth, openness and the sisterhood they showed to each other and gave to me.

2 Interview with Pauline Webb, Spring 1979, London.

3 Interview with Virginia Baron, March 1980, New York.

4 Personal letter from Hope Maitland to Sara Maitland, June 1980, emphasis original.

5 For this and for much of the historical detail that follows I am indebted to 'Their Prodigious Influence' by Dorothy C. Bass and 'American Women in Ministry' by Virginia Lieson Brereton and Christa Ressmeyer Klein, both in R. Ruether and E. McLaughlin (eds), *Women of Spirit* (Simon & Schuster, 1979).

6 Linda Maria Child, *Liberator*, vol. XI (July 1841), p. 118.

7 Bass, op. cit.

8 Brereton and Klein, op. cit.

9 Brereton and Klein, op. cit.

10 The Roman Catholic Church, however, did not open new ministries to women, but interestingly this period was marked by a surge of vocations to the religious life which can be seen as a parallel. Neither this surge, nor the increases of professional church workers in the Protestant denominations can be entirely attributed to the shortage of available husbands after the First World War although this may well have been a contributory factor.

11 Interview with the Rev. Martha Blacklock, Newark, New Jersey, summer 1979.

12 Ibid.

13 Interview with Daphne McNab, November 1978.

14 Hope Maitland is my mother. I have never interviewed her formally, but have frequently discussed this and related issues with her as the period of her involvement with the Guild nationally and my

involvement with this book have been similar. I think we have learned from each other in some sort of sharing.

15 More detail about Church Women United can be found in their own history book – *Just Because* by Margaret Shannon (Omega Books, 1977).

16 The *Christian Feminist Newsletter*, approx. monthly, c/o Sheelagh Robinson, 22 Forshore, Pepys Estate, London E4. Party Group, the Roman Catholic Feminists, and the Christian Women's Information and Resource Service all have newsletters or regular contact mailing available to women who are not members of these organisations.

17 Meeting with the Oxford Christian Feminist Group, winter 1979. Because I was there they did not have their usual meeting but attempted instead to describe their history and identity for me. This impression of the group is personal and I have therefore not tried to ascribe to named individuals any of the remarks or comments made.

18 'On Breaking the Rules: a Reply to J. M. Cameron', *New Blackfriars*, vol. 59, no. 703, December 1978, pp. 556 ff.

19 After the defeat of the November 1978 Motion Dr Una Kroll, one of the leading pro-ordination campaigners, suggested that these women's services would be a useful national exercise. The Oxford group attempted therefore to respond to an external appeal – it was not an idea generated within the group.

20 *A Time for Building* was published by the Catholic Information Office in response to *The Church in the Year 2000* in 1978.

CHAPTER 3   COMMUNITIES OF FAITH

1 Anonymous. Quoted in Marcella Bernstein, *Nuns* (Collins 1976), p. 302.

2 In fact this chapter deals almost exclusively with Roman Catholic nuns. The Orthodox nuns have a very different tradition and almost all of them are 'contemplative'. The Anglican nuns, because of their curious relationship to their church, tend to develop little that is markedly original or distinct from the Roman Catholic tradition. Their renewal has followed broadly similar lines. The increasingly closeness between Anglican and Roman Catholic religious communities is a sign of ecumenism which should not be ignored.

3 Alexander Pope, *Eloisa and Abelard*. It should not of course be overlooked that Pope himself was a Roman Catholic living in a predominantly Protestant and secular society – there were no religious communities in England at the time and his feelings about them were doubtlessly affected by this.

4 Mary Ewens OP, 'Removing the Veil', in R. Ruether and E. McLauglin (eds), *Women of Spirit* (Simon & Schuster, 1979), p. 272. I owe a more general debt to this article for my understanding of the development of the apostolic women's orders in the nineteenth century.

5 Letter to Henry Edward (later Cardinal) Manning. Quoted Shane

Leslie, 'Forgotten Passages in the life of Florence Nightingale', *Dublin Review*, vol. CLXI, October 1917, p. 181.

6 Kate Cumming, *A Journal of Hospital Life in the Confederate Army* (Morton, 1866), p. 178; emphasis mine.

7 Eg. Ruth Burrows, *Before the Living God* (Sheed & Ward, 1975). This is a good example because Ruth Burrows has remained a nun and indeed became a Mother Superior herself. The feeling of nuns who have left their orders is often, in this area, tinged with such bitterness that it makes less credible evidence.

8 Mary Daly, *Gyn/ecology: the Metaethics of Radical Feminism* (The Women's Press, 1979).

9 The whole story of Maria Goretti is extremely interesting. Traditionally martyrs have to die for the Faith: in her case she was deemed to have died for 'the Christian way of life'. This was undeniably a part of a conscious effort to make Catholicism more accessible to 'ordinary lay people'. Her murderer's conversion after years of prison, which he ascribed directly to her intercession, was taken as further proof of her sanctity – and because the case was so well known and frequently used by those opposed to the death penalty. Another women canonised in the same period was Joan of Arc (who was finally beatified in 1908). St Joan became a spiritual symbol of independent women – the English militant suffrage movement adopted her. The St Joan's International Alliance was formed under her patronage to further the rights of women in the Roman Catholic Church. The unusually rapid official recognition of Thérèse of Lisieux and Maria Goretti – both saints of the 'people', both representing peculiarly Victorian *feminine* virtues – cannot have been un-influenced by the fear of women's self-assertion (as a part of political unrest) which afflicted the Roman Catholic Church at this time. This is not to question the spiritual graces received by these two women, nor to deny the immense spontaneous popular devotion that their lives generated. It is to look at these things in an historic light. It is interesting that despite the emphasis on 'ordinary lives' and the growth of respect for the 'Catholic Mother in the Catholic Home', the Roman Catholic Church has not yet found an 'ordinary mother' suitable for canonisation. But these two virgins really were the next best thing: ordinary, bourgeois in background, young, innocent, and passionately obedient.

10 Additionally many male orders are devoted to parish work – to living as parish priests – and thus they did not have the shared and directed identity of women.

11 *Perfactae Caritatis*, para. 3.

12 Ibid., para. 4.

13 Ibid., paras 22 and 23 (reorganised by me).

14 Although not directly quoted these criteria are laid out in para. 2 of the document.

15 *Ecclesiae Sanctae* 11, para. 1. (*Ecclesiae Sanctae* was published in 1966. As with many of the other decrees of the Council, the theory was laid out in a primary document, which was followed up by a document laying

down the 'Norms' for interpretation. *Ecclesiae Sanctae* 11 was such a document, suggesting how *Perfectae Caritatis* should be used in practice.)

16 *Ecclesiae Sanctae* 11, para. 9.

17 *Ecclesiae Sanctae* 11, paras 3–10.

18 Ibid., para. 6.

19 *Perfectae Caritatis*, para. 16.

20 There are many reports of this struggle, e.g. Midge Turk, *The Hidden Life* (New English Library, 1972), which is by one of the nuns who left the order during the course of the events described below. Although she left her sympathies remain with the nuns, and against the Bishop.

21 Personal interview with English SHCJ nun.

22 *Signum* (information bulletin for religious, ed. Sr Mary Helena Desmond SHC, published by Catholic Information Office), January 1978 (see chapter 2).

23 *Probe* (Magazine of the National Assembly of Women Religious), April 1977.

24 Sr Ruth Duckworth SC, interview, London, Spring 1979.

25 Marcella Bernstein, *Nuns* (Collins, 1976), p. 222. Bernstein gives a large number of examples of American nuns (both from the USA and from Southern America) who are working directly in organised national politics – usually as radicals and 'women's issue' candidates.

26 *Probe* (op. cit.), November 1976.

27 Both the OFFICAL CELAM conference and the 'Mujeres Para El Dialogo' conference got a good deal of press coverage, particularly in the USA. The National Leadership Conference for Women Religious (USA) published a full report. The quotation, along with a short descriptive account, comes from *Probe*, May 1979. Sr Mary O'Keefe, *Probe*'s Editor, also filled me in extensively on the background to this and to nuns' involvement in the meeting point of racial and sexual oppression in Southern America in a personal interview in July 1979.

28 Demond Doig, *Mother Theresa: Her Life and Work* (Fontana, 1978) is a good account of her work, although, like most material, adulatory rather than analytical in tone. There is a tendency for conservatives to point to Mother Theresa as a proof that renewal is neither profitable nor popular. Indeed the Missionaries of Charity might be described as a 'radically conservative order'. However, it seems to be frequently forgotten that in order to form the Missionaries of Charity, Mother Theresa did precisely what other 'progressive nuns' are accused of doing – she left her old order, abandoned her habit in favour of contemporary local dress, and formed a new order based on simple shared life-style in small groups.

29 *Women Religious for ERA* pamphlet by NCAN (National Co-alition for American Nuns) is just one sample of the enormous quantity of ERA material produced by nuns in the USA in the last six years.

30 *Perfectae Caritatis*, para. 18.

31 Interview with Sr Mary Helena Desmond SHCJ and editor of *Signum*, October 1978.

32 Ibid.
33 *LCWR* (Leadership Conference of Women Religious – this is the USA version of the Committee of Major Religious Superiors, encouraged in *Perfectae Caritatis* and set up with the permission of the hierarchy), *Recommendations: Scheme of Canons on Religious Life*, December 1977, p. 23 (my italics). The document begins with the following statement, which sums up much of the 'consensus approach' of many contemporary nuns:

> This document is the final official report of the LCWR. . . . It has been forwarded to the pontifical commission under the aegis of the National Conference of Catholic Bishops. But the contents of the report do not represent the final word about the topics it addresses . . . underlying the topic are deeper questions about the identity and mission of women religious in the Church. The LCWR will continue to probe them – through the work of the task force on contemporary theology of religious life, through the regions and through the reflections of its members and their congregations.

34 Sr Mary Helena Desmond, op. cit.
35 LCWR *Recommendations*, op. cit., p. 25.
36 Sr Margaret Ellen Traxler, interview, July 1979.
37 Sr Mary Helena Desmond, op. cit.
38 *Signum*, June 1978.
39 The act of protest in the presence of the Pope, described in chapter 1, is an example of this. RC officials seem to have accepted with resignation that nuns are going to involve themselves in justice issues of all sorts – from global ecology, to individual law suits. They were outraged that nuns should turn their exposition of injustice inwards on the Church itself. This is a very commonly repeated pattern, not just for nuns. Women are encouraged, or at least not dissuaded from taking up justice issues, even justice in regard to women, outside the Church, but not to bring them home. At the time of the British anti-discrimination legislation, 1972–4, a priest told me that he very much supported my activity in the field; but when I pointed out that the Christian churches had requested to be specially exempted from the provisions of the proposed Act (a request that was granted, incidentally) he insisted that this was right and proper, and failed to see this as a justice issue.
40 CARA, 'Research Project Report', Autumn 1978.
41 Almost all the women who now live as nuns but outside canonical orders that I talked to mentioned the considerable advantages of this status in terms of freedom to develop as they wanted. The CARA report also pointed out the ignorance of diocesan offices about the existence of such groups. The apparent repudiation on both sides is worrying: with more pastoral contact it might be possible for the whole Christian community to make more use of the experiences of these women.
42 Sr Lora Anne Quinonez, Chairperson, LCWR, interview, July 1979.
43 Sr Ruth Duckworth, President of Committee of Major Religious

Superiors, typescript notes for unpublished article. Ruth Duckworth very kindly showed me the draft notes for this article. I wish she would write it, but thank her for sharing her ideas at such an early stage.

44 Mary Austin Doherty and Margaret Earley OSF, 'Women Theologise', *Women in Ministry: a Sister's View* (NAWR, 1972), p. 140.

45 Sr Ruth Duckworth, personal interview, London, Spring 1979.

CHAPTER 4   ORDINATION

1 Ordination formula for Deaconesses, *Apostolic Canons*: Epitome (10), 4th century AD. Quoted J. Danielou, *The Ministry of Women in the Early Church* trans. G. Simon (Faith Press, 1961). This rite, like some other early rites, is not only clearly an *Ordination* rite (rather than a ceremony for the 'setting apart' or dedication of Deaconesses), it also reflects the understanding of the early Church that women were ordained into a female tradition and an explicitly women's ministry.

2 Text cited from Arlene and Leonard Swidler, *The Exclusion of Women from the Divine Priesthood* (Scarecrow Press, 1976), p. xvii.

3 V. L. Brereton and C. R. Klein, 'American Women in Ministry' in R. Ruether and E. McLaughlin (eds), *Women of Spirit* (Simon & Schuster 1979), p. 302.

4 The word 'ordained' would not in fact be accepted by many of the Protestant denominations whose theology of ministerial leadership does not accept the concept. I am using it, with apologies, as the most accessible single word to describe all those who have been set aside for the 'ministry of word and sacrament' (howsoever understood) in all denominations.

5 Cited Elsie Gibson, *When the Minister is a Woman* (Holt, Rinehard & Winston, 1970), p. 21.

6 Ibid.

7 Margaret Blair Johnstone, *When God Says No* (Simon & Schuster, 1954), p. 37.

8 Brereton and Klein, op. cit., p. 303.

9 For example in 1965 Mary Lusk, a Church of Scotland Deaconess, after taking constitutional and legal advice decided to open the issue of women's ordination in her church not by requesting a general change in the rules, but by presenting her individual case. Based on the argument that the job she was doing – a University Chaplaincy – was normally associated with the ordained ministry, she requested ordination. Although the aim was to open the whole issue, the method (in this case unsuccessful at the time) was to speak of individual and particular talents, rather than essential nature.

10 The Rev. Ruth Matthews, personal interview, Autumn 1978.

11 Ibid.

12 Ibid.

13 Ibid.

14 The Rev. Ruth Matthews, 'On Ministry and Ordination', in Kenneth Wilson (ed.), *The Experience of Ordination* (Epworth Press, 1979), p. 142.

15 Rev. Ruth Matthews, interview, op. cit.

16 The Rev. Joan Martin, personal interview, New York, Summer 1979.

17 Ibid.

18 Ibid.

19 There have been numerous opinion polls in the USA on this subject – e.g. the Gallup Poll commissioned by the Quixote Center in 1978. Because of differences in constituency and the varying wording of the questions very different results have been forthcoming. An average figure is 60 per cent and this may be low. What all the polls agree on is that the acceptability of women priests is rising rapidly.

20 The Rev. Jeanette Piccard, personal interview, Summer 1979.

21 The elected Diocesan delegations to General Convention consist of two priests and two lay people. On controversial issues they vote by orders – lay votes and clergy votes counted separately. If the delegates are divided (in either section) that delegation's vote is not discounted but considered as a negative vote. It is thus possible, if properly divided throughout the diocesan delegations, for a very small minority to impose its will *negatively* on any issue.

22 The Rev. Carol Anderson, personal interview, New York, Summer 1979.

23 The Rev. Emily Hewitt, personal interview, Boston, Summer 1979.

24 The meeting of the Bishops at O'Hare Airport seems to have been confused. The possible grounds for invalidity (as opposed to mere irregularity) are traditionally wrong intention – the Bishop concerned did not mean to ordain the person or did not understand what ordination meant; wrong rite – that the prayers or other liturgical material were seriously faulty; and wrong matter – that the tools used for the sacrament were incorrect (this latter would apply, for example, if a priest used champagne instead of water for a baptism, or fruitcake instead of bread for the Eucharist). The rite at Philadelphia was deliberately conservative and correct. The Bishops appear to have had the right intention. The only possible grounds for invalidity would seem to be wrong matter: that it is as impossible to confer priesthood on women as it would be to confer it on a giraffe. Wrong matter was apparently not raised by the Bishops at all, and their decision on invalidity appears to have been made on the grounds that these orders were *very* irregular in their opinion, an argument which must be theologically faulty.

25 Alla Bozarth-Campbell, *Womanpriest* (Paulist Press, 1978), p. 150.

26 Despite having declared the Philadelphia ordinations invalid in 1974, the Bishops in 1976 expressed their own dissatisfaction with this opinion by their decision at Minneapolis. If the Philadelphia ordinations had been invalid, or even possibly invalid, then regularisation would have been impossible – conditional re-ordination

at least would have been necessary. The impression that the House of Bishops were swayed more by political climate than theological clarity cannot be escaped.

27 I have suggested in the previous chapter that nuns were used in this way in an earlier period.

28 Virginia Mollenkott, 'Topic: Religion, Author: Female. Outlook: Troubled', *Publishers Weekly*, Spring 1980, p. 54.

29 The Rev. Suzanne Hiatt, personal interview, Summer 1979.

30 This is in marked contrast to, for instance, the Rev. Alla Bozarth-Campbell's position, who insists that while sexism remains she must be known not as a priest but as a 'womanpriest'.

31 Pauline Webb, personal interview, London, Winter 1978.

32 The Rev. Carol Anderson, personal interview, New York, Summer 1979.

33 Cited, e.g., Carter Heyward, *A Priest Forever* (Harper & Row, 1976), p. 51.

34 Dr Una Kroll, *Christian Parity Newsletter*, November 1978.

35 For instance, it is interesting how many of the lay women in Synod are either employed by the Church or the wives of clergy. In the Church of England Handbook *Who's Who in Synod* for 1978 there are *no* lay people who could properly be described as working-class.

36 Draft manifesto for the Open Synod Group, February 1980.

37 All women are aware of the trap of saying 'surely we should be talking not about women but about human liberation' and then going on to ignore any questions that relate specially to women. So far as I know there are no points of tension about the ministries of *men*. There are two areas of genuine concern: (1) the relationship of women to the Church's ministries, and (2) the relationship between lay *people* and the clergy. Both these issues (feminism and clericism) were neatly ducked by the format, and even the title of this conference.

38 Personal interview, anonymous by request.

39 Dr Una Kroll, op. cit.

40 Not surprisingly in the wake of the disturbances in St Paul's in June 1980 correspondents to *The Times* have been drawing parallels between this campaign and the suffrage campaign of the Edwardian era. Did women get the vote because of militancy or because of their war service in the First World War? It is important to realise that this is not an either/or question. Even the most constitutional of the serious suffragists recognised the contribution of the militants. Mrs Fawcett, the President of the Constitutional Suffrage Organisation, gave a celebratory dinner for the first militants to be released from Holloway and said there, as she always said afterwards, that the attention they had gained for the cause in a week was greater than 'legitimate' measures had achieved in fifty years.

41 *Pacem in Terris*.

42 *Ibid.*

43 *Gaudium et Spes*, para. 29.

44 Rosemary Ruether, for example, expressed her combined emotional,

theological and philosophical problems with *Humanes Vitae* clearly: 'Such a request is simply a demand that I scuttle my interests, my training and in the last analysis my soul. This I feel is not only shockingly wrong, but for me psychologically impossible.' The rhythm method, she maintained, was a 'sexual version of the Chinese Water Torture' (cited Mary Daly, *The Church and the Second Sex* (Harper & Row, 1968), p. 133.

45 This old prohibition was reiterated in an official Papal statement as recently as June 1980.

46 Work on the Women's Diaconate proceeds. For instance, cf. J. Danielou, *Ministry of Women in the Early Church*, op. cit. and Felicitas Corrigan OSB, 'Women Deacons in the Early Church', *Clergy Review*, 1979.

47 Fran Ferder, *Called to Break Bread?* (The Quixote Center, 1978).

48 Anecdote by Rosemary Radford Ruether, personal interview, Evanston, Ill., Summer 1979.

49 Canon Mary Michael Simpson, personal interview, New York, July 1979.

50 Sr Lora Anna Quinonez, personal interview, Washington DC, July 1979.

51 Examples of women working from these alternative traditions could include women like Sue Harris whose article 'The Body is the Book' in Peter Moore (ed.), *Man, Woman and Priesthood* (SPCK, 1978) presents arguments which have not been properly answered. Marianne Kotoppo, *Compassionate and Free* (World Council of Churches 1979), in attempting to begin 'An Asian Women's Theology', also raises points from these traditions. Meinrad Craighhead OSB, *The Sign of the Tree* (Mitchell Beazley, 1979) uses visual imagery to raise questions around the spiritual expression of female biology, mythology and history.

52 Mary Daly, cited Mollenkott, op. cit.

53 Carter Heyward, op. cit., p. 84.

54 Carter Heyward, 'Priesthood', a sermon on the occasion of the ordination of Doug Clark, in Helen Gray Crotwell (ed.), *Women and the Word – Sermons* (Fortress Press, 1978), p. 80.

55 Ibid., p. 76.

CHAPTER 5 WOMEN IN THE BUREAUCRACIES

1 Song, 'I'm a Kept Woman in the Bureaucracy' from album *Sometimes I Wish* (Sister Unlimited Inc., 1976) by Carole Etzler.

2 David Perman, *Change and the Churches* (Bodley Head, 1977), p. 160.

3 *Lumen Gentium*, paras 1 and 8, extracts.

4 Anne Scheibner, 'The Church as Institution and Community', unpublished paper, 1979.

5 Ibid.

6 Matthew 16: 23 and Mark 8: 33.

7 *Signum*, January 1978.

8 The Conciliar Document *Perfecae Caritatis*, cf. chapter 3. On job

discrimination cf. *Gaudium et Spes* (1965) para. 29 where sex is specifically mentioned as a discrimination which must be 'curbed and eliminated as incompatible with God's design' (cf. chapter 4).

9 All figures provided by the Equal Opportunities Commission.

10 Not selected randomly – ACCM is responsible for the development of the Church's professional ministries, lay as well as ordained; the view of ministry here literally informs the whole Church. However, it is also reasonably representative.

11 *The Church of England Year Book* published annually by Church Information Office, Publishing Dept.

12 Rev. Ruth Wintle Dcs, personal interview, Autumn 1979.

13 Ibid.

14 Ruth Wintle mentioned this as a particular problem. It has been raised as an issue by a number of other women, usually in personal conversation. It would be interesting to compare job satisfaction of secretarial and service personnel within Christian institutions and secular ones, but that is not my brief.

15 Acts of the Apostles 6: 2–5.

16 Perman, op. cit., p. 155.

17 Telephone conversation with Mgr David Norris, February 1980.

18 Pauline Webb, personal interview, January 1979.

19 In a moving phrase a priest from Cork on the BBC Sunday Service in June 1980 spoke of the mentally and physically handicapped as 'the prophets of this generation'. If this is understood not as a sentimental platitude, but as a statement that those excluded, weak, apparently useless speak to us of the wholeness of the Body of Christ then there is a radical quality to the phrase which must not be lost.

20 Laity Commission report, published in *Briefing* (Catholic Information Office, February 1980).

21 Scheibner, op. cit.

22 Ibid.

23 The full text of Mary Daly's sermon has been reproduced in various places, e.g. E. Clark and H. Richardson (eds), *Women and Religion* (Harper & Row, 1977), p. 265.

24 Ibid, p. 271.

25 Emily Culpepper, 'The Women's Movement: An Exodus Community', *Religious Education*, no. 47, September/October 1972, p. 334. The very title of this paper suggests something of the impact that Daly's sermon had in the USA at that time. In retrospect it is seen as a significant turning point for radical feminist spirituality.

26 In all fairness it must be pointed out that this was precisely her intention. Between the publication of *The Church and the Second Sex* in 1968 and *Beyond God the Father* in 1975 Mary Daly's repudiation of Christianity, not just its institutional forms but its very theological, philosophical and symbolic base became total.

27 Interview with a group of women from New York City MCC Congregation, August 1979.

28 Interview with Dame Betty Ridley, Autumn 1979.

29 Ibid.
30 Ibid.
31 Matthew 10: 16–17. Honesty compels me to admit that in the RSV the last word is in fact 'councils'. The emphasis is my own.
32 Song, 'Minority Report' from album *Sometimes I wish*, op. cit.
33 Quotation and details from *Christianity and Crisis*, vol. 39, no. 10, 11 June 1979. The whole issue is devoted to the subject of homosexuality and contains both an article by and an editorial on Joan Clark.
34 This at least was the position of the Rev. Sally Dries, one of the Center co-ordinators with whom I spoke in August 1979. The whole issue of denominational loyalty among Christian feminists in the USA is complicated. However, in using the word 'ecumenical' in their title the Women's Center implies some denominational connections.
35 Fran Ferder FSPA, *Called to Break Bread?* (The Quixote Center, 1978).
36 J. Kennedy and G. H. Heckler, *The Catholic Priest in the United States* (Loyola University, 1972).

CHAPTER 6 LANGUAGE AND SPIRITUALITY

1 Psalm 137: 1–4.
2 *Children's Letters to God* (Collins, 1967).
3 Special thanks for this chapter are due to the women I shared this weekend with: Hilary Bloom, Polly Bluck, Jen Duncan, Jo Carcia, Helen Sands and Alison Webster. Together we had a gentle, spirit-filled weekend. I specially thank Alison Webster who read a draft of this chapter with careful attention and opened up for me some areas that I had failed to recognise.
4 *Parish Weekly Bulletin of the Episcopal Parish of St John's in the Village, New York*, July 1979.
5 Ibid.
6 See chapters 2 and 4.
7 Mother Thunder Mission, *Liturgy of Eucharist* (Mother Thunder Mission, P.O. Box 579, New York, 10011, USA, 1978).
8 An Order for Holy Communion, Alternative Series 3.
9 Formal canonisation – the declaration that an individual person, now dead, is in heaven – recognises various categories of sanctity: virgin, martyr, priest, monarch (oddly?), religious, etc. Doctor is that category for people who have made a special contribution to theological (intellectual) knowledge of God. Because the categories are in some ways deficient – administrator, parent and missionary, for instance, do not exist – some saints get rammed into rather unlikely categories: Joan of Arc's main claim to canonisation cannot rest on her virginity. Catherine of Siena, who was barely literate, was more a 'politician' than she was a theologian, but the lack of this category meant the Church had to find some other place for her. Her mystical experiences – swapping hearts with Jesus, for example – are rather alien to our generation, but her personal holiness and vivid articulation of

personal religious experience has gained for her the title of Doctor – showing the Roman Catholic Church in a more unitative, non-dualistic light than is usual, either in its treatment of women or its treatment of individual psychological experience.

10 Dame Julian's understanding that sin was 'behovely' – useful, even valuable, rather than damning – is a view that is very popular among women and other 'liberal' psychoanalytically influenced modern theologians. Her much-quoted catch phrase, 'All thing shall be well and all manner of thing shall be well', must be understood not as a passive optimism, but in the light of this belief – that God could and did use all of human experience, even the most negative aspects, for the progressive movement of the divine plan.

11 *National Catholic Reporter* (USA), 15 December 1965, p. 4.

12 Mary Levison, personal interview, Edinburgh, November 1978.

13 Mary Daly's God-as-Verb contribution (cf. Mary Daly, *Beyond God the Father* (Beacon Press, 1965)), although valuable in expressing an understanding of process, is limited because she apparently recognises only the verb 'to be': Judaism certainly, and Christianity at its best, recognise 'God-speaking' and 'God-doing' as inseparable from God-as-noun, or as fixed Aristotleian *essence*. 'God is love' is a God-as-verb statement, as much as it is a God-as-essence declaration. Christianity maintains that both transcendently and historically (in the Incarnation, the creation and the tradition) God and God-acts are not separate events. Although this is not always properly understood – let alone represented – it is the authentic Christian understanding; Mary Daly is often more 'orthodox' than she would like to be.

14 Eg. I Corinthians 14: 28. Paul's clarity about this does seem in contrast with much of the Charismatic movement today which seems to have an anti-intellectual bias and claims to justify this from Paul's epistles. He is clear about public worship: 'In church I would rather speak given words with my mind . . . than ten thousand words in tongues' (I Corinthians 14: 19) and, 'If I do not know the meaning of a language I shall be a foreigner to the speaker and the speaker a foreigner to me. So with yourselves: since you are eager for the manifestations of the Spirit, strive to excel in building up the church' (I Corinthians 14: 12).

15 Preface to the Rite for the Making of Deacons, Book of Common Prayer, 1662.

16 Ibid.

17 Elaine Morgan, *The Descent of Woman* (Souvenir Press, 1972).

18 Convenient access to much of the material on the sexist bias of language can be found in C. Miller and K. Swift *Words and Women* (Penguin, 1979).

19 Ibid., p. 87.

20 From the *Exsultet* – the ancient hymn of praise sung at the Easter Vigil in the Roman Catholic Church. It was a phrase much used by the early church theologians, e.g. Ambrose and Augustine.

21 Rosemary Radford Ruether in an interview I had with her in Evanston, Ill., in August 1979 said: 'It is not just that God is imaged as male, but

as male warrior elite. God is not imaged as a male garbage collector. It is important to keep a hold on this connection.'

22 USA National Education Association Representative Assembly 1974.
23 *The Times*, 23 October 1979.
24 Ibid.
25 The Rev. Dr Una Kroll Dcs, personal interview, London, Winter 1978.
26 Ibid.
27 The Rev. Kathryn Piccard, personal interview, Boston, July 1979.
28 Mother Thunder Mission, *Liturgy of Eucharist*, op. cit.
29 The Rev. Martha Blacklock, personal interview, Newark, NJ, July 1979.
30 The Mother Thunder Mission Liturgy does not include a Creed. But the *Wisdom House Liturgy of the Holy Eucharist* (Wisdom House, 4030 Raleigh Ave., Minneapolis, Minn., USA, 1977) and Leonard Swidler, *A Non-Sexist Eucharistic Text* and other similar texts all translate in this way.
31 Speech at the Catholic Renewal Conference, Loughborough, May 1978. This is what I understood Sr Irene Benedict (an Anglican nun) to be saying; owing to the appallingly rude, sexist and uncharitable reception of her speech it was difficult to hear it clearly. The general view, however, is quite a common one.
32 Leonard Swidler, 'Rationale Notes' to *A Non-Sexist Eucharistic Text*, op. cit.
33 Leonard Swidler, op. cit.
34 Apart from the Eucharistic rites from which I have already quoted there is a growing amount of material, e.g. Sharon and Thomas Neufer Emswiler, *Women and Worship* (Harper & Row, 1974), Irene Moriarty and Sandy Amundsen (eds), *Woman Soul Flowing* and Sally Dries (ed.), *Because we are one People* and *Sing a Woman Song* (all three: Ecumenical Women's Center, 1977 and 1978).
35 Alla Bozarth-Campbell, essay 'Transfiguration/Full Moon' for *Women Listening* (a collection of women speaking about their prayer life) as yet unpublished).
36 This is but one disadvantage of the split between science and theology. If evolutionary theory was truly absorbed and incorporated into Christian imagery, instead of merely recognised from a distance, Christians would obviously have much less difficulty with the idea of God participating in and *being* Process. Einstein recognised the theological implications of relativity and curved light even though the Church did not. His phrase 'The old man does not throw dice' has theological, ethical and political ramifications of immense proportions. If God is Truth it is extraordinary that Christians should not grasp that all searches after truth are potentially sources of holiness. Cf. Alla Bozarth-Campbell, *Womanpriest* (Paulist Press, 1978), pp. 206–11.
37 Edward Robinson, 'Interview with Meinrad Craighead OSB' (Religious Experience Research Unit, Manchester College, Oxford, 1977), published in *Studia Nuptica*, vol. 1, no. 1, Spring 1978, p. 21.
38 Meinrad Craighead, *The Sign of the Tree* (Mitchell Beazley, UK 1979).

39 Ibid., jacket cover description.
40 Edward Robinson, op. cit.
41 Cf. G. Russell and M. Dewey, 'Psychological Aspects' in Peter Moore (ed.), *Man, Woman and Priesthood* (SPCK, 1978). Although this line of discussion is used in the article in a virulently anti-feminist way (so that I have to take exception to the conclusions the authors draw) their presentation of the psychological arguments is interesting and open to different interpretations from theirs.
42 Sue Harris (Susannah Herzel), 'The Body is the Book' in Peter Moore, op. cit., p. 120.
43 Meinrad Craighead, interview in *Signum* (CIO) 1976.
44 *Sign of the Tree*, op. cit., p. 119.
45 Alla Bozarth-Campbell, *Womanpriest*, op. cit., p. 209.
46 Maria Boulding, *Marked for Life* (SPCK, 1979), p. 70.
47 Fran Ferder, *Called to Break Bread* (Quixote Centre, 1978), p. 38.
48 Monica Furlong, Lenten Series, *Church Times* (weekly 22 February–3 March 1980).
49 Both accounts can claim to be based in the Gospels. From Matthew, Luke and John come the best known accounts and anecdotes, but Mark – the most primitive of the Gospels – is also the most stark. His Jesus does not give up his spirit with noble resignation and trust; his Jesus does not speak to his mother, his fellows, or his enemies. Mark records only one phrase from the cross: the desolate, 'My God, my God why hast thou foresaken me'. And at the end, 'Jesus uttered a loud cry and breathed his last.'
50 Alla Bozarth-Campbell, 'Transfiguration/Full Moon', op. cit.
51 Ibid.
52 Proverbs 8: 30–31 (NEB translation which makes the meaning clearer than the RSV).
53 Maria Boulding, op. cit., p. 70.
54 Hugo Rahner, *Man at Play* (Burna & Oates, 1965) and C. S. Lewis, *Voyage to Venus* (Pan Books, 1953), pp. 198–202.
55 Anne Sexton, *The Awful Rowing Towards God* (Houghton Miffin, 1979), pp. 85–6.

CHAPTER 7   MOVING FORWARD – SOME CONCLUSIONS

1 Psalm 84: 5–7 (Book of Common prayer translation: I have altered the word 'ways' there to 'highways' (as in the RSV, the NEB and the Jerusalem Bible) because this makes clearer the travelling image. It is not the 'ways of God' meaning style of acts, but the paths of God to be travelled.)
2 Adrienne Rich, *On Lies Secrets and Silence* (Virago, 1980), p. 11.
3 Guillaume van der Graft, *Freedom Tastes of Pain* (USPG poster no. 19).
4 Carole Etzler, song, 'Sometimes I wish' from album *Sometimes I wish* (Sisters Unlimited Inc., 1976).
5 Matthew 10: 9–10.

6 John Bunyan, *Pilgrim's Song*. (The slight doubt that I occasionally feel at bowdlerising, or feminising, texts is completely absent in this case, because, with the exception of the Church of Scotland Hymnal, every other denominational and modern hymn book carries the grossly distorted and distinctly more sexist version of this hymn by Percy Dearmer. If this nineteenth-century corruption is so generally acceptable, I have no fears that the minor alteration of pronouns adopted here can give offence.)

INDEX

Abraham, 161, 190–1
Adam, 1, 166
Admission of Women to the Ministerial Priesthood, Declaration on the, 83
Advisory Committee for the Churches' Ministry, 132
Allin, Bishop, 137
Anabaptists, 128
Anderson, Carol, 100, 106
Anderson, Elizabeth Garrett, 12
Anglican Church, 60, 124, 145; *see also* Church of England
Anglican Communion: attitude to ordination, 85, 95, 98, 102, 108; Deaconesses in, 86; language of Prayer Book, 163; women priests in, 95–7, 108
Anglican Prayer Book, 168–9
Anglicanism, 96
Anstey, Sr Eleanor, 70
apostolic orders, 51–2, 54, 56–7
Aquinas, Thomas, 8, 11, 16, 177
Arian heresy, 162
Association of Women Preachers, 87
Augustine, 8, 177

Baptist Church(es), 124, 136
Baptist Union, 2, 84, 89, 167
Baptists, 32, 88–91
Baron, Virginia, 27
Belcher, Donald, 106
Benedict, Sr Irene, 173
Benedictine rule, 52, 158
Benedictines, 51, 159, 182
Bennet, Rev. Joyce, 2, 97
Bishops: advisers to, 135; Anglican,

163; authority of, 110, 129, 134; declare women's ordinations invalid, 101, 204; English compared to American, 106; Episcopal Church (USA), 3, 37; give women pastoral charge, 116; Lambeth Conference, 87; 'male chauvinist pigs', 37; MOW and, 109; National Conference of, 168; National Council of, 150; ordain women, 100; relationship with Mothers Superior, 58, 73; relationship with nuns, 57, 65–8, 75, 77; role in ordination, 85, 121; secular role, 134; support for women needed, 112
Bittner, Marrill, 100
Blacker, Thetis, 188
Blacklock, Rev. Martha, 35, 36, 172
Bliss, Dr Kathleen, 1
Boulding, Sr Maria, 182, 186
Bozarth-Campbell, Rev. Alla, 100–2, 120, 177, 182, 185
Breviary in English, 169
Burn, Kath, 113

Callahan, Fr William, 150
Calvin, 2
Calvinism, 128
canon law, 56, 60
canon(s), 57, 74, 76
Carthusians, 51
Catherine of Siena, 9, 53, 159
Catholic Herald, 169
Catholic Revival, 13
Central Committee for Women's Work, 145

213